ORGANIZATIONAL CHANGE

STUDIES OF URBAN SOCIETY

General Editor, David P. Street

Organizational Change

THE POLITICAL ECONOMY OF THE YMCA

MAYER N. ZALD

THE UNIVERSITY OF CHICAGO PRESS

CHICAGO & LONDON

Standard Book Number: 226-97850-8
Library of Congress Catalog Card Number: 77-101494
The University of Chicago Press, Chicago 60637
The University of Chicago Press, Ltd., London

TO

L. L. McCLOW

FRIEND

AND

COUNSELOR

CONTENTS

ILLUSTRATIONS

PREFACE

This book presents an analysis of the history of the Young Men's Christian Association in America and a case study of one urban Association, the YMCA of Metropolitan Chicago. The conceptual framework used to aid the analysis—developed as the study progressed—is that of the political economy of organizations.

The subject challenges the sociologist in at least two ways. First, because the YMCA appears to be such a bland organization—a gym and swim club for the middle class—there might seem to be little sociological merit in its investigation. Second, a study of a single organization would not seem to add much to the growth of a generalized body of knowledge. The blandness of the YMCA presents its challenge because historically sociologists have flourished on scrutiny of the nether regions of social life. Delinquency, narcotics, addiction, sexual relations, homicide, and mental illness are some of the social-problem topics that have been placed under the social scientist's microscope. The exposure and analysis of these areas of social life have helped remove the blinders of ignorance and have subtly titillated producers and consumers of sociological wares. Even when exposing less illicit areas of social life—for example, the operation of private wealth in community power structures or the power base of subalterns—sociological studies gain some of their force by their relation to private fantasy and motive and to hoped-for social change. This study, however, concerns an institution so much a part of everyday experience in America that it seems to offer little in the way of titillation or of nether-world exposure or even of complexity and subtle social process.

One challenge of this study is to show the deep intrinsic interest and complexity of the YMCA. As it happens, in many cities the YMCA is directly linked with urban change and ferment; thus its study appeals also partly by the knowledge it contributes to our understanding of agency adaptation to pressing social problems.

A second challenge is to show the continuing value of case studies at a time when many scholars have argued for a turn to comparative analysis. With these scholars I am well aware of the pitfalls of case analysis for developing tested propositions about organizations or for deriving any

xiii

generalizations whatsoever. Case studies, however, are still an appropriate vehicle for the study of social change. Even more important, case
studies are appropriate vehicles for the elaboration and development of
concepts and conceptual frameworks. While they rarely "test" theory,
they are invaluable in their development. Aside from the purely descriptive value of this study, one of its aims is to contribute a framework for
the analysis of organizational change and structure.

The fieldwork for this study extended over several years. My initial
contact with the Young Men's Christian Association of Metropolitan
Chicago was made in the spring of 1961, at the suggestion of James F.
Short. At the time, Short, in conjunction with Fred L. Strodtbeck, was
directing an intensive study of the Chicago YMCA's Youth Gangs
Project and was impressed with the YMCA's readiness to change and the
range of organizational problems that change was creating.[1]

Money was available to employ a research assistant for the summer
months, and so Patricia Denton Wallace and I began exploratory interviews in the Metropolitan office. The openness of the Metropolitan office
staff to candid discussion was seductive. (I had just completed a comparative study of the staff structure of correctional institutions for juvenile delinquents in which the guardedness and antagonism of one executive had almost ruined an important part of the study.) The candor and
encouragement of the general secretary (the chief executive officer of the
Chicago YMCA), Lloyd McClow, was especially important in two ways.
First, his willingness to discuss in detail the problems of his own position
gave a crucial vantage point from which to view the organization. Second,
his obvious support of the study made it extremely easy to gain access to
records and personnel. Our availability to examine the operation of the
Association fitted in with his and the board of managers' publicized commitment to examine the "total structure and function" of the Association.
And in the autumn of 1961 a formal proposal for study was presented to
the board of managers.

Between the fall of 1961 and 1964 several hundred hours of interviewing were conducted with board members, YMCA secretaries, and salient
professionals external to the organization. These included over twenty
hours of interview time with the general secretary, interviews lasting between one and four hours with thirteen executive secretaries and thirteen
board chairmen (from the same departments, all interviews conducted
separately), interviews of from one-half hour to two hours with the four-

1. Their research is reported in *Gang Delinquency and Social Process* (Chicago:
University of Chicago Press, 1966).

teen members of the executive committee of the board of managers, one hour to ten hours of interviewing with the nine assistant general secretaries in the Metropolitan office, and short discussions with many other staff members and lay volunteers. Longer interviews were also conducted with selected "line" professional staff. The interviews were loosely structured to focus both on the "career" of the interviewee and his perspectives on interunit and intraunit structures and relationships. Interviews outside the Chicago YMCA included interviews with relevant professionals in the Chicago Housing Authority, the Chicago Welfare Council, the president of George Williams College, and staff members of the National Board of the YMCA. The "outside" interviews focused on the position of the Association in relation to other organizations in Chicago and in relation to other YMCAs.

Beginning in the fall of 1961, project staff began attending meetings of staff and boards at the Metropolitan office. These included meetings of the board of trustees, the board of managers, the executive committee of the board of managers, and selected committee meetings (marketing, finance and operations, program, and others). We also attended meetings of the general secretary's cabinet (all executive secretaries and all assistant general secretaries) and of the Metropolitan staff, and two-day summer retreats of staff and laymen.

From the fall of 1963 until the summer of 1964 I switched from observer to participant-observer, serving as a member of the long-range planning committee of the board of managers. This committee, meeting monthly for three hours, considered the overall direction of the Association. The final fieldwork was done in November 1967, when I spent two weeks examining the changes in the Association over the preceding three years. Interviews were conducted in the Metropolitan office and in selected departments.

The fieldwork also included a questionnaire administered to all professional staff and to a sample of board members in the spring of 1962. When I began studying the YMCA I was working out of Selznick's general framework for organization analysis and combining it with an orientation toward the social psychology of professions. My first publication of the project (written with Patricia Denton) "From Evangelism to General Services: The Transformation of the YMCA,"[2] was cast in this mold, and the questionnaire emphasized dimensions relevant to attitudes and interpositional perception. The explicit political metaphor did not really begin to crystallize until the succession processes (described in

2. *Administrative Science Quarterly* 8 (September 1963): 214–34.

chapter 9) took place in the fall of 1962. But even then, I had not begun thinking of an organizational political economy and the full range of implications of the term.

Indeed, it was not until the spring of 1964, as I tried to pull together the threads of the study, that the political-economy theme appeared to have unifying strength. The potentiality of this framework for organizational analysis in general was then developed in seminars I taught at Vanderbilt University in 1965 and 1967. Most of the questionnaire material on attitudes and on perceptions seemed to be relatively remote from the more structural considerations of the political-economy approach. And so, though these data are interesting in their own right and remain to be fully developed, they have been only partially exploited in this volume.

Chapter 2 and 3 are a greatly expanded version of "From Evangelism to General Service on the Transformation of the YMCA," *Administrative Science Quarterly* 8 (1963): 214–34. Permission to use this material has been received from the Graduate School of Business and Public Administration, Cornell University. Chapter 9 is a slightly revised version of "Who Shall Rule, A Political Analysis of Succession in a Large Welfare Organization," *Pacific Sociological Review* 8 (1965): 52–60, and is reprinted with permission of the editor. Pages 17–19 in chapter 1 and pages 81–82 in chapter 5 are reprinted from my essay, "Political Economy: A Framework for Comparative Analysis," pages 223–24 and 226–27 in *Power in Organizations,* edited by Zald, © 1970 Vanderbilt University Press, with permission of the publisher. Table 8 is reprinted with permission from Clifford Carey, *Current Income of City YMCA's: A Study of the Sources and Change in Income from 1932–1953,* p. 17, Research Studies and Records Department, National Council of YMCAs.

Financial support has been received from several sources. Initially a small grant was received from the Research Council of the Social Sciences Division, University of Chicago. Two research grants from the National Institutes of Health (GM-10777 and M-6319[A]) supported the planning and field phases of the study. Analysis and writing were supported by a small grant from the Vanderbilt University Research Council and, finally, by a Career Development Award (1-K3-MH-34, 919) from the National Institutes of Health, United States Public Health Service. Amy Wexler Orum, Charles Kamen, and Mary Queeley helped in the collection and analysis of observations. Carolyn Mullins immensely aided in improving the manuscript's readability. And Suzanna Hershey typed the manuscript and compiled the index.

The list of people in the YMCA who were exceedingly helpful is too long to enumerate, but a special note of thanks is due Gerald Heyl, Solon Cousins, John Root, and Fred Replogle. They served liaison functions and provided access without which this study could not have been completed. Finally, I am indebted to Rolf Schliewen, James A. Wiley, David Street, and William Rushing for their critical and constructive reviews of the manuscript. In this last regard I am specially indebted to Gary Wamsley not only for his critical comments but for convincing me that I should not be modest in asserting the merits of the political-economy approach.

Part I
The YMCA in an Urbanizing Society: Finding a Niche

Introduction to Part I

The modern YMCA presents a rather bland front to the outsider. Its older physical facilities are usually located near the middle of a community's business center while newer suburban branches usually choose a fairly well-traveled highway, though not at the choice intersection. The membership of older YMCAs is usually heavily male. Some newer YMCAs, however, have as many female members as male; some, in fact, issue memberships only to whole families. Sitting in the lobby of older, residential-type YMCAs are often several "senior citizens," some of whom spend considerable time simply sitting in that lobby; the youth section, on the other hand, might well have a highly active group of ten-year-olds in the game room and a Hi-Y Club meeting across the corridor. In yet another area a part-time instructor may be teaching Spanish or flower arranging to young adults.

The niche occupied by most YMCAs in the organizational life of their communities can be characterized as that of a general service organization designed to facilitate the social, physical, and not-too-intellectual interests of community members. Apart from their inexpensive residences, YMCAs are formal organizations designed to assist community members in the constructive use of their spare time. YMCA's major services are activity- rather than product-oriented and are designed for the relatively well-adjusted rather than the maladjusted or deviant member of society. YMCA activities are interstitial to the central concerns of modern life, which revolve around school, family, and work. The numerous YMCA branches provide guided social and educational activities in exchange for member commitment and money as well as community legitimation and funds.

If the Association lacked an extensive history and if its staff and board commitments were restricted to providing the types of services listed above, there would be less of sociological interest in examining the YMCA. It is, however, precisely the organization's history and the

3

broader commitment of staff and boards that give the organization its internal dynamic and result in a changing niche for the organization. That history has developed a set of goals and organizational commitments which affect boards and staff. These commitments influence perceptions and reactions to the changing environment, continuously reshaping the organization.

1
Background

A 1954 Gallup survey indicated that of American males over the age of twenty-one, 25 percent reported a past membership in the Young Men's Christian Association.[1] Among cities with more than fifty thousand people in 1959, 96 percent had chartered YMCAs.[2] If an exact count were made, we would probably find that well over half the American male adults and a smaller, though still substantial, proportion of females had had some contact with the YMCA—perhaps spending a night in an ascetically furnished hotel room, serving as a camp counselor or group leader, or participating in a club program. The smell of the locker room, the arrangement of chairs in the lobby, and the log fire of a YMCA camp are part of the memories and backgrounds of a large segment of the American population.

THE YMCA IN AMERICA

The Young Men's Christian Association well exemplifies the adapted service organization, an organization which has changed with its environment. From its beginnings as an evangelical, proselytizing organization in the drapers' shops of London, it has become a worldwide association offering a wide variety of programs and services. In the process of change, it has all but dropped its evangelical revivalism and its overtly religious program. How does one account for the growth and spread of the YMCA, its ability to fit into a community niche, and its transformation from an evangelical to a general service organization? How is the YMCA controlled, and how does it change? And how can it adapt to the new consciousness of inner city problems which has emerged during

1. George Gallup, *YMCA Survey* (Princeton: American Institute of Public Opinion, 1956).

2. Clifford M. Carey, "Perspectives for YMCA Growth in the 1960's," *YMCA Yearbook and Official Roster,* 1959 (New York: Association Press, 1959).

the second half of the twentieth century? In attempting to answer these questions I will consider some quite general theoretical notions concerning the control of organizations and how they change. These concepts will be used to explain the broad historical transformation of the YMCA in America and to examine in depth one Association, the Young Men's Christian Association of Metropolitan Chicago, as it operated in the early 1960s.

As a large-scale organization, the YMCA presents a curious blend of characteristics. First, its contemporary goals of Christian character development are not clearly linked to any one kind of program or measurable outcome. Most organizations have more clearly defined goals and a more direct and observable link between goals and operating programs. (Some other organizations, of course, have diffuse and multiple goals—correctional institutions and universities, for example.)

Second, the Association in America includes within itself an occupational group characterized by many of the attributes of a profession—educational requirements for certification, an ethic of service to members and the community, a claimed base of knowledge and skill, training schools, and a monopoly over certain occupational positions. A profession and its professional organization are not usually coterminous with a particular bureaucratic structure; the professional community generally cuts across many organizations. In the YMCA, however, the YMCA secretary is considered a professional person and the Association of Secretaries (A.O.S.) is a standard-setting professional group totally within the YMCA movement.

Third, the American YMCA is composed of bureaucratic elements while yet embodying aspects of a social movement. Owing to its Christian evangelistic origins (a missionary zeal and spirit are part of the organization's basic mandate), highly involved and committed staff and lay members are likely to perceive themselves as part of a Christian movement for a better world. The symbols and rhetoric of legitimation include reference to this missionary spirit; nevertheless, the routinization of charisma and the development of career lines, accounting systems, and division of labor have proceeded rapidly.

The YMCA's broad goals, its "social-movement" qualities, its incorporation of a profession coterminous with the organization, its ubiquity, and finally its long history of change provide fertile ground for investigation. Because the organization departs in many ways from the usual structure of large-scale organizations, analysis of (1) the YMCA's special characteristics, (2) the problems these characteristics do or do not engender, and (3) the way they intermesh with some of the more usual features of organizations should contribute to a clarification of both organizational theory and thinking about organizations in general.

This study *is* partially intended as an organizational ethnography, describing an organization which is based in a changing urban environment and which presents an interesting amalgam of organizational characteristics;[3] too few descriptions of organizations and organizational change are written with language and concepts relevant to social science. Equally important, however, I shall not only describe the YMCA but also develop an analytic framework that should facilitate explanation and analysis of the directions of change in any large-scale organization whatsoever. For the YMCA, the central analytic problem is twofold. First, what are the forces—external and internal—that hold the YMCA within its particular niche in American communities? Second, what are the pressures for change and for moving into a redefined niche within the network of organizations and groups? In even more abstract terms, I shall examine those elements of the interchange between an organization's environment and its internal structure that determine which interchanges are selected and developed.

The framework here used is what I call the "political economy of organizations." It is my contention that use of this framework will advance both the comparative study of organizations and the study of organizational change. The political-economy approach can be used in studying any large-scale organization, but it is especially useful for studying the YMCA. In its long history the YMCA has shifted from a social-movement organization with religious appeal to its members to an organization whose appeal is based largely on services rendered. Sociological literature usually treats social-movement organizations

---

3. Although the YMCA has deviant characteristics, this study is not framed within the logic of deviant-case analysis. Deviant-case analysis has maintained a substantial and properly prestigious place in the sociological literature, setting limits for variation in key factors and clarifying the conditions under which the "normal" occurs. The best-known deviant-case analysis in the organizational literature is, of course, Seymour M. Lipset, Martin A. Trow, and James S. Coleman's *Union Democracy: The Internal Politics of the International Typographical Union* (Glencoe, Ill.: Free Press, 1956). The strategy of deviant-case analysis requires that the case differ markedly on a limited number of characteristics. Usually the deviance is seen as a dependent consequence of some other set of variables, and the research task is to search out the causes of that dependence. (It is possible to begin with deviance in an independent variable and then to seek dependent consequences.) Here the focus is not primarily on the deviance, per se, of the YMCA.

separately from "formal" or "bureaucratic" organizations. A good theoretical framework for the study of complex organizations ought to encompass both, however, and the political-economy framework easily encompasses both social-movement and formal organizations.

Second, the YMCA represents a magnificent case of organizational change and adaptation. Because of its history of change, one should not retreat, as is the American custom, to an explanation based on leadership alone. One is forced by the case to examine the interaction between environment, internal organization, and political life. As Associations adapted to the American scene, internal political conflicts emerged both nationally and locally over whether the YMCA was to be a general evangelical agency or an agency for young men only; whether it was to be overtly and simply a religious organization or whether it was to meet all acceptable needs, including those (such as physical recreation) that were foreign to fundamentalist and puritanical conceptions of the moral life; whether it was to include all classes and religions or to be restricted to a narrow social class and group; and finally, in our times, whether it should confront race relations and problems of the inner city or whether it should rather remain a general service organization for well-adapted citizens. These "choice" situations were created by the urbanization, industrialization, and growth processes of the larger society which, at different points in time, made different age, sex, and socioeconomic groups available for organizational participation. Each goal and policy choice was intimately tied to underlying economic choices and dilemmas (for instance, scarcity of resources, compatibility of program directions with personnel and facilities). Each goal and policy choice had to be shaped through interlinked national and local polities constituting power systems of various shapes, with contending groups holding different values and conceptions of the YMCA.

Finally, the breadth and pervasiveness of the YMCA in America deserves explanation. The YMCA has carved a niche for itself in most urban communities. It has a network of users and funders, competitors and critics, that sustain its contemporary position. During some periods in American history the YMCAs have been highly valued, and the community has sustained their operation well. At other times Associations have been threatened with extinction. And at still others they have existed in a state of stable transaction with their environments. The growth, change, and variety of American communities present a range of alternatives for YMCAs. The political-economy approach can facilitate explanations of transformations and differences of niche.

ORGANIZATIONAL ANALYSIS AND POLITICAL ECONOMY

The social change accompanying the processes of urbanization and industrialization presented the YMCA with opportunities for serving young men and other groups. Physical recreation programs, vocational courses, and escape from isolation and wretched hotels have long constituted the bases upon which the YMCA has built a program. Whereas in early days board members debated the introduction of physical recreation, in our own times they have debated the use of federal funds for poverty-related programs. Such is the independence of local Associations that some have rejected the use of federal money whereas others have wholeheartedly embraced it. How can we explain the long-range transformation of the American YMCA and, within a given time span, the differing propensity of local Associations for change?

To explain the directions taken by organizational change, whether of the YMCA or any other organization, we need an appropriate analytic framework. The direction of organizational change is a function of many factors. External sources of change include market demands; competition with other organizations; the values, attitudes, and knowledge of potential members; the requirements set by the law of the larger society; and the like. Internal factors include shifts in the authority structure, the relative differentiation of tasks and responsibility, and the values and perception of key executives and factions. The difficulty in explaining change is not the identification of factors causing or associated with change but rather the development of a framework for classifying, ordering, and relating these factors.

This is a difficult task since, at this time, no coherent theory of organizational change exists, nor is there any coherent framework for developing a taxonomy of organizational change elements. The political-economy approach is a middle-range conceptual scheme designed for use both in comparative studies and in analysis of organizational change. Here the emphasis is on its utility for studying organizational change. Since anyone brash enough to introduce yet another jargon should be held responsible for justifying it, I will briefly survey contemporary approaches to organizations, especially those relevant to the study of change.

Current Organizational Theory

There are, of course, numerous empirical studies, essays, and theoretical syntheses concerned with organizational change. Empirical studies of change by social scientists have often focused on the adaptation of groups to each other and on the consequences of this adaptation for organization effectiveness. These studies have been set largely in a social psychological framework. Robert Guest's study of the effect on productivity and "morale" of changing leadership in a branch plant of a large industrial firm is one of the better studies of this genre.[4] Guest uses Homans's "sentiment-activity-interaction" framework for analyzing change. Elliott Jaques's *The Changing Culture of a Factory,* although it does not use Homans's system, is in the same vein.[5] Both Jaques and Guest deal primarily with interpersonal and intergroup relations. Although aware of both the outside world and the larger organizational structure, they take as their object for analysis the microsystem of parts of the organization.

Some studies in the social psychological tradition (that of Mann and Hoffman, for example) use technological change as the independent variable and individual and group change as dependent variables.[6] These studies, however, focus on the explanation of individual, rather than organizational, change. Moreover, even those social psychological studies which examine the consequences for organizational effectiveness of interpersonal relations accept in essence the particular goals and organizational niche of the organization; the broad directions of organizational change are thus outside their scope.[7]

Not only are many studies unconcerned with organization as organization; several emerge from such a value-laden perspective that it is difficult to separate fact from wishful thinking. The essential task of the social scientist—to search for knowledge—is thereby lost in a haze of participant-democracy verbiage. Thus Warren Bennis's *Changing Organizations,* while in part demonstrating an awareness of the nature of social systems, begins by assuming that social scientists know enough about organizations to assist in changing them and that a democratic structure and process is inevitable.[8] Indeed, his second chapter is entitled "Democracy Is Inevitable." While there may be some long-range trends (such as the increasing proportion of professionals in organizations)

4. *Organizational Change: The Effect of Successful Leadership* (Homewood, Ill.: Irwin-Dorsey Press, 1962).

5. London: Tavistock Publications, 1951.

6. Floyd C. Mann and L. R. Hoffman, *Automation and the Worker: A Study of Social Change in Power Plants* (New York: Holt, Rinehart & Winston, 1960).

7. Some social psychologists recognize that major sources of change are external to the organization. See Daniel Katz and Robert L. Kahn, *The Social Psychology of Organization* (New York: John Wiley & Sons, 1966), p. 449.

8. New York: McGraw-Hill, 1966.

that bring about a collegial structure and greater orientation toward participation, the extent and location of any movement toward democratic structure will vary, and the difficulties in understanding organizational change must remain.

There are, of course, many histories of individual organizations, from department stores and railroads to social-movement organizations and churches. Yet many of these suffer from a total absence of theoretical apparatus. One of the best is a comparative study of the rise of the decentralized corporate firm. Alfred Dupont Chandler, Jr.'s *Strategy and Structure*[9] attempts to discover why certain leading firms (Sears, Roebuck; General Motors; Du Pont; and Standard Oil of New Jersey) independently switched from functional departmentalization to a structure of divisional decentralization. Difficulties in organizational control and coordination growing out of product multiplication, market diversification, and inventory control are seen as key causes. Chandler's central thesis is that a strategy (for example, how a company chooses to define its major market and products) calls forth a structure. Yet Chandler's theoretical apparatus is relatively unspecified and underdeveloped. Because he does not specify variables and concepts clearly, his framework is of little use to those studying other kinds of organizations.[10]

In brief, the social psychological works are inadequate for analyzing change because they select inappropriate (for our purposes) dependent variables; the historical works are inadequate because they are relatively atheoretic.[11]

---

9. Cambridge: M.I.T. Press, 1962.

10. Furthermore, his lack of theoretical specification and sophistication has led some to question his analysis. In "Decentralization and Control: Problems in the Organization of Department Stores," (Ph.D. diss., Harvard University, 1966), Harvey Sapolsky has argued that Chandler largely misread the level of decision discretion involved in the organizational reformation of Sears, Roebuck. Specifically, the entire product line was controlled through a central merchandizing office; only the amount of space allocated to different product groups was left to local discretion. Sapolsky concludes that Sears bought the language of decentralization without buying actual decentralization.

The difficulty inherent in the "strategy before structure" formula is that the reverse is also true. Previous structures and market position can provide opportunities for a new strategy: structure and strategy together can cause administrative problems which require new structures, and so on. Although Chandler provides an imaginative discussion and comparison of the change processes in the four cases (see his chap. 6), he makes no further theoretical elaboration. For my purposes, therefore, his work is wanting.

11. In recent years social psychological approaches to social interaction have focused on power and exchange as crucial dimensions of analysis. These works tend

Work of a more sociological nature is too closely focused on internal structure, scant attention being paid to external pressures toward change or to overall organizational change. Theories and studies of internal organizational structure are more numerous than those of organization-environment relations. The works of Barnard,[12] Gouldner,[13] Blau,[14] and Dalton[15] are among the most distinguished studies in a long line of research and theory focusing primarily on the internal structure and operation of organizations. Many of these works discuss the internal control of organizations, raising such questions as: (1) Under what conditions will subordinates accept attempts to influence them? (2) What conditions favor rule systems? (3) Under what conditions is formal authority consistent with informal? (4) Under what conditions does one group or position have more influence or power than others? Some of these studies consider only *who* has control, ignoring both organizational effectiveness and goal attainment. Others (notably those of Tannenbaum and his colleagues) study the relationship of control structure to organizational effectiveness, but they are limited because they assume goals as given. Control is viewed only as it reflects on the ability of an organization to achieve or control its goals; the joint interdependence of goals and control structure is not considered.[16]

---

to analyze interaction between people in relatively homogeneous relations; they treat the emergent exchange and power relation rather than relations imposed by roles and position in the larger social system. Thus they do not provide the analysis of structural relations of power and exchange needed for a political-economy approach. The social psychological works, by and large, are characterized by a more rigorous approach to definition and theory construction than are the works of political scientists. Yet I have found the insights and concepts of political science more useful for my work than those of social psychologists. The more recent social psychological works focusing on power and exchange are George C. Homans, *Social Behavior* (New York: Harcourt, Brace & World, 1961), Peter Blau, *Exchange and Power in Social Life* (New York: John Wiley & Sons, 1964), and John Thibaut and Harold H. Kelly, *The Social Psychology of Groups* (New York: John Wiley & Sons, 1959).

12. Chester I. Barnard, *The Functions of the Executive* (Cambridge: Harvard University Press, 1938).

13. Alvin W. Gouldner, *Patterns of Industrial Bureaucracy* (Glencoe, Ill.: Free Press, 1954).

14. Peter M. Blau, *The Dynamics of Bureaucracy* (Chicago: University of Chicago Press, 1955).

15. Melville Dalton, *Men Who Manage* (New York: John Wiley & Sons, 1959).

16. Basil S. Georgopoulos and Arnold S. Tannenbaum, "A Study of Organizational Effectiveness," *American Sociological Review* 22 (1957): 534–40.

One central concern of this study, however, is with the manner in which goals are shaped and given direction by prevailing control systems and, conversely, with the way in which goal changes bring about shifts in internal allocations of physical facilities, prestige, and power. Moreover, a major problem with much organization theory is its reductionistic nature; it considers the internal structure of organizations or some aspects of structure (for example, supervisor-subordinate relations) without studying the organization qua organization. Organizations have collective identities and systemic properties; they can and should be considered as whole systems insofar as their components are integrated. This study takes precisely such an approach.

Since I am using the phrase *political economy,* it is well to inquire how economists and political scientists study organization. The type of economic analysis used here is more akin to the older school of institutional economics than to modern analytic economics. Price theory and the theory of the firm in analytic microeconomics primarily relate the variables of price, demand, and cost to supply schedules and the variables of fixed and variable costs to production decisions and profits, respectively. They are essentially bodiless theories, ignoring the internal processes, problems, and structures of organizations that bring about different kinds of organizational choices.[17]

On the other hand, economic historians and historians of business enterprises do begin to delve into the organizational body when they relate technology, capital, and market constraints on the overall organization of industries and firms. Their works, however, are somewhat divorced from economic theory and are of little use for comparative analysis.[18]

Not only is analytic economics of little value for this study, studies of organizations by political scientists have also been of little use. While eminent political scientists have argued that large-scale organizations

17. Some economists, Edith T. Penrose, for instance, have recognized this bodiless quality of the theory of the firm. Her *Theory of the Growth of the Firm* (New York: John Wiley & Sons, 1960) primarily examines problems and limits of the management cadre as they constrain organizational growth. Even for Penrose, however, the body of the firm is treated only as it constrains the time and energy of the managerial group.

18. However, these works are indispensable for gaining a sense of the environmental dynamics of organizations. See, for instance, Melvin G. De Chazeau and Alfred E. Kahn, *Integration and Competition in the Petroleum Industry* (New Haven: Yale University Press, 1959).

represent a fertile field for political analysis,[19] their remarks have remained largely programmatic.

When political scientists have made empirical studies of large-scale organizations, they have usually turned to psychology or sociology for their conceptual apparatus. Herbert Simon and his colleagues, for example, have been largely interested in explaining the decisions and perception of middle-level managers.[20] While the phrase "coalition" appears in the index of *A Behavioral Theory of the Firm,* there is little analysis of coalition process, composition, or change in the book. Such analysis is scanty, partly because, for Simon and his colleagues, "coalition" signifies mainly the willingness of an individual to join a firm. More important, however, political process is also neglected in this work simply because the analysis of one decision at a time makes it extremely difficult to locate coalitions, since the finding of stable coalitions depends upon the examination of choices and alliances over time. In part the absence of politics results from restricting the unit of study to hierarchic organizations. Just as nation-states range from monarchies to republics, from totalitarian dictatorships to multiparty democracies, so large organizations range from almost anarchical religious orders to hierarchic extensions of one-man rule, from democratic voluntary associations to loose confederations of giant bureaucracies. Decision theory misses their structural variation.

When political scientists have studied bureaucratic organizations in toto rather than simply one decision, they have utilized what appears to be general sociological concepts as their tools. In this vein Herbert Kaufman has marvelously described the forces molding the geographically dispersed United States Forest Service into a single, homogeneously acting organization.[21] Interestingly enough, however, political science seems to have played little part in his analysis.

Only in studying the control of voluntary organizations (such as labor unions, the American Medical Association, or the Grange) in the national political system have political scientists used political concepts and

19. Robert A. Dahl, "Business and Politics: A Critical Appraisal of Political Science," *American Political Science Review* 53 (1959): 1–34; Earl Latham, "The Body Politic of the Corporation," in *The Corporation in Modern Society,* ed. Edward S. Mason (Cambridge: Harvard University Press, 1959), pp. 218–36.

20. James G. March and Herbert A. Simon, *Organizations* (New York: John Wiley & Sons, 1958); Richard M. Cyert and James G. March, *A Behavioral Theory of the Firm* (Englewood Cliffs, N.J.: Prentice-Hall, 1963).

21. *The Forest Ranger: A Study in Administrative Behavior* (Baltimore: Johns Hopkins Press, 1960).

analysis. Such studies have analyzed the factors shaping pressure group policies and operation of the internal political system.[22] Although they need not be democracies, however, voluntary organizations are distinguished from other organizations precisely in the existence within them of electoral systems. They generally have formal constitutions and resemble aggregates of interest groups. Political scientists seem to have spent less time studying organizational structures which are less pluralistic and openly political. The task, then, of understanding the polity processes of complex organizations remains.

Since the mid-1940s one group of students of organization have attempted empirical analyses that take the total organization as the object for analysis and focus on both external dependencies and internal power process. The works of Philip Selznick and his followers have several characteristics which are relevant to our search for a framework for comparative and change analysis.[23] Their approach is goal-oriented, focusing on the external social base of the organization and examining the interdependence of, and conflicts among, groups—both within and without the organization.

Because Selznick and his students select, from the universe of organizations, those whose goals usually have social values apart from providing economic gain to their staff or owners, his studies show an overarching concern for the analysis of goal attainment, the pressure to goal displacement, and the autonomy of elites to preserve goals. In *Administrative Leadership* Selznick takes as a central problem of institutional leadership the protection, maintenance, and promotion of value.[24] Organizations or parts of organizations not embodying values are expendable, needing neither "institutional statesmen" nor protection.

Selznick's students have been less concerned than he with the creation

22. Oliver Garceau, *The Political Life of the American Medical Association* (Cambridge: Harvard University Press, 1941).

23. For Selznick, see *TVA and the Grass Roots* (Berkeley: University of California Press, 1949); *Leadership in Administration: A Sociological Interpretation* (Evanston, Ill.: Row Peterson, 1957); and his article, "Foundations of the Theory of Organization," *American Sociological Review* 13 (1948): 25–35. Relevant works by his students are Charles Perrow, "The Analysis of Goals in Complex Organizations," *American Sociological Review* 26 (1961): 854–65, and "Organizational Prestige: Some Functions and Dysfunctions," *American Journal of Sociology* 66 (1961): 355–41; Burton Clark, *The Open-Door College* (New York: McGraw-Hill, 1960), and "Organizational Adaptation and Precarious Values: A Case Study," *American Sociological Review* 21 (1956): 327–36.

24. P. 28.

and maintenance of an autonomous elite to protect values; nevertheless, they share his concern with the interaction of goals and internal structure and with the organizational maintenance requirements which can bring about goal deflection.

Perrow, studying the relation of operative goals (or tasks) to authority, is to the point.[25] He suggests that, as an organization's major tasks or problems shift, the locus of power generally shifts to different groups within the organization. In a hospital, for instance, when the major task is to gain and maintain capital funds, the board of directors will probably dominate. If, on the other hand, the central concern is to marshal technical skill, those professions specializing in that knowledge will gain ascendency. Finally, if the organization has difficulty coordinating and meshing its many complex parts, administrative skills will be stressed. Perrow suggests that these problems differ in their impact for different kinds of organizations (for example, a large coal corporation, with its heavy investments in land and fixed assets, will probably be largely dominated by its board, whereas a space age electronics firm will probably be dominated by scientists) and for one organization over time (hospitals, for example, have often shifted from trustee to medical and finally to administrative domination). Furthermore, Perrow's analysis indicates that each succeeding ascendant group brings a different set of decision criteria to bear on the operating problems of the organization and redefines its goals.

The theoretical framework of such works is characterized by a focus on goals and goal displacement, external and internal dependencies, power or authority structure, and intraorganizational conflict. It is also characterized by an attempt to have as the object of analysis organizations and their problems *as such* (or, at minimum, the interpenetration of major components) rather than some lower-level component. In terms of analytic style and the conceptual framework employed, these works are closer to political science and political sociology than to industrial sociology or the human relations school or, for that matter, to studies assuming the Weberian model of bureaucracy. Their emphasis on power, dominating elite, and group conflict represents a sometimes explicit, though more often implicit, concern with the political process in a large-scale organization. Furthermore, because their concern is with both the internal and external dependencies of an organization, they often focus

25. "Analysis of Goals."

on income sources, production, and the internal competitive processes determining the allocation of resources within organizations.

What has often been implicit is what I will make explicit in examining the YMCA's political economy. I contend that the use of an explicit political-economy framework will substantially advance the analysis of organizational change and structure.

The Concept of Political Economy

In its most generic sense, political economy studies the interplay of power (oriented toward goals) and productive exchange systems.[26] As I use the term, political economy is neutral to the question of the market's value as a mechanism for registering preferences, producing goods, and distributing income. In its nineteenth-century meaning, of course, political economy referred to that system in which politics or government was so ordered as to encourage the free play of market forces in determining the allocation of resources. In its more general sense, however, political economy refers only to the form of the relation between political and economic structures and processes.

When applied to nations, the term refers to description and analysis of the interplay between the institutions of government and law, fortified by coercive power, and the economy; that is, the system of producing and exchanging goods. James Willard Hurst's monumental *Law and Economic Growth: The Legal History of the Lumber Industry in Wisconsin, 1836–1915,*[27] for example, relates the manner in which government's initial desire for rapid economic development brought about legal policies relating to the disposal of public lands in Wisconsin; he demonstrates how the laws of property and contract led to certain patterns of private use; and finally he shows how changing goals and conceptions of the public good influenced property-use regulations and the use of state funds (for conservation) in relation to this property.

As this capsule summary of Hurst indicates, political economy encompasses more than study of a power structure as it affects economic structure. Also involved is study of the *ends* valued by polity actors as they affect the political and economic processes. In these terms laissez-faire

---

26. This focus on power as the defining element of politics and exchange as the defining element of economics parallels that of James Buchanan, "What Should Economists Do?" *Southern Economic Journal* 30 (1964): 213–32. Needless to say, power helps to define the terms of exchange, and advantages gained from exchange can become elements of power.

27. Cambridge: Harvard University Press, 1964.

economics was a normative system of political economy which strove to maximize overall production of material goods (regardless of the apportionment of those goods within society). By allowing market forces to determine profit and production, society would capitalize on the benefits of the division of labor.

Both in political science and sociology, conceptualization (though not empirical study) of the polity has focused on this goal-determining aspect of government and the political process. Norton Long, in a prescient analysis entitled "Aristotle and the Study of Local Government,"[28] points to the value of analyzing community constitutions, that is, the study of community rule and the ethos or values of dominant groups as a way of answering the central questions raised by Aristotle for the study of politics.

In sociology Talcott Parsons has also focused on the political process as the major arena of goal determination and allocation for a society.[29] His relevant point is that study of an organization's political economy must be concerned with the goal-shaping activities of organizations and the organization-shaping aspects of goals as they are embodied in an organization's dominant groups.

Beyond study of an organization's goals and power, the political-economy approach requires an analysis that focuses on the interaction of values and goals of power and control groups with (1) the *external* supply of money and other incentives and the demand for services of clients and funders and (2) the internal allocation of men, money, and facilities to accomplish tasks.[30] Economies, whether within nation-states or organizations, require a division of labor related to the state of the practical arts (technology). Organizational economies, however, unlike those of

28. In *The Polity* (Chicago: Rand McNally, 1962), pp. 222–41. James Wilson notes that too many political scientists seem to have understood only part of Long's message. Including himself in this category, Wilson comments that he and his professional peers have, by and large, studied the structure of power in local communities without studying the consequences of uses of power (i.e., that which the power system produces). Except for Williams and Adrian, who concentrate on community ethos and its effects, few studies by political scientists have been concerned empirically with the problems of value maximization in politics. See James Q. Wilson, "Problems in the Study of Urban Politics," *Essays in Political Science,* ed. Edward H. Buehrig (Bloomington: Indiana University Press, 1966), 113–50.

29. *The Social System* (Glencoe, Ill.: Free Press, 1951).

30. An essay by Tom Burns has been invaluable in shaping my perspective. See his "Micro-Politics: Mechanisms of Institutional Change," *Administrative Science Quarterly* 6 (1961): 257–81.

societies, do not proceed by market processes; instead, the mechanisms for allocating men, facilities, and money are carried out either by intergroup bargaining or by hierarchical assignments.[31]

The term *economy* should not be conceived narrowly as limited to the exchange of money for goods and services. Rather what is exchanged is a number of goods, or incentives, that bind men to each other. Following Barnard[32] and (derivatively) Wilson and Clark,[33] a wide range of incentives can be explicated. Men are bound to organizations by promises of values fulfilled and of friendship and prestige, as well as by monetary contracts for the exchange of goods and services.

To say that this analysis is guided by the major political and economic factors in an organization does not rule out attention to many traditional concerns of the sociology of organization; professions and professional socialization, role relations and role conflict and even the "fit" between personality and role can be included. Basing this analysis on political economy, however, suggests that these more traditional concerns must be subordinated and intermeshed with a dominant concern for the political economy. For me the attitudes and values of professional staff are not important as indicators of satisfaction or morale or even as a reflection of organizational ideology: they are important only as they articulate with the process of goal and direction formation. In a sense, then, the political-economy approach abstracts for analysis two key sectors of a social system. Processes of socialization and pattern maintenance are not dismissed but are treated only as they affect the political economy.

Although the general thrust of this approach has been stated, its major components have not been indicated. Because the political concepts applied to nation-states are more closely analogous to internal organizational analysis than are economic concepts, analysis of the YMCA's polity will be somewhat more theoretically vigorous than will the analysis of the economy.

Economy. Analysis of an organization's economy divides neatly into the relations with the economic environment (demands for service,

31. The range of alternative structures for registering choices regarding the allocation of goods and services is discussed by Robert A. Dahl and Charles E. Lindblom, *Politics, Economics and Welfare: Planning and Politico-Economic Systems Resolved into Their Basic Social Processes* (New York: Harper & Bros., 1953).

32. *The Functions of the Executive*, pp. 143–81.

33. James Q. Wilson and Peter B. Clark, "Incentive Systems: A Theory of Organizations," *Administrative Science Quarterly* 6 (1961): 129–66. See also J. Q. Wilson, "The Economy of Patronage," *Journal of Political Economy* 69 (1961): 369–80.

prices of labor and other input factors, structure of supply, etc.) and internal economy (internal division of labor relative to technology, product, and geographic market, rules governing the allocation of resources, etc.). Analysis of the economic environment for an organization such as the YMCA is more complicated than similar analysis for either a business corporation or an out-and-out welfare organization. The YMCA's economy combines elements of both. First, like a business, it offers for sale services on which it hopes to make a profit (albeit a discreet one). Second, some programs are expected at minimum to carry their own weight. Third, some programs are subsidized with profits from other programs and with contributions from board members, the Community Fund, and public fund-raising drives. Even a subsidized program is not a straight charitable or welfare financial arrangement since the direct consumer is normally expected to pay part of the cost. Thus the organization's ability to finance itself is conditioned not only by its ability to sell services but also by its ability to convince contributors that its services are worthwhile. It must convince contributors that its services are better than, or different from, similar offerings of other organizations. Furthermore, its ability to sell one kind of program may directly affect some other program. To give but one example, if the organization appeals to philanthropic foundations and contributors on the basis of service to delinquent gangs in the neighborhood of one of its branches, the offering of that service may affect income from residents and health clubs, for "normals" may prefer to avoid contact with delinquents.

The YMCA must also compete in labor markets for professional, clerical, and service personnel (maids, cafeteria workers, maintenance people). Nonprofessionals are recruited from the local labor market of unskilled and semiskilled workers. Professional personnel are recruited from a complex arena consisting of the professional staff of other cities, college graduates interested in "service" and agencies of the physical education type, and those specifically motivated by the religious and social appeals of the YMCA. The organization also must compete with other service organizations for the time of volunteers and board members. Sources of income and personnel, and their distribution, represent some of the organization's historic commitments to specific types of programs and groups. To understand the directions of change is to understand these commitments and how they are changing.

The internal economy is concerned with accounting for and allocating funds, personnel, and facilities within the organization. And it is concerned with the coordination and distribution of program skills and services to meet the requirements of technology and task definition as well as the demands of the market.[34] The internal economy processes money received from consumers and contributors and presents to employees models of right behavior (that is, models of behavior meriting a reward from the organization). Who gets what, how, and when are political, as well as economic, questions.

The Chicago YMCA's Metropolitan Association includes thirty-seven local operating departments with claims on the dollar; the Association employs a central staff which maintains accounting records, manages the endowment funds, loans money to departments in debt, and has legal responsibility for the disbursement of funds. If allocations were made solely on the basis of earning power, rich departments would get richer and poor, poorer—with the poor, clearly, eventually being eliminated. Given the organization's mission, earning power is only one criterion for disbursements.

In addition to an internal economy of money, there is also an internal labor market, a system of personnel allocation. The distribution of personnel and the career lines within the organization both reflect goals and influence the formation of goals; decisions affecting personnel are linked to the internal prestige system. The structure of the polity is important to the internal labor market, for the person who controls personnel decisions controls the allocation of a scarce resource of the organization.

Polity. I have suggested that the economy interacts with the polity in shaping organizational direction. The polity is the total system of an organization's influence or power; it includes both the institutionalized and authoritative patterns of decision control as well as the less regular (and even "illegitimate") but systematic, influence processes. Analysis of polity focuses on the purposes behind decisions, the channels through which influence is exerted, the characteristics of influence holders, and the forces affecting changes in all three.

The examination of polities requires two essential, interrelated analyses, one of "constitution" and the other of an organization's power systems. An organization's constitution is its fundamental normative structure. The constitution of an organization—or, for that matter, of any enduring social system—is a set of agreements and understandings which

34. The division of labor in an organization such as the YMCA is relatively simple. (For instance, in comparison with an organization like General Motors, its list of job titles is relatively short.) Thus analysis of the internal economy of the YMCA need not focus extensively on technology, division of labor, and related factors which generate power and control distributions.

define the limits and goals of the collectivity as well as the responsibilities and rights of participants standing in different relations to the organization. The term *constitution* is often used both in a narrower and in a broader sense than I am using it here. Narrowly, it refers to a more specific, usually written, set of agreements on the structure and rights of parties. More broadly, the constitution sometimes refers to a total pattern of organization and the relationship among its parts.[35] In the sense in which I am using it, the constitution of an organization is more limited than the pattern of social organization, since it refers to a conceptually defined normative order; the pattern of social organization contains elements which are neither normative nor conceptually defined. By constitution I refer to a historic and conceptually defined normative order.[36]

I consider the power system the actual means by which decisions are influenced. There need not be much difference between the constitution and the actual power system, but it is a fundamental postulate of sociology and political science that, in a changing society, there is likely to be a continuous state of tension and adjustment between them. An organization's constitution defines both the constraints on and opportunities for the exercise of power.

What is meant by the actual power system? The use of the term *polity* here indicates that we wish to include more than simply those who formally or informally make decisions that are implemented in the organization. In its most inclusive form, polity refers to the whole web of groups and individuals that possess resources to sanction decisions. This is an excessively inclusive definition, since every potential member deciding whether or not to join becomes a power wielder and thus part of the polity (just as, with business corporations, each potential or actual stockholder's deciding to buy or sell his stock certificate could be con-

35. E. Wright Bakke's concept of an "organizational charter" is somewhat similar to that used in this study although it focuses less explicitly on political process. See his "Concept of the Social Organization," in *Modern Organization Theory,* ed. Maison Haire (New York: John Wiley & Sons, 1959), pp. 16–75.

36. The notion of constitution used here is broader than that used by Arthur Stinchcombe in "The Sociology of Organization and the Theory of the Firm," *Pacific Sociological Review* 3 (1960): 75–82. He writes, "By an 'organizational constitution' I mean a stable and legitimate distribution of power and responsibilities of people and sub-units in the determination of organizational policy. Within an organization this constitution, like the constitution of a state, determines the form of political life." My notion is broader than this, since, as here conceived, constitutional norms also specify collective ends.

sidered a power wielder). Following the usage current in political science, I use the term to refer only to those groups or positions having an active and somewhat organized influence on the process of decison making. Certainly upper-level staff are included within the boundary of a polity. Also included would be groups holding major sanctions, such as unions or professional associations. The boundary blurs as we approach the individual voter (that is, one who registers preferences relatively passively and without direct interaction with decision makers), but interest groups which speak for an articulate mass interest are certainly part of the polity. Similarly, within organizations individual workers become important to the political process as their interests aggregate to affect decisions.

Although discussed only briefly in this study, there also exists an external political aspect to organizations. Organizations have various alliances with, and commitments to, outside organizations, groups, and individuals which limit and shape (directly and indirectly) goals and policy choices. Furthermore, the normative order of the larger society and its institutions acts as a "cultural constitution," shaping and limiting internal behavior.

Our primary focus is upon the interplay of staff groups with boards and local branches with the Metropolitan office. Each group and unit controls resources relevant to operating decisions and operating effectiveness; each group has traditional rights and privileges which limit the ability of other parties to make decisions. The relationships among these groups and units have evolved as the organization confronted a changing environment and changed its goals.

As was noted earlier, variations in organizational rule are as great as, or greater than, variations in the forms of nations. Before the analysis of organizational polities can be complete, we must develop a framework which encompasses the broad variety of political structures and processes. For instance, we must analyze the political implications of succession and the rules governing succession, from crown prince systems to organizational coups d'état; we must study factions, coalitions, and social movements within organizations, as well as the development of quasi-judicial procedures for adjudicating claims of members and the structural and ideological conditions of organizations that call forth such systems. Since this study utilizes a political framework to analyze just one organization, propositions on the political economy of organizations in general are largely eschewed. But many of the succeeding chapters (especially those dealing with the Chicago Association) will describe the political-economic variation one might expect to find in broad comparative studies.

In this study the concepts of an organizational political economy serve as a broad framework to orient and guide rather than as a specific model to generate hypotheses.[37] As we trace the YMCA's change from a religious, evangelical agency to a broadly secular, social service agency, these "sensitizing" concepts guide our explanation of how the YMCA fits into a community niche—into a position in the welter of groups, individuals, and organizations making up the community—how it is controlled, and how it changes. A consistent focus on the political and economic aspects of the YMCA will yield an efficient and illuminating explanation of the organization and its change process. The explanation will be efficient in explaining parsimoniously the central features of the dynamics of organizational change; it will illuminate by exposing and exploring aspects of organizational life rarely treated in sociological works.

37. Since the framework developed after most of the data had been collected and because this study is essentially a historical case study, I have not attempted to elaborate general propositions systematically. Further, even my own framework has been but briefly elaborated. I have attempted to introduce only enough of the framework to guide the reader into the case materials on the YMCA. A prospectus for a more fully developed framework is given in the concluding chapter. At that point fairly general political-economic propositions are developed to account for the level and forms of organizational conflict found in the YMCA.

2
Growth and Change: Programs and Clientele

In the middle of the nineteenth century, the YMCA was a slender reed planted in the unstable ground of evangelical revivalism. It was to become a pervasive institution rooted in the diverse services it offered to a broad range of clientele.

The general proposition elaborated here and in the next chapter is that the YMCA attachment to revivalistic and other direct religious programs proved to be an unstable source of membership and financial support. Only as it provided a variety of general service activities—especially recreational facilities and inexpensive residence—was an adequate economic support base established. At the same time, a shift away from direct religious program was occurring in response to an increasingly secularized society.

The transformation of clientele also reflects the great transformation of the Association in the urban context. Urban society made available for organization many clientele groups aside from young men.

Further, the transformation of program and of clientele required a transformation in the internal division of labor and in organizational perspectives of the Association.

ORIGINS AND INITIAL SPREAD

The Young Men's Christian Association originated in 1844 with a few young men led by an eighteen-year-old who worked in a London draper's shop.[1] George Williams (later Sir George Williams) and his friends felt

1. The historical material is drawn primarily from three published works: C. Howard Hopkins, *History of the Y.M.C.A. in North America* (New York: Association Press, 1951); Owen E. Pence, *The Y.M.C.A. and Social Need: A Study of Institutional Adaptation* (New York: Association Press, 1939); and Luther L. Doggett, *History of the Young Men's Christian Association,* vol. 1, *The Founding of the Asso-*

that the young employees, living crowded together in the dormitory provided by the shop owners, lacked spiritual guidance and were thus prone to the temptations of the teeming city. A period of industrialization and commercial growth, this was also an era of vast, cityward migration and uprootedness. Most of the shopworkers were young men newly arrived in London. The Association's first programs, held in the dormitory after the shops had closed for the day, included Bible readings and prayer.

The program's enthusiastic reception prompted Williams and his coworkers to spread their idea to other shops. Recognizing their need for a central meeting place, they approached the owner of their draper's shop for aid. He and other businessmen provided the early capital to rent space for a meeting hall, a small tea shop, and a reading room. Lists of reputable boarding houses and job opportunities were kept and posted.

Some of the organization's initial concepts were crucial for later development. First, Williams, believing that clergymen had little influence on the young men, turned to indigenous lay leadership: the YMCA was to depend on young men to save and lead other young men into the paths of righteousness. Secondly, Williams and his friends did not wish to form a new denomination or to choose among the old; they intended only an association which would serve all Protestants. By providing constructive fellowship as well as direct religious teaching, they felt they could be most effective in leading young men to a more Christian way of life.

This early ecumenism and the emphasis on a passive, or at least background, role for the clergy constituted an early polity commitment crucial for understanding later developments. It dictated a minimizing of theological and ritual concerns in the Association's life. It also prevented any single denomination from dominating the Association and determining its directions.[2]

Their emphasis on association and fellowship was also crucial, for while Christian righteousness and morality would always constitute ultimate goals, the key to their attainment was not participation in church activities but rather association with wholesome young men. Wholesome activity could be redefined for each generation; furthermore, wholesome

---

ciation, 1844–1855 (New York: International Committee of Young Men's Christian Association, 1896).

2. The interdenominational orientation was not original with the YMCA; all of the major American Protestant benevolent associations founded during the 1820s and modeled after the English benevolent societies were interdenominational. See Gilbert H. Barnes, *The Anti-Slavery Impulse, 1830–1844* (New York: D. Appleton-Century, 1933), pp. 17–18.

activities and relations could substitute for religious participation itself. The organization's indirect associational techniques encouraged the early development not of facilities for direct religious activities (that is, chapels) but rather of general facilities designed to permit a myriad of casual activities.

The first YMCAs were clearly commercially based. Membership was recruited from among clerks, and the businessmen who supported the organization were overwhelmingly from commercial firms.[3] Both clientele and supporting groups were classbound.

Although certain categories of men were denied voting privileges in the YMCA (namely, those not converted to an evangelical denomination), any man could become a nonvoting member and use its services. This lack of exclusiveness, part of the organization's constitution, is important for the American case because it favored the YMCA's later receptivity to women and to other age groups. The organization was not formed either to preserve male prerogatives or to foster an exclusive set of young men's activities; such an exclusionism would have made more difficult or even prohibited many later changes.[4]

I have mentioned several aspects of the early organizational structure and operation which helped to shape later operation. Before discussing the American YMCA's growth, I must also discuss an essentially environmental factor important to the Association's early growth. The impetus for the YMCA's formation arose not only from a perception of young men's needs but also from the sense of a growing return to religion. The 1840s constituted a period of religious revival which was in part a reaction to the disorganization attendant upon urbanization and industrialization.[5]

3. Both Doggett and Galen Fisher argue that the YMCA grew out of the low church dissension and was directed almost exclusively at the middle class. See Doggett, pp. 21–22; Galen Fisher, *Public Affairs and the YMCA: 1844–1944, with Special Reference to the United States* (New York: Association Press, 1948), p. 24. Both the Chartist and Christian Socialist movements bypassed the YMCA. That the working class was not involved in the English YMCA can be documented by citing a negative case: there is not a single reference to the YMCA in K. S. Inglis's definitive work, *Churches and the Working Class in Victorian England* (Toronto: University of Toronto Press, 1963).

4. The lack of exclusiveness may be overstated. Services to females and to others than young men were hotly debated at different points in the YMCA's history. The Association remained largely for males.

5. Reinhard Bendix, *Work and Authority in Industry* (New York: John Wiley & Sons, 1956); chapter 2 deals with Britain. For America, see William Warren Sweet, *Revivalism in America: Its Origin, Growth, and Decline* (New York: Charles Scribner's Sons, 1944).

The timing of the Association's formation gained it the support not only of those served (the young draper's clerks) but also of those ready to perceive it as part of the broader revival movement; in other words, a support base was easily mobilized out of society's general readiness to support evangelical movements.[6] In economic terms, there was increased demand for the programs of evangelical and revivalistic organizations. The concept of religious associations for young men was not in itself new; Cotton Mather recorded his membership in such a group in 1716,[7] and David Nasmith (founder of the London Missionary Society) founded similar organizations in the early 1830s in both England and the United States.[8] Many of the earlier organizations had died away, however, or later merged into the YMCA, which thrived in the seedbed of revivalism.

This brief discussion of the YMCA's origins provides the background for analyzing the growth and change of the YMCA in the United States. Although differences existed between the English and the American YMCAs even during the earliest period, the fundamental similarities are nevertheless strong.

GROWTH IN THE UNITED STATES

The conditions in the United States which favored the growth of the YMCA in many respects paralleled those in England. Growing urbanization and uprootedness characterized the population. In both cases the Protestant denominations were often in conflict with each other. In both cases the societal environment encouraged associationalism.[9] At the same time there were important differences; the American movement grew more rapidly and wandered farther from its religious course.[10]

The first American YMCA was founded in a characteristic fashion. A letter from an American college student visiting in England appeared in a Baptist weekly published in Boston (*The Christian Watchman and Re-*

6. Mayer N. Zald and Roberta Ash, "Social Movement Organizations: Growth, Decay, and Change," *Social Forces* 44 (1966): 327–41.

7. Clarence P. Shedd, *Two Centuries of Student Christian Movements* (New York: Association Press, 1934), p. 2.

8. Richard C. Morse, *History of the North American Young Men's Christian Association* (New York: Association Press, 1913), pp. 2, 11.

9. Not all societies do. See Arnold Rose, *Theory and Method in Social Science* (Minneapolis: University of Minnesota Press, 1954), chap. 4, "Voluntary Associations." See also Edward Banfield, *The Moral Basis of a Backward Society* (Glencoe, Ill.: Free Press, 1958).

10. Doggett, pp. 171–72.

flector for 30 October 1851).[11] This letter praised the work and described the organization of the London YMCA. A retired sea captain,
long committed to aiding young men, read the letter and concluded that
such an organization could meet the needs of young men in the rapidly
growing and somewhat disorganized Boston area. Captain Sullivan was
subsequently instrumental in founding two Boston YMCAs. During the
same time and through a similar process, a YMCA was founded in Montreal. In other cities similar organizations—with different names and
often with no knowledge of the London YMCAs—were being founded.
The programs of these groups were often identical with those of the London and Boston YMCAs, even when their members had no knowledge of
the YMCA.

It is virtually impossible to know why so many organizations affiliated
with the YMCA when other organizations disappeared. In some cases,
members may have learned of the YMCA through the Boston Association's initial mailing of ten thousand copies of its constitution to people
in other cities and towns. The Boston constitution was directly modeled
on that of the London organization.

This mailing had a wider effect than simply to bring prominence to the
YMCA. First, certain provisions of the constitution solved organizational
problems that may have plagued many of the other young men's organizations. For example, provision for interdenominational representation
defined the YMCA's relation to denominations. Second, the Boston
YMCA's program clearly served the needs of a widespread clientele
group.

Although some of these factors were crucial, it is equally important
that the YMCA appeared at precisely the most propitious time for rapid
growth. As we have seen, associations for young, religiously oriented men
were not at all new, but the rapid urbanization of these decades favored
an associational ferment. In addition to the YMCA, many other benevolent societies were formed during the period 1830–60.[12] By 1856 there
were fifty-six organizations in America directly modeled on the London
Association.

11. William B. Whiteside, *The Boston Y.M.C.A. and Community Need* (New
York: Association Press, 1951), p. 17.

12. See Sweet, pp. 159–60. Because so many associations for young men were
founded separately and later merged into the YMCA, the question of priority and
"birthdate" had long troubled the Association. At the 1904 world conference, a
document was issued stating that the London Association was the alma mater of
all others, and the date of its founding, 1844, should be considered as the average
for the foundation of the Association (Hopkins, p. 21).

Membership and Chartered Associations

The growth of the American YMCA must be measured along several dimensions—the number of Associations, the number of members, the growth of facilities, and the growth of professional and nonprofessional staff. Furthermore, especially in its earliest stages, the organization's relative stability must be examined.

The two most graphic indicators of the American Association's growth are the number of Associations and the number of members at different points in time. Table 1 presents data on these items as listed with the national office of the YMCA.

The overall picture (with some exceptions) is of continuing growth, from 2 Associations in 1851, to 1,476 at the turn of the century, to 1,819 in 1962. Membership figures show a similar, rapid growth. More interesting for our purposes is the decade-to-decade variation in the organization's growth. In particular, the earliest period was one of rapid growth and marked instability. During the years of the panic, 1857–58, and the accompanying revival, many new Associations were formed, with the result that the 1857 national convention listed 98 Associations.[13] The Associations of this early period were very unstable, however, and Hopkins asserts that only 3 of 30-odd southern Associations continued to operate throughout the war, and of the northern Associations, only about one-fourth were still operating at the war's close.[14] Even after the war, many existed on flimsy foundations. Pence sampled the *Yearbook* listings for 1860, 1870, 1880, and 1890 and found that well over 40 percent of those sampled were not listed at the beginning of the following decade.[15] Since many Associations would have begun and completed their life cycles wholly within a ten-year period, his figure most probably underestimates turnover.

After the Civil War there was an immediate upsurge in Association activity. The more than 700 Associations existing in 1871 had increased to more than 1,200 in 1878. After this point the actual number of Associations declined slightly, not passing the 1878 mark until 1889.

Growth in membership has clearly outstripped the general population growth from the beginning. This was true even after the YMCA had become firmly established during the last decades of the nineteenth century:

13. Hopkins, pp. 81–84.

14. Because of this instability the data in table 1 for the earliest years must be taken as estimates. Ibid., p. 98.

15. Pence, p. 48.

from 1940 to 1957, for example, YMCA membership increased by 92 percent while general United States population increased only 23 percent. Traditionally, of course, the YMCA has been located in the areas of largest growth—metropolitan areas—but its growth has also been favorably affected by its changing program, which (as will be shown) has brought about a substantial shift in the organization's clientele.

By the beginning of World War I, YMCAs existed in almost all large cities. There were YMCAs in 94 percent of cities of fifty thousand or more inhabitants, 76 percent of cities of between twenty and fifty thou-

TABLE 1

GROWTH OF THE YMCA IN THE UNITED STATES

	Number of Associations	Number of Members	United States Population (in millions)
1851.........	2	....	24.1
1856........	56	....	28.2
1866........	90	15,498	36.5
1876........	982	84,392	46.1
1886........	1,066	132,803	57.9
1896........	1,448	263,298	70.9
1900........	1,476	268,477	76.1
1912........	2,421	597,857	95.3
1920........	2,194	868,892	104.3
1930........	....	1,034,109	123.1
1940........	1,292	1,323,076[a]	132.0
1950........	1,688	2,088,361	151.2
1957........	1,799	2,427,610	170.3
1962[b]......	1,819	2,885,766	185.7

SOURCES: Data for the period 1866–1900 are from Pence, p. 47; for the period 1912–62, from selected *Yearbooks* of the Young Men's Christian Association of North America (New York: Association Press).

NOTE: The data are subject to several sources of error. (1) Through 1930 they include information on Canada, inflating the numbers of Associations and of members by approximately 5 percent. (2) Until 1940 they do not include females, leading to an underestimation of membership. (3) The membership figures represent those on the rolls at the end of the year; members terminating during the year are not included. For instance, during 1956 there were 3,044,896 individuals who were members *at some time* during the year, a figure 30 percent higher than the numbers of individuals who were members at the end of the year. (4) The figures also do not include nonreporting Associations whose figures are unknown by other means (previous year reports). Historically, it has been the smaller Associations that did not report. In general there has been an increased rate of report filing as Associations developed permanent staff and achieved stability. (5) Overreporting would come from failure to eliminate terminated members from the rolls. My best estimate is that even in the latest years the figures presented in this table are on the low side.

[a] Includes number of women reported in 1941.

[b] 1962 is used as a cut-off date in these and later tables to carry the history to the midpoint of the field study.

sand, and 48 percent of cities of between ten and twenty thousand.[16] Even earlier, in the late 1880s, YMCAs had begun to spread within the larger cities as city Associations added branches and as new programs were defined.

Growth of Facilities

The expansion in membership and number of Associations was obviously accompanied by a growth in facilities. A new YMCA's first facilities were usually rented rooms above a store in a downtown location. Usually these rooms functioned as a reading room, two offices, an auditorium, and classrooms for Bible study. Since evangelism was the major work of early YMCAs, the physical facilities could not totally encompass YMCA activities. Members were often on the streets distributing religious tracts or holding tent revivals. (An early publication of the YMCA Central Committee, the forerunner of the National Council, contains directions for holding tent revivals and gives the prices of tents of various sizes.)

After the Civil War, YMCAs began to build their own facilities. In 1867 only one Association owned a building. During the following decade 14 buildings were constructed, and from 1877 to 1886, 33. The decade 1887–96 saw even more expansion; 159 buildings were erected. By 1900, 359 buildings were YMCA-owned.[17]

The first buildings included stores on the ground floor to provide rental income, but they lacked dormitories. Dormitory space for about fifty young men had been planned for the first Chicago YMCA building in 1867; it burned down, however, and the smaller building which replaced it did not include a dormitory. In the 1870s, following the New York YMCA's example, new city buildings increasingly included dormitories rather than stores. Dormitories provided a substitute means for raising income more compatible with organizational goals and constituting norms. Around 1900, dormitories became the rule for new buildings, and stores were no longer included.

Gymnasiums were another characteristic aspect of early YMCA facilities. Even when a YMCA did not own its own building, it became increasingly likely that it would include a gymnasium in its rented facilities. Table 2 presents data on the number of Associations reporting gymnasiums and physical directors. Before the Civil War, leaders of the YMCA, believing that lack of physical exercise was debilitating, had discussed the need for gymnasiums. But not until the late 1880s and 1890s did the

16. Ibid., p. 127.   17. Ibid., pp. 89, 92.

gymnasium and physical program become a dominant part of organizational growth. Many of these gymnasiums were simply large, rented rooms fitted with body-building equipment such as weights, pulleys, and rowing machines. That the gymnasium "took" during the decade 1886–96 is beyond dispute. Both the gymnasiums and the dormitories, which developed rapidly after 1900, represented major facilities and program commitments defining the niche that the YMCA came to hold. How these were assimilated to the organization's goals is discussed more fully later.

TABLE 2

ASSOCIATIONS REPORTING PHYSICAL WORK
1866 TO 1900

	Gymnasiums Reported	Physical Directors Reported
1066.........	0	0
1876.........	2	3
1886.........	101	35
1896.........	495	220
1900.........	507	272

SOURCE: Pence, p. 75.

The Growth of the Secretariat

The renting of rooms for meetings and for reading required the hiring of staff to supervise them. The first full-time employee was a librarian for the Boston YMCA. The first full-time *secretary,* a staff person responsible for supervising the total organization program, was hired by the Philadelphia YMCA in 1857.[18]

The first secretaries were usually young men with no special religious or professional training; often they were not high school graduates.[19]

18. The identity of the first secretary indicates exceptionally well the organization's base in commercial occupations and the YMCA's relationship to upward mobility in the commercial world. John Wanamaker served as secretary for three years, 1857 to 1860, before beginning a not unsuccessful business career. George Williams also became a very wealthy merchant.

19. See A. G. Knebel, *Four Decades with Men and Boys* (New York: Association Press, 1936), pp. 15–45, for an autobiographical description of the process of becoming a secretary. Knebel's case is typical. About 1882, at the age of fourteen, he began attending classes and activities at the YMCA while working as a store clerk in Waco, Texas. He would often spend four or five nights a week at the YMCA. The local secretary eventually asked if he wanted to become a YMCA secretary in

They were chosen for their devotion to the organization, their religious sincerity, and their interpersonal skills. At various times the requirements for certification as a YMCA secretary have been raised, first to two years of college, then to a college degree including thirty hours of specialized work relating to YMCA programs and history.[20]

Table 3 presents the number of secretaries for selected years. The mushrooming of professional personnel after 1890 can be attributed both

TABLE 3

NUMBER OF SECRETARIES
SELECTED YEARS

Year	Number of Secretaries
1873	53
1880	178
1890	977
1900	1,399
1913	3,853
1919	5,076
1920	4,500
1928	5,475
1930	4,610
1935	3,332
1940	3,779
1950	3,741
1956	3,776
1962	3,863

SOURCES: For 1873–1900, Pence, p. 95; for 1913–62, *Yearbooks*.

to the growth of the city Association and to the rise of the foreign mission and student movements. World War I gave even greater impetus to personnel growth as the YMCA became heavily involved in providing services to the armed forces. After World War I many of the additional personnel were retained in the expanding student and city Associations. The depression, however, cut sharply into the YMCA's ability to support salaried personnel, and from a high of over five thousand secretaries in

Corsicana, Texas. Knebel was, at that time, being given increasing job responsibility by his employer, a local hard-goods merchant. After much self-debate Knebel took the job and, with only a short apprenticeship at the Waco YMCA, became the secretary in Corsicana.

20. For a history of the secretaryship see Hopkins, pp. 148–78, 505–624. See also Pence, pp. 93–101.

1928 the YMCA by the end of 1934 had lost over 40 percent. Since that time the number of full-time professional staff employed has stabilized at slightly below four thousand despite the Association's continued growth. (This point will be discussed more fully below.)

It is clear that the rapid increase in professional staff after 1900 grew not from the continual spread of professional managers to all Associations but rather from the proliferation of subspecialties. There was actually a decline in the number of *general* secretaries (a general secretary is the chief professional of a single Association) between 1893 and 1900, although simultaneously the total number of secretaries became greater. The decline in the number of general secretaries is explained in part by the fact that in 1891 the national organization determined that it would henceforth recognize only one Association in each city. The effect of this decision was that, although a metropolitan-area YMCA previously unaffiliated with the others in its area could remain autonomous, no new YMCAs within a city would be recognized and suburban associations were encouraged to affiliate with the large city associations. Furthermore, many small town and rural county Associations were having difficulty existing at all.[21]

By way of contrast, between 1873 and 1900 the listing of types of secretaries grew from one to over twenty. The types of work were sometimes classified by skill (such as superintendent or secretary of gymnasium work or boys' work) and sometimes by agency classification (such as Army and Navy secretary or railroad secretary). Clearly a diversified organization had developed.

Interestingly, up to 1900 no separate record was kept of the number of religious secretaries, since everyone was assumed to be a religious worker. As the YMCA developed a functional structure with more specializations, however, religious work became a separate department within the organization. In 1904 twenty-five religious workers or directors were listed, and by 1914, seventy-eight. About the time of the depression, the YMCA began to reorganize along age-sex lines (work with boys, with women and girls, and so on). Both the reorganization and the depression issued in the termination of separate religious-work departments. By 1940 the number of direct religious programs was much smaller than in 1900. (The number listed as attending Bible classes was roughly the same, but many other religious programs had disappeared in spite of the organization's five-fold increase in membership.)

21. Pence, p. 94.

Although the number of YMCA secretaries has tended to remain the same in spite of continuing growth in membership, the ratio of staff to members has not dropped. The organization has compensated by increasing its use of part-time workers and specialists. Certainly college students are less expensive group leaders than full-time employees. Further, the growth of an enrollment economy focusing on specific activities rather than on generalized participation demands the utilization of specialists to

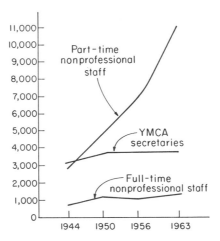

Fig. 1. Personnel trends in the American YMCA. "Nonprofessional staff" refers to personnel holding program or administrative jobs; not included are service and maintenance personnel such as office help, maids, cafeteria workers, and maintenance men. This figure, an extension of one published in Richard E. Hamlin's *A New Look at Physical Education* (New York: Association Press, 1959), p. 41, is based on data drawn from *Yearbooks* for the appropriate years. Earlier information on nonprofessional personnel is not available.

guide these activities. The effect of this enrollment economy on personnel related to program can be seen in figure 1, which shows dramatically the rapid growth of part-time personnel.

Although the YMCA has increasingly used paid leaders and teachers for specific activities, it also has continued to use large numbers of volunteers. Some relevant trends may be seen in table 4, which gives the numbers and percentages of different types of leaders for selected years. The most interesting column is the last one. The highest rate of growth is in the paid leader category, which shows a 300 percent increase.

If paid leaders and volunteers supervised similar numbers of groups, the trend shown in table 4 might not have great import, for the differences in growth rates are not large. But paid leaders, teachers, and YMCA staff supervise, on the average, many more groups than do volunteers. Indeed, when a group is led by its own officer, two or more officers often are listed as leaders. The data given in table 5 are relevant.

It is quite apparent that paid personnel supervise more groups per person than unpaid volunteers. Thus the trends shown in figure 1 and table 4 also mean that a larger proportion of YMCA groups are led by paid leaders. These trends indicate not only the growth of an enrollment econ-

TABLE 4

LEADERSHIP OF GROUPS, SELECTED YEARS

GROUP LEADER	1950		1955		1962		1962 AS PER-CENT OF 1950
	Number of Leaders	Per-cent	Number of Leaders	Per-cent	Number of Leaders	Per-cent	
Group's own officer..........	35,703	44.2	65,744	45.2	95,296	43.8	267
Adult volunteer....	31,263	38.7	59,910	41.2	87,253	40.1	279
Paid leader........	7,390	9.2	12,558	8.6	22,266	10.2	301
Teacher...........	2,463	3.1	2,479	1.7	6,438	3.0	261
YMCA staff member[a]	3,834	4.8	4,747	3.3	6,431	2.9	168
Total..........	80,653	100.0	145,438	100.0	217,684	100.0	270

SOURCES: Data for 1950 and 1962, *Yearbook, 1963*, p. 44; data for 1955, *Yearbook, 1956*, p. 35.
[a] Includes secretaries, junior secretaries, and full-time program and administrative staff.

TABLE 5

TYPES OF LEADERS AND NUMBER OF GROUPS LED, 1955

Group Leader	Number of Leaders	Percent	Groups	Percent	Number of Groups per Leader
Group's own officer......	65,744	45.2	45,709	25.1	.695
Adult volunteer.........	59,910	41.2	56,081	30.9	.936
Paid leader.............	12,558	8.6	33,895	18.6	2.699
Teacher...............	2,479	1.7	5,200	2.9	2.097
YMCA staff member[a] ...	4,747	3.3	40,949	22.5	8.625
Total	145,438	100.0	181,334	100.0	

SOURCE: The *Yearbook, 1956*, p. 45.
[a] Includes secretaries, junior secretaries, and full-time program and administrative staff.

omy, but the slow transformation of the YMCA from an association of members to a payment-based service organization. Furthermore, as more and more part-time paid leaders and other personnel are used, the distinctively Christian image of the Association is bound to decline, for these part-time staff are more heterogeneous in background and less socialized to the YMCA outlook. (Of course, the two volunteer categories start from a much larger base.)

THE CHANGING CLIENTELE

In discussing the YMCA's growth, I have largely avoided discussing the transformation of its goals. This topic must be of central concern, however, as we consider clientele change and internal conflict. Here clientele changes are discussed as they relate to social class and to age-sex composition.

Although it is clear that the YMCA was begun by members of the white-collar and commercial occupations for work among their own kind, formal YMCA constitutions did not generally specify the social class of their constituencies. Montreal's written constitution, paraphrasing the London constitution, stated that the Association's object should be the improvement of young men's conditions

> especially in connection with the study of the scripture—the union of young men, of various churches, in this and other plans of usefulness—and the providing of means by which young men, coming as strangers into the city, *may be brought under religious influence among their own class.*[22]

The written constitutions adopted by early American Associations, however, did not contain this class exclusion.[23]

In the United States the initial focus on the middle and lower middle classes was modified in several directions. Although its membership might consist primarily of men drawn from the white-collar classes, its emphasis on revivalism and evangelism nevertheless involved the YMCA with all classes. Before 1890, Associations participated heavily in welfare and relief activities, often serving to coordinate work with the needy. Furthermore, the YMCA's evangelistic activities inevitably issued in lower-class contacts (for example, pairs of young men would visit jailhouses to evangelize the prisoners).

22. Italics mine.   23. Hopkins, p. 18.

As long as the organization focused on evangelical and welfare-type activities, it could claim a mission to all classes of men. With the decline of active evangelism in favor of Bible study and general character-development programs, however, the Association found itself confronting the difficulties of mixing socioeconomic groups. These difficulties were intensified by a basic change in general society. Whereas, in the past, Protestant laymen had sought to assimilate the lower classes to their own norms, after the 1870s, the difficulties in assimilating immigrants had begun to overwhelm the dominant Protestant groups who reacted with a self-protecting retreat.[24]

TABLE 6

OCCUPATIONAL DISTRIBUTION OF YMCA MEMBERS, CIRCA 1900
(Percent)

	Brooklyn	Hartford	Chicago
Laborer (unskilled)	3	. . . .	2
Mechanic (skilled laborer)	19	34	10
Student	10	21	6
Clerk	57	33	50
Merchant	7	. . . .	. . . .
Manager	15	. . . .	. . . .
Professional	4	. . . .	9
Miscellaneous	. . . .	12	8

SOURCE: Hopkins, p. 239.

By 1890 local YMCAs were quite consciously directing their programs at "preoccupying and preventive work among the better classes."[25] Secretaries and laymen alike decried the absence of the lower classes in the YMCA's ranks; in only a few cases, however, such as the railroad YMCAs, which were paid for by the companies, and other YMCAs serving special industrial groups, did Associations actually tailor their program for work among blue-collar groups.

Unfortunately, there appear to be no systematic studies of Associations' memberships before the 1890s. Table 6 presents the occupational distribution, around 1900, of members of the Brooklyn YMCA, the Hartford YMCA, and the Chicago Central YMCA. Skilled labor was

24. Joseph Gusfield, *Symbolic Crusade: Status Politics and the Temperance Movement* (Urbana: University of Illinois Press, 1964).

25. Hopkins, pp. 194, 202; Pence, p. 68.

strongly represented in the Hartford YMCA but other working-class occupations were not. The Brooklyn YMCA included only a very small percentage of either skilled or unskilled laborers. The Central YMCA probably cannot be considered typical of Chicago YMCAs at the time. Regarding national occupational distribution the 1910 *Yearbook* notes:

> We have a growing but limited contact with working men. Today more than one-third of our members are industrial workers—yet this is less than two per cent of the workers between 16 and 44 years of age in the United States and Canada. The masses of these workers are in the great industrial cities where the strongest Associations are found. But in the same cities, only 20 per cent of the membership is drawn from the industrial workers who form 75 per cent of the population. In other words, we get four-fifths of our membership from one-fourth of the constituency.[26]

The figures show that industrial occupations accounted for a larger proportion of the total national membership than of the city membership; this was due to the existence of the railroad YMCAs, which though located mainly in cities, were not considered part of the cities' Associations. The pattern shown in table 6 was if anything accentuated in later years. In 1920 it was claimed that 23 per cent of the total membership of the American Association was from industrial occupations, but by 1930 the figure had dropped to 12.6 percent.[27]

In 1947 a constituency study reported that craftsmen and foremen or their children constituted 16.3 percent of the YMCA membership, versus 18 percent in the occupational distribution of the society, while unskilled workers formed only 8.1 percent of the membership, versus 21.4 percent of the occupational distribution; nonfarm laborers constituted 1.8 percent of the membership versus 8.1 percent of the distribution.[28] In short, roughly twenty-six percent of the membership was drawn from the "working class."

These figures suggest that the YMCA has not altered significantly the socioeconomic composition of its membership. In economic depressions poorer members decline more rapidly than wealthier members as a proportion of the total. There are, of course, great variations among branches (departments), in their socioeconomic composition. A predominantly middle-class membership is maintained when a city has only one central department, or a central department and branches in middle-class areas.

26. P. 82.   27. Pence, pp. 151–52.   28. Hopkins, p. 724.

But a branch located in a formerly middle-class area that has become working-class or a branch located in a working-class environment tends to mirror its environment (with a slight upward drift). When branches have both residences and program facilities, there are both class and age differences between the residents and the program members.

More than class composition, the age and sex composition of the YMCA membership has altered radically, over the past half-century.

TABLE 7

AGE AND SEX COMPOSITION OF CITY YMCAS IN AMERICA

	Total	Under 12	12–17	18–29	30 and Up
		Males			
1900.........	268,477	11.0%[a]		89.0%[a]	
1912[b]........	597,101	23.0		77.0	
1919[b]........	739,438	24.6		75.4	
1930.........	1,034,109	8.0%	22.4%	46.3%	23.3%
1940.........	1,224,410	12.7	28.4	34.5	24.4
1950.........	1,840,273	19.1	26.0	28.0	26.9
1957.........	1,939,977	25.8	23.8	16.6	33.7
1962.........	2,187,646	26.6	23.2	15.2	35.0
		Females			
1941[c]........	98,666	13.5%	32.7%	29.7%	24.1%
1950.........	248,088	18.0	43.9	19.1	18.9
1957.........	487,833	22.1	40.9	15.8	21.2
1962.........	698,120	25.4	37.3	12.4	24.7

SOURCES: For the years 1930–57, Clifford M. Carey, *"Perspective for YMCA Growth in the 1960's"*; for other years, *Yearbooks.*
[a] Estimated.
[b] Data given for boys (below 18) and men only.
[c] No data prior to 1941.

Table 7 presents these shifts in age and sex composition. The first great transformation occurred with the shift to serving teen-agers and, later, youngsters under twelve and females of all ages.

Until 1900 less than 20 percent of the membership fell into the lower age groups. Both the growth and the great transformation of membership since the 1930s have resulted from the inclusion of females of all ages and of males over thirty and under twelve. As late as 1930 the YMCA still concentrated on its original clientele group; 46 percent of its members were between eighteen and twenty-nine years old. By 1957, however, the total number of young men in this category had dropped from over 460,000 to about 300,000—in spite of a 180 percent growth in membership overall.

Although the addition of boys to the membership began after the Civil War, work with them had actually been discussed before the war. The evangelistic emphasis seemed to preclude youth work, however, and it was rejected. Only after the war, when active evangelism had yielded to a combination of character building and religious development, did work with teen-agers begin. Even then this work was conceived as a prelude to working with them as young men. In 1901 the organization claimed 30,000 boys, chiefly from twelve to seventeen years old. By 1913 this figure jumped to 132,000, an increase of over 400 percent, and by 1920 the organization claimed approximately 200,000 members under eighteen. Programs for grade-school boys were initiated after World War I. By 1960 the proportion of members between eight and twelve years of age was larger than that for any other narrow age range.

Just as programs for teen-agers and grade-school boys were originally departures from the key clientele groups of the YMCA, so was work with women and girls. From the earliest days and until 1900, local Associations often had women's auxiliaries whose purpose was not to serve women but to aid the Association in its work.[29]

The women taught Bible classes, prepared baked goods for fund-raising affairs, organized relief work, assisted with tent revivals, and so on. Some local Associations admitted women to membership; the Scranton, Pennsylvania, YMCA, for example in the mid-1870s, claimed that one-third of its members were women. Furthermore, in the 1880s and 1890s, many city Associations initiated gym classes for women. Service to women was frowned upon by the International Committee, however, and national policy even stated that work with women was a departure from the organization's true purpose. Whether or not national policy hindered local Associations, many local Associations involved women either as members or in auxiliaries. A survey completed in 1930 reported that of 914 Associations reporting, 586 worked with women.[30] Finally, in 1934, with a change in national policy, a census was taken, and 275 Associations reported over 57,000 female members. Thenceforth, service to

29. Ibid., p. 241.

30. The survey was requested by the YWCA and conducted by Dr. John Shenton, according to a personal communication from Clifford Carey, 20 December 1967.

women expanded rapidly, and as Associations spread to the suburbs, they increasingly served both sexes and all ages.

To summarize, these data indicate that the YMCA has steadily increased the number of age groups served and the extent of female participation. Further, the increased participation of both women and older men has been accompanied by a decline in participation by the groups initially served. The membership of men from eighteen to thirty has substantially declined, and the twelve-to-seventeen-year-old group, which in the early 1900s was defined as a key group, has at best held its place as a proportion of total members. Read another way, these changes in membership composition represent shifts in the demand functions of different segments of the population for YMCA programs. Simultaneously, over its more than a century of operation, there has been a dramatic shift in the YMCA's fundamental program. The purpose of this study, ultimately, is to account for these shifts. As I shall try to show, they relate, in part, to some of the organization's fundamental financial difficulties.

THE TRANSFORMATION OF FINANCIAL SUPPORT

The growth and transformation of YMCA programs and membership has been accompanied by a transformation of the organization's sources of financial support. Indeed, the search for sources of financial support compatible with the organization's basic goals and constitution has, in turn, influenced the shape of that constitution.

During its formative years the YMCA sought funds and support in the same manner and from similar sources as Protestant churches. Members paid a fee, businessmen subscribed to sustaining memberships of larger amounts, and collections were taken at public affairs and various kinds of fund-raising events. These sources did not provide much financial stability, and since the YMCA received much of its early support from the devout, it was always in competition with the churches for money. Although the YMCA had had strong support from many Protestant denominations, these denominations may well have wondered whether money contributed to the YMCA might not be spent better by the church.[31]

Even more important, recruitment of members was sharply affected by the ebb and flow of revivalism and by the state of the business cycle. The YMCA was "selling" only the opportunity to participate in a noble enterprise, and members received few perquisites, services, or privileges for belonging.

---

31. Knebel, p. 50, writes of hearing a Sunday sermon in which the minister berated congregation members who gave to the YMCA rather than to the denomination.

One solution for many YMCAs was to promote a public, profit-making lecture series. The Star Lecture Series was very profitable to many Associations before the Civil War, but when the public lost interest, the YMCA discontinued the series.[32] In the late 1870s vocational courses offered a new means for attracting potential members. Young workers, both white- and blue-collar, could take courses that would advance them on the job. By 1900 there were 15 educational secretaries; by 1912, 142, and by 1919, 201. The YMCA began withdrawing from this function as public schools initiated their own night-school and adult work-study programs. In 1940 there were only 139 educational secretaries and by 1947, 82.

Over the long run, a more important factor in changing the YMCA's economy and polity was the development of the gymnasium. The case of the Dayton, Ohio, YMCA illustrates the gymnasium's importance in stabilizing finances and membership. The Dayton YMCA began in 1858 but went out of existence at the beginning of the Civil War. In 1870, a year of religious revival, it was started again. Frequently in financial straits, the operation often had to borrow money, and in 1878 the board of directors discussed closing again. The Star Lectures had raised some money, but the organization had few members (in 1871, sixty-nine young men; in 1872, forty-two; in 1874, only three; in 1885, around fifty). Certainly one difficulty was the lack of any incentive to induce a young man to buy a membership. The Association felt that membership should not convey special privileges; without special privileges, however, there was little motivation for joining. The point became moot in 1885 when the secretary of the Dayton YMCA recommended serving the physical needs of young men. Before remodeling Dayton's facilities into a gymnasium, he received pledges from three hundred young men to pay ten dollars each per year for the privilege of using it.[33] The gymnasium proved to be an excellent means of recruiting members.

The construction of residences also assisted in stabilizing income, but the gymnasiums and the residences have stood in different relationships to YMCA goals and program. The emphasis on physical recreation was considered ungodly by some, while its advocates viewed it as an essential tool in fulfilling the organization's purposes. On the other hand, the provision of clean and decent lodging for single men at less than current

32. Hopkins, p. 196.

33. *The Story of Twenty Years in the Life of the Young Men's Christian Association of Dayton, Ohio, 1870–1890* (Dayton, Ohio: YMCA of Dayton, 1890).

market prices[34] was seen as an acceptable part of the organizational mission. Indeed, in the rapidly growing cities, provision of decent housing was seen as a real benefit to young men who otherwise would have had to live in firetraps and unruly neighborhoods. The propriety of the YMCA's maintaining residences was questioned only by those who viewed them as tending toward development of a building and institutional philosophy and away from a more community-centered and/or evangelistic outlook. This issue, however, was never as sharply focused as that relating to physical recreation.

Regardless of the relation of residences and gymnasiums to the YMCA's basic conception of goals, their addition contributed to the development of a diversified economy for the organization. Economically, the YMCA was not a membership organization, since many nonmembers paid for services; nor was it a business organization, since contributions and membership fees constituted an important part of its finances. It was also not a welfare organization in the traditional sense, for it did not concentrate on the poor or deviant; users' fees represented a substantial part of the operational cost.

The YMCA's economic diversification, begun toward the end of the last century, has continued. For 1953, Carey listed the following distribution of income sources for all departments: dues, 12 percent; program fees, 12.6 percent; "club services" (including residence, food service, etc.), 43.7 percent; contributions, 21.8 percent; endowment income appropriated to operations, 2.2 percent; miscellaneous, 7.7 percent.[35] Almost half of the YMCA's 1955 income was drawn from business operations, slightly under a quarter from contributions and endowment income, and the remainder from membership dues and program fees.

There was wide variation in income sources among cities of different sizes. Smaller cities are considerably more dependent on contributions for

34. To minimize criticism from hotel owners, YMCA residences have generally provided ascetic facilities priced far below the respectable market. (They have competed with "flea traps," rather than middle-class establishments.) To maintain their attractiveness to customers, however, the standard of decency has shifted upward. The first residences were dormitories housing as many as sixty men in a large room. Narrow rooms lacking private baths and lavatories constituted the second phase. Only the most recent buildings have included private baths and lavatories. These changes have had their effects on architecture, including a progressive widening of the residence corridor.

35. Clifford M. Carey, *Current Income of City YMCA's: A Study of the Sources and Change in Income from 1932–1953* (New York: Research Studies and Records Department, National Council of the YMCA, 1955).

income and less dependent on business features. Indeed, many smaller communities have neither residences nor cafeterias. These differences between communities of different sizes are illustrated in table 8. While membership and program income constitute a slightly smaller portion of total income in the very largest cities, the major systematic difference in income source reflected in table 8 is the larger role of club service (business) income and the smaller role of contribution income in the larger as contrasted with the smaller cities. To cite just the extremes, for cities under 25,000 population, only 28.6 percent of income resulted from business operations; for cities over 500,000 population, 57.1 percent

TABLE 8

PROPORTIONATE SOURCES OF INCOME BY CITY SIZE, 1953
(Population in Thousands)

	Under 25	25–50	50–100	100–250	250–500	Over 500
Membership fees....	15.7%	17.3%	16.1%	16.1%	15.5%	10.9%
Program fees.......	10.6	11.9	12.2	15.7	8.9	7.6
Business...........	28.6	37.1	41.2	40.9	51.5	57.1
Contributions.......	38.6	26.9	21.6	20.4	16.8	12.3
Endowment........	1.4	1.6	1.6	.6	1.7	2.9
Other.............	5.1	5.2	7.3	6.3	5.6	9.2

SOURCE: Carey, *Current Income of City YMCA's: A Study of the Sources and Changes in Income from 1935–1953*, Research Studies and Records Department (New York: National Council of YMCA's, 1955), p. 17. Reprinted with permission.
NOTE: Based on stratified sample of "non-abnormal" cities.

(twice as much proportionally) was drawn from such features. The reverse holds for contribution income: for smaller cities contribution income represented 38.6 percent of total income, in contrast to the largest cities, where such income represented only 12.3 percent of the total. This difference in income dependency probably has a real influence on the internal decision processes and authority structure of Associations: clearly, an Association in a small community is more dependent on contributors' and board members' goodwill than is one in a large community. We would expect a board of directors responsible for raising much of an Association's income to have a greater say in organizational affairs than one responsible for raising a smaller proportion of income.

Although contribution income represents less than one-fourth of the total YMCA income, YMCAs have become increasingly dependent on one particular contributor, the Community Fund, or Community Chest. The YMCA did not welcome the growth of the Community Chest movement, with its emphasis on one large campaign and centralized allocation of funds. First, these drives utilized a technique which the YMCA had been the first to master—the quick, intensive campaign with organized prospect lists and competitive teams. Second, and more important, the YMCAs were uncertain about their share of the funds. On the one hand, most Chest agencies were secular, and the YMCA considered itself a distinctively religious organization; on the other, most of the early Chest agencies were poverty-relief and working-class organizations, whereas the YMCA's clientele lay elsewhere. But the pressures to join the Community Chest mounted, and a study done in 1927 demonstrated that those YMCAs belonging to the Chest were receiving more contribution income

TABLE 9

INCOME SOURCES OF CITY ASSOCIATIONS, 1926–62

	1926	1936	1946	1956	1962
Membership fees....	11.2%	13.9%	14.6%	15.3%	18.5%
Program fees.......	15.1	12.2	13.1	15.8	17.9
Business income....	42.3	45.1	46.8	38.0	32.0
Contributions......	22.5[a]	20.9	16.8[a]	21.5	21.5
Endowment........	2.0[a]	2.3	2.0[a]	2.5	2.8
Other.............	6.9	5.6	6.7	6.9	7.4

SOURCE: *Yearbooks* for appropriate years.
[a] Estimate: contributions and endowment income were reported together for these years.

than before they had joined.[36] (The report of the study does not indicate whether Chest YMCAs were matched with non-Chest YMCAs.) By 1940, 49.7 percent of contribution income was received through the Chest, and by 1950, with more cities engaging in Chest drives, 62.3 percent derived from this source. In 1953, 23.9 percent of *total* YMCA income was drawn from local Chests; the Community Chest quite clearly had become a new and potentially important wielder of influence over the YMCA.[37]

Although a larger proportion of contribution income has been coming from Chests, contribution income as a proportion of the whole has been stable. Table 9 presents sources of income for selected years since 1926. From 1926 to 1962 income categories have been fairly stable in their

36. See Hopkins, pp. 601–3.

37. Incidentally, although the Community Fund contribution to the Chicago Association is an important source of funds, it has not represented more than 5 per cent of current income in recent years.

proportional contribution to the whole. Business income has become a smaller proportion of the whole, and membership fees have become a larger proportion. In large measure, these shifts are related to suburbanization of the YMCA, because new branches in the suburbs have largely been built without cafeterias or hotels. Second, the increase in program fees reflects both the growth of segmental participation in the Association through classes and through such facilities as summer camps.

In a few words, then, the emergence and growth of the YMCA in America, and its adaptations might be summarized as follows. Originally developing within the tide of evangelical revivalism that swept the United States, the YMCA first attracted support as a result of its commitment to interdenominational Protestantism. Its broadly defined goals and loosely defined means permitted different staff members and laymen to interpret its mission variously. Consequently, it could leap into new endeavors consonant with those goals. When young men needed libraries, the YMCA provided them; as public libraries emerged, it dropped them. The same held true for the YMCA's provision of vocation and citizenship courses.

Over the years the YMCA has transformed itself from a religious and social-movement support economy (one offering potential supporters participation in a movement aimed at changing people or the world) to a mixed economy based mainly on services provided for a fee. Such an economy was conducive to a more stable organizational base and one fitted to a changing, urbanizing society. The city Associations found revivals an inadequate base, and the gymnasium and the dormitory gradually formed the basis of a building-centered program. The enrollment economy that eventually emerged tied the organization to clientele demands.

Such a summary, however, stressing as it does the role of economic factors, is obviously one-sided. It was an ongoing, essentially political, selective process that shaped the directions of change and dictated the alternatives foregone. To interpret the Association's history without reference to the political would be a gross distortion.

3
The Evolution of Organizational Polity

The great transformations in program and clientele described in the last chapter occurred in response to a changing society. The demands of the environment, however, were filtered through an organizational polity. *Some* demands were rejected by the organization. For example, although some pro-abolitionist local Associations applied pressure by threatening to withdraw from the national organization (as some eventually did), the YMCA as a whole took no stand on the abolition of slavery. Since that time the organization has continued to avoid embroilment in controversial issues. To understand the YMCA's gradual transformation into a general service organization, as well as the process by which some demands were rejected while others were embraced, we must examine some of the crucial aspects of its polity. By understanding polity as it evolved we can better understand the constraints on the directions of transformation.

Three aspects of polity were of particular importance in this regard. They can be stated in terms of organizational choices. The first choice concerned the basic definition of organization goals: Was the YMCA to be an association for evangelism, or was it to be an organization for Christian service to young men? The choice of the latter goal shaped the Association's development throughout the latter part of the nineteenth century. The second choice involved the relation of local YMCAs to one another and to the national organization: Were the Associations to be essentially autonomous but cooperative, or was the national organization to be a rule-making, governing body? The third choice delineated the professional staff member's relationship to the lay board member: Was control of the organization to remain in the hands of laymen, or was the professional staff to dominate as they began to operate a large and diverse enterprise?

The resolution of these three issues affected the basic structure of the polity and, therefore, the Association's response to its environment. Without attempting to reconstruct fully the history of a particular choice, I shall consider the issues as they arose within the organization, the way in which the issues were resolved, and some of the immediate consequences of the solutions.

FROM EVANGELISM TO GENERAL SERVICE

The choices that shape later development of an organization most profoundly are often those made during the period of formation—before institutional forms and commitments, which strongly limit freedom to select alternatives, have developed. The most crucial choice an organization can make—crucial in terms of defining its niche—is that of its basic work: Who are to be the target groups? What is to be done? What means are to be used? In brief, what are the organization's basic goals?[1]

Goals are not necessarily either explicit or recognized. Furthermore, an abstract statement of purposes may be only loosely linked to operating programs. Nevertheless, an organization's choices of target group, ends desired, and means for achievement are major components of organizational constitution and determine the basic character of the organization. These choices contribute to defining a network of the organization's relations to its environment, the organization's ability to motivate participation, and the frames of reference within which members in decision-making positions scan both the organization and the environment.[2]

Choices of goals are filtered through the components of the organizational social system. In the YMCA changing goal definitions were sometimes reflected in parliamentary debates and majority votes; at other times they were reflected in the career decisions of key personnel; at still other times they were reflected in building architecture. Since local Associations were usually autonomous, policies and recommendations of national conventions and of the national staff never fully determined local decisions. Goals were continually being developed in hundreds of communities as each local Association adapted to its particular niche. To an important extent the influence of national recommendations was always filtered by local perceptions and environmental conditions.

1. For a discussion of the ambiguity of conception of goals and the crucial role goals play in organization analysis, see Charles Perrow, "Organizational Goals," *International Encyclopedia of the Social Sciences* (1968). See also Mayer N. Zald, "Comparative Analysis of Organizational Goals: The Case of Correctional Institutions for Delinquents," *Sociological Quarterly* 4 (1963): 206–30.

2. James D. Thompson and William J. McEwen, "Organizational Goals and Environment: Goals Setting as an Interaction Process," *American Sociological Review* 23 (1958): 23–31.

A niche-shaping choice is a decision or line of action that determines an organization's basic relations to clients and supporters—what services it offers to what groups. The American YMCA's basic niche-shaping choice—the choice between general evangelism and Christian service to young men—was made early. It was crucial because it determined the organization's relation to the Protestant denominations that had given it much support, the organization's ability to find a stable continuing support base, and the direction of future goal modifications.

Although the YMCA had begun as a service to and by young men, as it spread across the United States it began to resemble an organization for general evangelism. Particularly in such western cities as Chicago, where denominational development was minimal and community flux substantial, the YMCA served as a center for general evangelism closely linked to religious revivals. Although service features were provided (for example, reading rooms and lists of boarding houses), its major effort was expended on distributing religious tracts and holding evangelistic meetings. This was a period of widespread lay evangelism and lay ministry, a period in which a preacher's sincerity and commitment were more important that his professional and theological training. Thus the Association's early structure, with its emphasis on lay participation, clearly blended well with the times. Indeed, before the Civil War the YMCA appeared to be shifting away from its specific concern with young men and toward becoming a general evangelical agency.

At the national convention in 1859, William C. Langdon, the president of the convening committee of the National Confederation, argued against the YMCA's becoming a general evangelical agency because (1) the YMCA would lose its distinctive missionary service to young men if it immersed itself in general evangelism, and (2) the churches would support a young men's organization but not an organization that was, in essence, competing with them for commitment and participation. The YMCA's rapid spread, however, was due to its participation in the general revival accompanying the panic of 1857 and 1858. Langdon offered resolutions that would have directed the YMCA away from general evangelism, but these were voted down by an overwhelming majority, and he subsequently resigned his post. So strong was the revival atmosphere at the convention that, in Hopkins's opinion, had appropriate leadership been available, a new Protestant denomination might have been formed on the spot.[3]

3. Hopkins, pp. 69–70.

Eastern as well as western YMCAs participated in the revivalist spirit. After the Civil War, however, the eastern Associations focused more on service to young men (erecting buildings and providing gymnasiums, etc.) than on evangelism to the whole community. The New York YMCA was one of the country's strongest, and the headquarters of the International Committee (the national executive committee for the confederation) was located in New York. Robert McBurney, the general secretary of the New York YMCA and the dominant figure in the nineteenth-century American YMCA, was committed to the concept that the YMCA should serve young men. His position gradually prevailed. The New York building included many meeting rooms, athletic facilities, and reading rooms, whereas Chicago's was dominated by a large hall for evangelistic meetings. As time passed, more and more Associations modeled their architecture on the New York rather than the Chicago design.

The changing state of the YMCA's general evangelistic work can be illustrated with brief sketches of two of its most active proponents. Dwight L. Moody, one of the most famous nineteenth-century evangelists, began his career as a religious worker when he became the Chicago YMCA's secretary. Convinced that the Association could not operate as a full-time, evangelical agency, he voluntarily resigned to become a full-time evangelist. Moody remained a friend of the Association and became president of the 1879 international convention. During that year, while answering questions at a meeting of secretaries about what YMCA functions might be most effective in reaching young men, Moody is quoted as having said,

> There are many ways of reaching young men; I would recommend a gymnasium, classes, medical lectures, social receptions, music, and all unobjectionable agencies; these are for week days. We do not want simply evangelistic meetings. I have tried that method in Association work and failed; so I gave it up and became an evangelist. You cannot do both and succeed.[4]

Moody seems to have said that the YMCA was not and could not be a church, a not uncontroversial opinion, since many local Associations considered themselves to be part of a new universal church. A flaming example of such sentiment is that of George S. Fisher, who went to Kansas in 1886 as state secretary. (State secretaries functioned to guide local Associations and develop new ones in communities that had none.)

4. Quoted in Morse, p. 123. Morse was not an unbiased recorder of Moody's words, since he strongly favored forgoing general evangelism.

Fisher was a powerful preacher, emotional and fundamentalist, and with the aid of extreme evangelical supporters, had soon transformed the Kansas YMCA. By 1889 Kansas had thirty-one general secretaries (as against nine when Fisher took office); the budget had risen from $4,400 to $15,000 and in 1888 there were 844 conversions as compared with roughly half that number the year prior to Fisher's arrival.

Although by 1889 the International Committee was on record as opposing general evangelism as a proper YMCA technique, there seemed to be little action the committee could take in the face of his evident success. Nor was there much pressure to remove him; certainly, by one definition of organizational goals, Fisher was accomplishing YMCA purposes. Pressure to remove Fisher began to mount, however, when it appeared he was threatening the Association's relationship with the Protestant denominations. In 1889 Fisher began recruiting missionaries for the Sudan. During the preceding decade, the YMCA had developed a pact with the major denominations' mission boards which provided that the YMCA would not engage in general evangelism (that is, it would work only with young men) and would enter foreign countries only by invitation of a denominational mission board. Fisher's independent actions were an obvious threat not only to the YMCA's relationship with the denominations but also to the YMCA's other foreign endeavors. Fisher continued his campaign despite considerable pressure against him. The Ministerial Association of Kansas threatened to boycott the YMCA, and a resolution condemning independent ministries was overwhelmingly passed at a national convention. Finally, in 1891 after great pressure from outside the YMCA and threatened with the loss of many large donors, Fisher resigned his position.[5]

Whereas Moody voluntarily resigned because he perceived the organization's proper focus as inimical to evangelism, Fisher was forced to resign because he insisted on an interpretation of the organizational mandate basically inimical to the organization's political and economic relationships with established denominations. Had the YMCA been a true sect, with its supporters isolated from denominational influence, Fisher's actions would not have threatened the Association's political and economic structure.

From the viewpoint of goal transformation, it is instructive to contrast the Fisher situation in 1891 with that of the 1859 international convention, where Langdon was forced to resign his post when he attempted to restrict YMCA's focus to serving young men. Although some Associa-

5. Fisher's history is related by Hopkins, pp. 350–54.

tions (as in Kansas) concentrated on general evangelism, most perceived their primary task as work with men under forty. This task and the YMCA's cooperative relationship with the denominations were framed in five principles (set forth in 1888 by McBurney as settled principles):

> First, the work shall be for young men and boys only. Second: The welfare of the whole man—body, soul and spirit—should be promoted by the energetic development of the physical, intellectual, social and spiritual departments of our work. Third: Points of doctrine controverted by evangelical Christians are to be avoided, and the simplicity of the gospel adhered to. Fourth: Churches to which our members belong have a prior claim on their sympathy and labors. Fifth: When questions of moral reform become political party questions, our Associations as such, can have no relation to them.[6]

The first and second points defined the organization's goals and target populations whereas the fourth point reassured the churches regarding the Association's Christian designs. Points three and five enabled the organization to maintain a continuing consensus when faced with denominational and ideological controversy. These points were also integral to the essential pragmatism which has always dominated the YMCA's world view. It is clear from the Kansas incident that if McBurney by *settled principle* assumed complete consensus, he was somewhat precipitous. Nevertheless, these principles received wide support in the Association's activities.

With the surrender of general evangelism as a major goal, the organization could maintain a less competitive relationship with the denominations. With its emphasis on fourfold works providing for the physical, social, mental, and spiritual welfare of youth as a guideline, the YMCA could accept and reject programs (in Moody's words, "all unobjectionable agencies") without being restricted to programs specifically religious in content. Furthermore, the focus on serving young men essentially bypassed social gospel concerns with changing society, centering instead on assimilating individuals into the ways of right living.

Giving up a mission of general evangelism, the YMCA still had to decide whether it was going to provide general services to all young men, or just those who were members of "acceptable" Protestant denominations.

For over sixty years (from the late 1860s through the 1930s), a perennially debated question at annual conventions was whether active (voting) membership was to be extended only to those belonging to evangeli-

6. Morse, p. 146.

cal denominations (the Evangelical Test, also known as the Portland basis) or, whether voting membership was to be open to anyone of sound moral character who subscribed to the general tenets of Christian ethics. A restriction to evangelical membership would exclude Jews, Roman Catholics, and other nonevangelicals. The definition of *evangelical* was also hotly debated.[7]

In 1869 the American Association had chosen to restrict active membership to those from evangelical churches, and although this was not made retroactive, no new charters were to be issued to Associations not using the Evangelical Test. Numerous factors were involved in this early decision. First, it was made during an era of doctrinal controversy among Protestant denominations; in particular, the orthodox denominations were hostile to the growth of Universalism and Unitarianism. The Boston YMCA, engaged in sharp competition with the Association organized by the Boston Unitarians, led the fight for orthodoxy and even threatened to withdraw from the national organization if the Evangelical Test were not maintained. Since the Boston Association was one of the strongest, its loss to the organization would have been crucial. A further threat, this to the earlier, English-based denominations, was posed by the Lutheran and Roman Catholic growth which accompanied increasing immigration. The adoption of the Evangelical Test assured the Protestant nature of the Association.

The consequence of this adoption was to solidify the link between the YMCA and the established Protestant denominations. It appears that local Associations rejecting the Evangelical Test were less likely to gain the wholehearted support of these denominations within their communities, and since these denominations were often the largest and wealthiest, their support could be crucial.

Use of the Evangelical Test for active membership also bound the board and staff somewhat more closely to religious definitions of program. Morse, for instance, argued that the movement was more likely to recruit secretaries from Associations using the test than from those not using it. (There are no adequate statistics bearing upon this assertion.)

Because the Evangelical Test focused on religious affiliation, however, it proved a barrier to the organization's attempts to reach the nonevangelicals and the unchurched. On the one hand, Catholics and Jews and, on

7. For a historical review of the "Evangelical Test" and the debate over it, see J. Quincy Ames, *The Evangelical Test: A Review of the History of an Important Policy of the Young Men's Christian Association in North America,* Monograph no. 1, The Changing Young Men's Christian Association Series (New York: Association Press, n.d.).

the other, unchurched working-class members were ineligible for full participation. By the turn of the century the Association had begun to reconsider the test and in 1931 finally repealed it. The "Paris basis" permitted anyone—including Jews, Buddhists, and Catholics—who agreed with the organization's general purpose to become a voting member. The repeal brought the YMCA's formal constitution into line with the actual operation of many local Associations that had long accepted memberships wherever they could recruit them, and within which voting rights had long since become unimportant. The repeal of the Evangelical Test and adoption of the Paris basis were thus a symbolic transformation rather than a change in operating procedure. To assert that the test and its repeal, however, were primarily symbolic is only to acknowledge the lack of an effective enforcement procedure. The test's existence certainly affected the Association's image within communities and the behavior of both members and others.

This broadening of goals and target groups (some might consider it a return to original goals) was basic to the organization's long-range adaptation. Fundamentally, it reflects an organizational consensus that emerged as individual Associations shaped their positions within communities, established relations with the major denominations, and related to each other and to the developing national bodies. Some sort of consensus on goals had to develop if the organization was to survive, for its basic structure permitted only a partial imposition of goals from a central authority.

FEDERATED NATIONAL POLITY

Emerging out of the Protestant denominations, with their emphasis on the community of believers, and diffusing through the brush fire of revivalism (yet lacking a central charismatic leader to impose his authority on local Associations), the YMCA as a national organization developed a federated polity.[8] The federated structure permitted maximum and continuous adaptation to local opportunities and pressures. Conversely, however, that structure permitted local and state Associations to ignore, with relative impunity, the judgments of national bodies.

This polity, which bound together local Associations, such as city, student, and railroad Associations, emerged and changed in response to

8. For one discussion of the difference between federated and corporate structures see David L. Sills, *The Volunteers* (Glencoe, Ill.: Free Press, 1956). The corporate structure is basically one in which the constituent units are "owned" and controlled by the parent, or central, body. The federated structure is one in which the central body is controlled by the units, which enter voluntarily into the larger association.

numerous economic and ideological pressures. Three stages in this process can be roughly delineated. By the end of its first decade in America, the YMCA had reached tentative agreement on a confederation of Associations. From the end of the Civil War until the 1920s, an internecine war was waged over the national organization's growing powers; finally the local Associations' dominant role was reasserted.

First Phase: Confederation

The difficulties inherent in forging a national organization from local Associations appeared in the very first attempts to establish such an organization. Many Associations did not wish to surrender authority over their affairs to a central body. In 1854 representatives of nineteen Associations met in Buffalo to discuss the possibilities for some sort of interassociational organization. Some delegates wanted only annual conventions, whereas others thought a stronger, continuing alliance, modeled after the new European alliance, was necessary. Initially the delegates were willing to vote only for annual conventions in which common concerns would be discussed; finally, however, a voluntary constitution was accepted. The Articles of Confederation established that the Confederation of North American Y.M.C.A.'s would have no authority over the affairs of any Association and that a Central Committee would be established with duties limited to disseminating information and arranging conventions. Although the Central Committee could make recommendations to local Associations, the latter would be free to reject the recommendations. Further, the Central Committee could not levy dues on an Association without its consent. The Central Committee would consist of eleven members, five to be selected from the Committee's city of residence, but from different Protestant denominations, and six to be selected from Associations in other locales.

The impetus for confederation issued from the social-movement and revivalist character of the Associations. The original founders had had a sense of participation in a larger Christian movement, and some formal linkage among the Associations seemed inevitable if they were to participate in a broad national—even world—movement. But the difficulties of distributing power and defining relations among units posed roadblocks to confederation. First the larger Associations (Boston, for example) felt entitled to a proportionately larger number of votes, but their proposal was voted down. Secondly, some Associations feared a loss of autonomy. The New York Association, for example, apparently feared that the local Associations would become branches of the Boston Association, parallel to the English situation in which the London Association was the parent organization for Associations in other cities. Only after substantial persuasion and a firm guarantee that no further constitutional provisions were anticipated would the New York Association join.[9]

The first confederation held annual conventions until 1861, when the Civil War broke out. During this period the Central Committee conducted correspondence and advised new Associations. After the Civil War the rapid growth and expansion of YMCA work was accompanied by the emergence of the International Committee (it evolved from the Central Committee) as a power and organizational center in its own right. It was empowered to charter new Associations, to raise money for its own programs, and to encourage and assist the formation of new Associations, including the supervision and financing of the latter.

Second Phase: The Growth of the International Committee

Immediately after the Civil War steps were taken to increase the permanency, continuity, and responsibility of the International Committee. The committee's headquarters were permanently located in New York, and the local Associations agreed to take a collection at annual conventions for the support of the committee. Furthermore, they agreed to allow the committee to publish a quarterly journal. Had the committee's task been largely restricted to giving advice and disseminating information, it is likely that the model of the first confederation would have been maintained. Beginning in the 1870s, however, and accelerating through the 1880s and 1890s, three programs developed which were directly related to the International Committee: college student work, foreign missions, and railroad work. These programs substantially enlarged the International Committee's staff as well as the number of Associations directly financed through the committee. Consequently, it developed an elaborate superstructure which it had to finance independently of, and often in competition with, the local Associations. Indeed, the proliferation of programs and staff financed by different program subcommittees eventually fostered considerable competition within the International Committee.

College student work was of two types. Antedating the development of denominational centers on college campuses, the YMCA had established student Associations on many campuses. Often attached to the faculties, these Associations carried out the YMCA's fourfold task—but usually with greater religious fervor and (in later years) with greater commit-

9. Hopkins, p. 62.

ment to the social gospel, than the city Associations. The YMCA's second campus endeavor was the Student Volunteer Movement, a late nineteenth-century Peace Corps, drawn from religiously committed students who became foreign missionaries to the dark continents as part of the movement to Christianize the world.

The development of railroad work resulted from the spread of railroads across the nation. The International Committee's first paid employee, Robert Weidensall, was a theologically trained shop foreman with one of the railroads at the time he was hired to organize railroad Associations. These YMCAs were usually financed by the railroad companies themselves. The YMCA was viewed by the company as good business, resulting in improved morals and better employees. In all cases the railroads provided facilities, including dormitories that could be managed by the YMCA. Initially, the companies often provided operating expenses as well, but the workers gradually provided an increasingly large share of these expenses. Both the campus Associations and the railroad YMCAs brought the International Committee into increasing conflict with the local Associations and state conventions. (State conventions were an intermediate form of organization, run by state committees and financed by the Associations within the state and by the International Committee.) The local Associations and state committees had assumed that any YMCA activity conducted within their territory should be supervised and coordinated with the local units. The International Committee could not, however, simply relinquish both the railroad and the student work to the local and state organizations. With respect to the railroad Associations, many companies preferred to work with the International Committee, which could speak for the whole Association, negotiating the organization of branch Associations for a whole railroad company rather than negotiating for each branch separately. Although the International Committee relinquished the operation of railroad branches located in cities to local Associations, it still retained a committee on railroad work which, due to pressures from the railroad, resulted in dual supervision of the railroad branches. This work by the International Committee was widely viewed as a violation of local autonomy.

The conflicts over student work arose from attempts by the students and by the International Committee's secretaries for student work to insulate themselves from the perspectives of their state and local Associations. In addition, the campus Associations were both more pietistic and more likely to preach a social gospel than were the state and local Associations; supervision by the more conservatively pragmatic state and local Associations could only hobble the campus Associations. Consequently, when attempts were made to link the student movements with the city Associations, the student leaders threatened to withdraw from the national polity.

Aside from these conflicts over supervision, however, the International Committee's growth also required an immense year-to-year financial campaign. Initially, the International Committee had raised much of its support from among its own members. J. P. Morgan, the Dodge family, and later the Rockefellers were among the best-known major supporters of the committee's endeavors. But the proliferation of its work across the country required it to compete in local communities for funds.

And the conflict went beyond supervision and financing. The chaotic growth of the International Committee, under the direction of powerful and aggressive leaders committed to their own programs, gradually caused local and state organizations to feel that the International Committee was not accountable to the founding Associations: committee secretaries were charged with concealing budgets and fund sources and with taking action and launching programs without consulting with or receiving a mandate from the local Associations.

The national polity that emerged during this second phase was a mixture of corporate and federated elements. On the one hand, local Associations retained their autonomy; they owned their own property, financed their own activities, hired their own staff, and adopted programs as needed. On the other hand, an independent center had developed which spoke to the nation (President Harding invited the International Committee to hold a fund-raising drive in the White House for its overseas work), conducted massive programs, and packed the national conventions. The state conventions and committees also had become power centers. State committees appointed their own personnel and, once well established, raised their own budgets. Much like the larger metropolitan associations, they were nodes of power and influence.

In interpreting this phase of the national Association's development, I am tempted to characterize the International Committee's growth as primarily a growth of centralized power. The committee was effectively run by five men, all living in New York, who raised 50 percent of the committee's funds, selected personnel, and promoted McBurney's conception of the YMCA wherever they could. But the primary change lay not in the centralization of authority: rather, a national organization had developed, separate from and independent of, the city and state Associations.[10] A dual national polity emerged: a federation of local Associations and state committees as well as a massive, inchoate central organization.

Third Phase: The Resurgence of the Local Association

The International Committee's growth and its extensive field program were challenged by some local Associations. Under the leadership of Wilbur Messer, general secretary of the Chicago YMCA (one of the largest in 1899), resolutions were passed at national conventions re-affirming the territorial rights of city Associations and asserting their control over branches within their territory. The passing of resolutions, however, did not solve the national polity's basic structural problems. The local Associations remained effectively unrepresented on the International Committee: further, the annual conventions were too large to allow effective policy discussions and were dominated by the International Committee.

Through the first two decades of the nineteenth century and inter-rupted only by World War I, there was agitation for change in the structure of the national organization. Finally, after numerous negotiations, special committees, and conventions, a special reorganization plan was adopted which placed the governing of the organization in the hands of a National Council elected by delegates to triennial conventions; the delegates themselves would be chosen by the voting membership. Furthermore, the National Council would choose its own executive committee (the General Board) from among its members. The local Associations would support, on a proportionate basis, the National Council's work, although committees of the National Council were given permission to raise certain budgets independently.

The purpose of these formal constitutional changes was to return control of the national Association to its constituent elements; to unify the relationship among state, local, and national agencies; and to establish a sounder financial base. The changes in formal structure, however, seem not to have altered significantly the local Association's relationships to the national organization; within a few years the same complaints were heard again: the local Associations could not control the budgets and policies of the National Council's agencies. Hopkins concluded that a real unification of the organization had not been achieved.[11]

It is difficult to assess the impact of formal constitutional changes per

10. Ibid., pp. 141–45.   11. Ibid., p. 445.

se on the local Association's relationship to the national organization, but several forces eventually brought about a retrenchment and curtailment of the national organization's work. Beginning in the 1920s, there was a precipitous decline in the number of campus YMCAs. On the one hand, the major Protestant denominations increasingly formed their own student associations; on the other, many universities assumed the student activity functions of the YMCA under their own aegis. Furthermore, supervisory conflicts and rigidities in methods of working with these Associations inhibited the institution of new ways of working with students. In any event, between 1920 and 1940 the number of student Associations declined from 731 to 480. This decline is particularly significant in that the number of institutions of higher learning nearly doubled and the number of students receiving higher education more than doubled during these two decades.[12] Where the Associations had included nearly 94,000 student members in 1921, by 1940 the total had declined to around 51,000 members.

The railroad work also suffered setbacks beginning with the Great Depression. As the railroads retrenched, they either curtailed their support, discontinued their branches, or relinquished them to the city Associations. In 1920 there were 244 Associations with 111,652 members; in 1940, 126 Associations with 93,941 members; and in 1963, 87 Associations with 81,158 members.

A similar process occurred with the foreign work. The expressed object had always been to encourage foreign Associations to become self-supporting. Although the American organization continued to support several overseas secretaries, there was, nevertheless, a gradual but substantial reduction in national organization staff as foreign Associations became self-supporting. Thus by the close of the depression period the national organization's three great program arms had been greatly reduced and no new programs had replaced them.

The number of secretaries attached to different types of Associations provides one index of the International Committee's relative role. As table 10 shows, during the twentieth century the numbers of secretaries attached to student and railroad work have drastically declined, whereas professional staffs of city Associations have increased proportionally.

Furthermore, the depression led to a rationalization of organizational functions. Major contributors looked less kindly on multiple solicitations,

12. Ibid., p. 646. The trends reported by Hopkins were from a special study of student associations. The annual reports indicate an increasingly precipitous decline, from 764 student associations in 1920 to 186 associations in 1940.

and the need to reduce staff led to a retrenchment in central rather than marginal functions. With the reduction in staff a series of agreements on jurisdictions was more easily obtained and has abided.[13]

At about the same time, state and regional executives began to be appointed jointly by the general secretary of the National Board and the state and regional committees. With more consultation and with joint appointments, the state and national organizations became relatively well

TABLE 10

SECRETARIES IN DIFFERENT TYPES OF ASSOCIATIONS FOR SELECTED YEARS

	1912	1919	1940	1947	1956	1962
City Associations....	64.5%	64.1%	74.0%[a]	65.0[a]	82.8%[a]	83.2%[a]
Student............	4.0	2.9	2.0	2.0	1.6	1.5
Railroad...........	17.1	10.9	5.0	3.0	2.5	1.5
Army and navy.....	2.1	2.2	3.0	3.0	1.6	1.2
Town and country...	1.8	4.1	3.0	3.0	3.7	3.9
General agency State and area....	3.4	5.9	2.7	3.3	3.1	3.2
International Committee[b].....	6.1	7.6	3.2	3.9	3.4	3.7
Other[c]............	1.0	2.3	5.7	15.7	4.0	1.0
Total number of secretaries........	4,093	5,511	3,779	4,058	3,708	3,863

SOURCE: *Yearbooks* for appropriate years.
NOTE: Each column totals 100 percent.
[a] Includes "colored" Associations.
[b] Called General Board after 1923. includes overseas secretaries as well as those employed domestically.
[c] "In transition," "Training agencies," "Instructors in training schools," "Miscellaneous"; high in 1947 due to end of war.

unified in providing local Associations with service functions and consultation. Of course, for smaller Associations these service functions could be vital. Much more than for the larger metropolitan Associations, small Associations depended on the state committees for recruitment of personnel and financial advice and support. Nevertheless, by the end of the 1930s the autonomy and jurisdiction of the local Associations had been reasserted. Rather than continue as an independent agent in its own right, the national organization gradually returned to its originally intended function as a service agency for the local Associations.

The YMCA's history as a national organization makes clear the local Associations' importance in shaping the niche-making characteristics of the American YMCA. Although the International Committee exerted

13. Ibid., pp. 449–51.

pressure to define work along certain lines, it was the ability of local Associations to command the support of their own communities that accounted for the YMCA's staying power and defined the characteristics of its contemporary niche. The failure of the student Associations to retain their campus positions is but one indicator of the importance of the Association's local community basis. The fact that local Associations often made policy decisions contrary to International Committee policy (such as accepting women into membership) which later became organizationwide trends is another such indicator. The adaptability of local Associations and the directions their adaptation took were sharply influenced by the kinds of men recruited for YMCA boards and staff and the relationships between them that emerged. These characteristics and relationships contributed to a pragmatic, service-oriented definition of YMCA work.

LAY CONTROL AND THE SECRETARY

In the development of the YMCA's polity, at both the local and national levels, one central value, derived from the dominant ideology of America and the structure of major Protestant denominations, has been that of democratic congregationalism. Congregationalism emphasizes the autonomy and self-determination of local Associations. Democratic congregationalism emphasizes control of local Associations by the voting membership and their representatives; under this concept, goal setting and policy formation are dominated by a "council of elders" rather than by professional staff.

The organizational niche that the YMCA gradually assumed was conditioned by democratic congregationalism. In particular, the dominant orientations of both staffs and boards, as well as the relationships between these groups, must be understood if we are to explain the selections from among alternative opportunities which have characterized the YMCA program. As the Association shifted from evangelistic goals, many alternative programs and target groups were proposed. Some thought the YMCA should assume a settlement house role and help the downtrodden. Others, inspired by the late nineteenth-century social gospel movement, suggested that the YMCA take a more active part in social reform; it should serve as a forum for the discussion of major social issues and aggressively pursue the good, Christian society. That the city Associations largely rejected these alternatives in favor of general services to individuals and building-centered activities was a function both of the emerging organizational economy and the orientations and relations of staff and boards.

Although the early voting members of the YMCA were predominantly young men, the boards of directors, as the Associations acquired buildings and the original members grew older, increasingly resembled those of other private bureaucratic organizations in America: namely, they were dominated by businessmen drawn from Protestant denominations. From the historical studies it is difficult to locate YMCA boards within local status structures, but it appears that in the late nineteenth century they were more likely to be drawn from among the newly moneyed than from among the older, established families. Furthermore, it appears that they were more likely to be drawn from commercial and merchandising occupations than from industry and manufacturing. Hopkins asserts without qualification that the YMCA was dominated by the business classes and that it was allied with "individuals and social groups that were the chief beneficiaries of the rampant individualism of the 'gilded age.' "[14]

Had the YMCA's boards been isolated from policy formulation or involved primarily in fund-raising activities, they might have had less effect on the choice of alternative programs. An Association's structure, however, heavily involved laymen in organizational affairs. Four aspects of a secretary's relationship to his board are crucial for understanding the importance of board member orientations for policy and program selection. (1) The secretary did not command a skill or knowledge base that established his greater wisdom in organizational affairs. (2) The secretary had no allegiance to, or identification with, professional groups outside his own organization. (3) The YMCA's historical development as a layman's association issued in organizational structures and ideologies asserting the board's rights as predominant. (4) The secretary's personal disposition typically led him to have acquiescent relations with authority figures.

Knowledge Base

Although secretaries might be highly competent in managerial skills, in ability to program and conduct activities, in group process, and in knowledge of fund-raising techniques, these skills never achieved legitimation as a base for independent decision making. Many board members might also command one or another of these skills. Indeed, highly involved lay-

14. Hopkins, p. 392.

men of long experience might know much more about a particular area of operation than a neophyte secretary. Furthermore, the secretary did not generally command the authority of theological doctrine or the cloak of ministerial position. When in the 1880s and 1890s Protestant ministers began to develop new interpretations of the gospel and of Christian ethics, the YMCA remained relatively untouched. Only in the student Associations and at the national staff level was the social gospel prominently featured. (To note a current issue, although many southern ministers have lost their posts because of their commitment to greater racial equality, I have been unable to find a single such case in the YMCA.)

Profession within Organization

Not only did the individual secretary not command the respect of greater wisdom or knowledge, he was also not part of an independent profession. YMCA secretaries formed a professional association in 1871, but membership has been drawn solely from within the YMCA. The secretaries thus lacked an independent, collegial knowledge base that could serve as a criterion against which they could measure their Association's policies. Other professional associations (such as those for social work, medicine, engineering) provide the professional with an independent source of operational standards. But although the Association of Secretaries (A.O.S.) might encourage discussion of good practices, the range of alternatives and the legitimation of their independence has been less pronounced.

Emphasis on Role of Laymen

The Association's developmental process historically placed great emphasis on the role of the layman. Some, in fact, pronounced the role of the layman to be "the distinctive genius" of the Association. As the YMCA acquired larger numbers of staff members and of programs, the secretaries' tendency to take a larger role in policy formation became pronounced. McBurney and others, however, warned of the growth of "secretarialism"—the tendency of secretaries to do themselves what they should instead be asking laymen to do.[15] McBurney himself resigned his voting position on the New York YMCA's board of directors, and all officers both of local Associations and of the national organization were selected from among laymen. Furthermore, local Associations developed a committee structure designed to involve laymen in policy making for each subarea of organizational activity as well as for overall direction.

15. Morse, p. 81.

For instance, if a local Association had a separate boys' work section, the Association's board would also have a committee on boys' work. The committee structure, then, reinforced the ideology of lay work.

Typical Personality of the Secretary

The early transformation of YMCA goals was accompanied by a transformation in the recruitment base for secretaries. Whereas the earliest secretaries had often had some theological training and some had even been ordained, by 1887 roughly four-fifths of the secretaries were drawn from white-collar business occupations.[16] The earliest secretaries, too, had usually been good orators, skillful at platform evangelism; as the Associations began to operate large buildings with extensive staff and committee structures, however, general administrative skills became more important.

Although a shift in the recruitment base certainly occurred, some characteristics of YMCA secretaries' personalities seem to have remained constant. Even when Associations recruited ministers into the secretaryship, they were generally men who emphasized a simple morality of clean, upright living rather than a concern for theological distinctions. Dwight L. Moody, not a minister but nevertheless the YMCA's greatest evangelist, impressed people by his evident (though often ungrammatical) sincerity. Most YMCA evangelism, though not intellectual, was not of the highly emotional fire-and-brimstone variety either. In short, neither intellectual nor millenarian concerns, whether theological or ideological, were ever dominant characteristics of the secretary.

The first secretaries were usually trained, if at all, through an apprenticeship to previously established secretaries. Later, training institutes were held, and finally training schools were established for the preparation of secretaries.

Without detailed analysis of personal biographies, it is difficult to assess the model personality of a YMCA secretary. In 1960, however, Roy Grinker and his collaborators published a detailed psychodynamic analysis of the personalities of the George Williams College student body.[17] (George Williams College, then located in Chicago, is a major training institution for YMCA secretaries and other youth workers.) Their description closely approximates the impression of the secretary

16. *Yearbook, 1887*, pp. 33–39.

17. Roy R. Grinker, with the collaboration of Roy R. Grinker, Jr., and John Timberlake, "Mentally Healthy Young Males (Homoclites)," *Archives of General Psychiatry* 6 (1962): 405–53.

one gleans from extensive reading of YMCA history. Grinker found that the George Williams College student had very little psychopathology (so little, in fact, that he was awed by their normality). Typically from the lower middle class, these students perceived their families as relatively happy and their parents as consistent in discipline and attitudes. They showed little adolescent rebelliousness and generally had rather low aspirations for material wealth. Although they were not verbally constricted, they showed considerable interest in sports and other physical activity and tended to release tensions in these ways. Although they perceived their families as relatively happy and integrated, Grinker judged that they were often closer to their mothers than to their fathers and that the YMCA became a substitute for the masculine world.

The relevant aspects of Grinker's narrative are those that reveal both the low level of intellectual concern and the general respect for authority he found. As one examines the Association's history, one is struck by the secretaries' great willingness to accept the values and policy orientation of their boards of directors in spite of holding, generally, more liberal social and political views themselves.[18]

These four factors—the secretary's typically limited knowledge base, the existence of a profession within the Association, an ideology of lay involvement, and the secretary's characteristically acquiescent disposition—have each contributed to the Association's identification with business interests and to a selection of program alternatives compatible with those interests. The YMCA's identification with conservative businessmen was at its height in the late nineteenth century. In the twentieth century, members and secretaries of the student movement searched for and adopted more radical perspectives on social reform. Furthermore, in the 1930s and earlier, local Associations sometimes tried to provide a neutral forum for the discussion of labor-management conflicts. By way of compromise, the YMCA's approach to social issues, to poverty, and to programs other than those of general service to individuals has employed a twofold strategy. On the one hand, to maintain the attachment of business groups which have long supported the organization, local Associations have ruled out doctrinal and political controversy; on the other, in their approach to the poor they have followed a policy of "assimilative reform."

18. Hopkins, p. 456. Hopkins cites a study by E. C. Torrence, "A Study of Association Viewpoints and Policies on Social Problems," (M.A. thesis, YMCA Graduate School, Nashville, 1934) which shows statistically significant differences in political and social attitudes between boards and staff.

Had the YMCA held very specific goals, the avoidance of doctrinal and political disputes would not have become a central concern for the organization, for such issues would not have been part of its normal agenda. Given the looseness and generality of goals, however, conflict and debate over goals and religious doctrine could have occurred as different groups attempted to define goals. The avoidance of taking a stand in such disputes effectively narrowed the scope of the organization and was necessary to maintain the interest and commitment of dominant business groups.

The YMCA did not simply become a country club for the lower middle class; instead, it held out to prospective members the opportunity to become like its dominant members. Through club programs, vocational training, night law schools, and so on, it offered an opportunity to join the "better classes." In discussing the temperance movement Gusfield has termed such programs, which offer the target group the opportunity to join the morally "sound" group, "strategies of assimilative reform."[19] In developing such a strategy the YMCA retained the interest and commitment of its dominant support group, developed programs consistent with its original goals, and found many opportunities to promote its own growth.

This strategy of assimilative reform has contributed to the organization's basic mission of moral uplift and reform. To justify the YMCA's existence as a partly philanthropic organization, its board and staff members point out that it offers programs of character and skill development (for both social and occupational purposes) to persons who could otherwise not afford them. Acceptance of this strategy limits the directions of organizational change but is compatible with the character of board and staff personnel.

GOALS AND THE DEFINITION OF NICHE

Over the last century, we have seen, the YMCA has shifted from an evangelistic organization, closely linked to the Protestant evangelical denominations and serving primarily young men, to one utilizing a highly secularized program and serving all age groups (indeed, having lost ground among its original target population) and both sexes. A growing organization, the YMCA has shaped a place for itself in most cities. During the same period it has developed a diversified financial support base which includes contributions, business features, and membership and program fees. Structurally it is characterized by its emphasis on the local

19. Gusfield, pp. 6, 68–69.

Association's autonomy and the importance of lay involvement in the organization's decision making. These structural characteristics are important for understanding the organization's directions of change.

Equipped with some of the historical material as background, we are now in a better position to understand the YMCA's adaptive processes as it has redefined its niche. Since the YMCA was not organized as a church and was not limited to evangelism, the declining demand for evangelistic activity freed local YMCAs to search for other programs consistent with their very broad goals. While individual staff members, boards, or local Associations might develop a firm and inflexible commitment to one specific program or mode of operation, the federated relationship among Associations permitted some to search for alternatives even while others, including the International Committee, were condemning the departure from "accepted" practice. Thus, laymen and secretaries were in a position to create new programs responding to their perception of need, or demand.

Simultaneously with the search for alternative programs, old ones could be discontinued without disrupting the Association's overall operations, for by the end of the nineteenth century no single concept of program dominated the Association. The YMCA has initiated numerous program activities in response to its perception of the needs of the time, and many have later been discontinued as other, more specialized agencies, having either a closer relationship to the clientele or better funding or administration, have entered the field. As noted previously, YMCA reading rooms and libraries yielded to public libraries; employment services initiated at the organization's founding were discontinued as public and private employment agencies developed. Vocationally oriented night school courses were dropped when public and private technical institutes began to serve the same clientele.[20] (Although night law schools and certain other vocational programs continue to exist, the YMCA's adult education program has gradually been reoriented along avocational rather than vocational lines.)

20. Several private universities began as part of the YMCA vocational training program. Northeastern University in Boston, Roosevelt University in Chicago, and the Detroit Institute of Technology are among the better known of ten colleges and universities which later separated from their founding YMCAs. The early history of these and other colleges is given in Paul E. Williams, *The YMCA College* (Saint Louis, Mo.: Educational Council of the Young Men's Christian Association, 1938). Both political problems (such as the clash of constitutional norms) and economic problems (such as fund raising for growing universities) led to their separation from the YMCA.

The YMCA has reacted to competition by discontinuing unwanted programs and seeking either new clientele groups or new program activities for which there is a demand. The organization has not been indiscriminate in this process of rejection and selection: the programs most quickly dropped have been those less compatible with its normal clientele, normal modes of funding, and basic strategies of assimilative reform and service to the relatively well-adjusted. As a membership association, the YMCA easily developed a moral justification for its enrollment economy: participants should want to pay for services. Much like psychoanalysts, many YMCA secretaries and board members have believed that services are only valued and effective when the client pays for them. Of course, this belief has solidified the organization's ties to a "service" rather than a "welfare" orientation and mode of operation.

The enrollment economy has particularly affected the operations of local Associations. The International Committee, on the other hand, initiated extensive missionary efforts funded primarily along philanthropic lines; wealthy backers became particularly involved in the student movement and in the overseas missionary work. Even after the major Protestant denominations had founded campus associations, the national organization continued to support the student movement because of its commitment to the style of interdenominational work represented by the campus associations. The local Associations, however, have been less willing to fight losing battles. During the latter part of the nineteenth century, when the Charity Organization Societies began assuming responsibility for and coordinating relief to the poor, local Associations seem to have left the field rapidly.

Although the YMCA was primarily based on the middle-class segment of the population, and although it had had a diversified enrollment economy to a greater extent than other organizations concerned with welfare problems, YMCA personnel were not insensitive to the needs of the poor, nor were they unaware of the need for new types of agencies. The public parks movement was supported by the YMCA, and for many decades Springfield College in Massachusetts (a YMCA affiliate) was a major trainer of public park workers. Similarly, in some cities YMCA personnel worked for the creation of councils of social agencies. But what is important is that, although local Associations recognized such needs (or demands) and opportunities and worked to meet them, only certain kinds of needs were met within the YMCA's structure. Most typically, the Association programed to meet needs which involved individual or group services to the relatively well-adjusted members of the society and which could be met with the kind of staff it possessed without alienating financial supporters.

With the rise of the American city the YMCA developed as an evolving general service agency available to serve new needs as they arose. At the beginning of the twentieth century it was probably the largest and most general community agency devoted to community and individual betterment. Its role in American communities was sufficiently prominent that Josephus Daniels described it as "a clearing house for American Christianity."[21] And when Woodrow Wilson dedicated the Pittsburgh Association's building in 1914, he is quoted as having said, "You can test a modern community by the degree of its interest in its YMCA."[22]

As public schools have assumed broader functions, including provision for physical recreation, as the institutional church has developed, in some ways imitating the Associations, and as both public and private welfare agencies have increased in number, size, and scope, the YMCA has perhaps declined as an agency facilitating occupational mobility and as a teacher of leisure-time activities and skills. Nevertheless, the generality of its goals, its readiness to seek out new target groups, and the continued demand for its services have allowed it to continue growing in membership and size.

I have argued that the very breadth and generality of the YMCA's organizational goals have contributed to its great flexibility and adaptative strength. This breadth of goals and general Christian commitment have indeed allowed it to rush in to take on new tasks when an incontrovertible need was perceived, as in service to soldiers in World War I. One should not, however, ignore the other side of the coin; the very breadth of goals may have contributed to partial, halfhearted meeting of new needs as they arose. Lacking a wholehearted commitment to a single program or goal, the YMCA may have met only partially the demands which presented themselves.

A case in point contrasts the YMCA's youth involvement with that of the Boy Scouts. The Boy Scout movement began in England in close connection with the YMCA; indeed, in England it was considered an integral part of the YMCA. The two decades from 1900 to 1920 saw the incorporation in the United States of the major youth-serving agencies.[23] The

21. Hopkins, p. 484.   22. Ibid.

23. Has any sociologist really explained how the youth demands for service arose? Youth seems to have become "available" to these organizations during these decades. Probably a rise in the number of students remaining in school past a certain age provides the major explanation (see Pence, p. 225). Boys Clubs of Amer-

YMCA assisted the Boy Scout movement in establishing a national organization. Edgar M. Robinson, the boys' work secretary of the International Committee, worked for six months almost full time on the formation of the national Boy Scout movement in 1910. He believed that the Boy Scouts should organize separately and, having become self-supporting, withdraw from direct involvement with the YMCA. By 1919, there were 460,000 Boy Scouts in America whereas the YMCA included roughly 200,000 members in the same age group.[24] Although this decade saw a substantial increase in YMCA boys' work, it is clear that the Boy Scouts' specialized and standardized mode of operations attracted even more members. Indeed, the Boy Scout movement appealed to YMCA secretaries, many of whom joined the Boy Scout staff.

An even clearer example of the advantages of specialization emerged in the late 1930s. During the late 1930s and early 1940s, boys under ten began to be available for youth organizations (the Boy Scouts' major age range was from eleven to thirteen and that of Explorer Scouts fourteen and older), and both the Boy Scouts and the YMCA initiated programs for this younger group. The Boy Scouts organized the Cub Scouts while the YMCA initiated a variety of clubs and recreational programs. Between 1940 and 1957 the Cub Scouts grew from 195,000 to 1,806,000 (a 900 percent increase), and the total youth membership of the whole Scout movement—Cub Scouts, Boy Scouts, and Explorer Scouts—grew from 1,106,000 to 3,460,000.[25] During the same period the YMCA's under-twelve membership grew from 155,000 to about 500,000 (a 300 percent increase) while its total under-seventeen membership increased from about 502,000 to approximately 960,000.[26] The YMCA was indeed serving the newly available population, but in comparison with its major "competitor" it was not penetrating as deeply. It appears that the very breadth of organizational programs prohibited it from focusing organizational effort on new target populations.

---

ica, Boy Scouts of America, Camp Fire Girls, Girl Scouts, Boy Rangers of America, Boys Brotherhood Republic, Pathfinders, Big Brother and Sisters Federation, Junior Achievement, and Order of DeMolay are only a few of the organizations established in America during this period.

24. Hopkins, pp. 468–69.

25. *Statistical Abstract of the United States, 1958* (Washington, D.C.: Government Printing Office, 1958), p. 292.

26. Carey, *Perspectives on YMCA Growth* (1959).

Part II
The Chicago Association

Introduction to Part II

In introducing this discussion of the Chicago YMCA, it is tempting to develop a fugue-and-counterpoint theme to the foregoing description and analysis of the transformation of the national movement. A fuguelike echoing of the national movement is certainly to be found in the Chicago Association's growth and processes of transformation. The city's prodigious growth during the second half of the nineteenth century provided fertile ground for the YMCA's broad variety of programs and activities.[1] In its earliest days the Chicago Association suffered the same instability as other local Associations. Founded in 1854, it died out in 1856 only to be started again in 1858. During 1858 and 1859 its program consisted of noon prayer meetings, the provision of a library and reading room, lectures by clergymen, an employment service, a referral service for respectable boardinghouses, and a program of visiting the sick.

The YMCA's first building was built in 1867, only to be burned down in 1868, built again in 1869, and burned again in the great Chicago Fire of 1871. Finally in 1874 a building was constructed that lasted for a number of years. By 1884, as the city expanded, branches (departments) were being opened. Some of these survived; others did not.

The Chicago Association's history offers counterpoint to the national movement in its resistance to transformation from evangelism to general service and in its preference for federation rather than centralized direction by the national organization. In the early 1870s, as we have seen, under the influence of McBurney, the International Committee, and the New York YMCA, there began to emerge a consensus on the fourfold work restricted to serving young men. The Chicago Association, however, either opposed or was ambivalent about this view, which was accepted by many local Associations. The Association was heavily committed both to the distribution of mission tracts (in many languages) and

1. See Emmett Dedmon, *Great Enterprises: One Hundred Years of the YMCA of Metropolitan Chicago* (Chicago: Rand McNally, 1957), for a history of the Chicago Association. Dedmon's book was commissioned by the Chicago Association for its centennial celebration.

to general evangelistic work in the city, among the poor and among all age groups. Evangelism was the Chicago Association's chief concern during a time when character development was becoming the dominant goal for the national movement as a whole. (Although the 1867 building had included a gymnasium, it had been provided primarily as a safeguard against the allurement of unsavory recreation places. The Association considered the gymnasium a distraction from the YMCA's true mission and leased its operation to a separate club.)

Dwight Moody was not the only evangelist associated with the Chicago YMCA. Billy Sunday, previously a volunteer worker, was employed as religious director of the Chicago Association from 1888 until 1894, when he left to become a full-time evangelist.

The debate over evangelistic versus service-oriented goals issued in open conflict among board members in 1880, finally resulting in the resignation of the general secretary in 1887, when it became evident that the service-oriented board members were winning the debate.

In 1878 the Chicago Association had eight hundred members and by 1885, over three thousand. By 1900 the Chicago and New York Associations were the country's largest (New York City had two large Associations, the Brooklyn Association and the New York Association).

In the Association-shaking debate over federalism versus centralization, Chicago served as a counterpoise to the East Coast Associations, the International Committee, and the committee's general secretary, Richard Morse. The leading proponent of a federation and of restricting the International Committee's role was Loring W. Messer, Chicago's general secretary from 1888 until 1923. As leader of the largest Association outside New York, Messer was the chief spokesman for those who felt that Morse and the International Committee were gathering too much power to themselves.

The Chicago Association's internal evolution also provides an echo and counterpoint of economic and political change as the program evolved and the Association grew. For one thing the amount and proportion of income resulting from religious activities declined as the proportion of fees from classroom activities, general membership, and physical program increased.

Less obviously, the Association's growth and transformation of goals appear to have brought about a subsequent transformation of the Association's control mechanisms and underlying polity. Under Messer each branch (department) was managed by a committee which was part of the board of managers; there seems, however, to have been little central bookkeeping or financial control. When Messer retired, his business manager, William T. Parker (general secretary from 1923 to 1939), instituted more centralized bookkeeping procedures, set up depreciation reserves, and enforced other accounting rules designed to promote departmental solvency. Such policies issued in a centralization of financial control in the Chicago Association. Parker was succeeded by Frank Hathaway (general secretary from 1939 to 1954). Although Hathaway was a strong leader, drawn from the business operations of the organization, he made a point of encouraging the relative autonomy of individual departmental boards of directors within the Chicago Association. Thus in effect he was encouraging the centrifugal power forces in the Association.

A few brief facts may help set the stage. In 1961 the Young Men's Christian Association of Metropolitan Chicago had thirty-seven departments scattered in most areas of the city and in several suburbs. These departments ranged from the massive YMCA Hotel, just south of the Loop, with over two thousand rooms and an annual budget of more than $2,200,000, to a small storefront branch in a sparsely settled suburb, Palos-Orland, some twenty miles from the downtown area, with an annual budget of about $20,000.

Aside from the thirty-seven departments, the Association owned twelve camps and operated a laundry. Each department's program was designed to meet the needs of the local community, these needs being defined by staff perception of response to different mixes of program offerings. Thus programs varied widely across the metropolis, depending upon the facilities offered and the socioeconomic composition of the community. Indeed, change in the socioeconomic composition of the local community was a major impetus to organizational change.

There were some 265 professional staff members, over 1,000 full-time nonprofessional employees, 700 part-time professional and nonprofessional employees, and 80 George Williams College students on a form of work-study program. Altogether, the Association listed more than 2,000 employees. The annual expenses of the Association were over $16,000,-000.

The YMCA claimed 133,000 members in 1961, 33 percent more than six years before. Also, many thousands of nonmembers used the facilities and participated in programs. Indeed, the YMCA recorded 12,000,000 participants in formal programs that year and many more used facilities in less formal ways. Five million participants were recorded in supervised program events.

The real estate of the Association was owned by the board of trustees, which delegated its operation to a board of managers. In turn the board of managers appointed the local boards of directors and a general secretary, responsible for staff supervision.

My first purpose in part 2 is to describe and analyze the Chicago Association's political economy in the mid-twentieth century. My second purpose is to show the consequences of the basic political economy for other aspects of the social system—executive roles, program supervision and innovation, and some crucial policies and their implementation. The foregoing brief history and description is intended only as background for the more detailed analysis of the 1950s and 1960s which follows.

4

Polity

Adam Smith and Alexis de Tocqueville knew, as a later generation of
scholars seem to have forgotten, that societal institutions and formal
structures are based on a substratum of opinions and sentiments. Without supporting sentiments among key groups and members of the society,
political structures, offices, and mechanisms cannot endure.[1] Just as the
phrase *societal or national polity* directs us to view the mobilization,
utilization, and institutionalization of power in terms broader than the
formal structure of government, so the phrase *organizational polity* also
requires a broad view of structure and political mechanisms in complex
organizations. This chapter describes the Chicago YMCA's constitution
and the polity that operates in relationship to that constitution.

An underlying theme in this discussion of the organization's basic
polity is that there exists a set of constitutional norms which limit and
direct the uses of influence and power. In any social system constitutional
norms (written or not) are those sets of legitimate, institutionalized
norms which limit and direct the uses of discretion.

Constitutions regulate behavior along at least four normative dimensions. First, constitutional norms vary according to the norms binding
individuals into the organization (that is, according to the "contract," or
terms of exchange existing between the organization and its individual
members). These norms of exchange determine the amount of energy,
time, and commitment that the organization can expect from different
members. They also determine the extent to which organizations have
discretion over various areas of members' behavior. "Incentive theory"
and "compliance theory" have their major interest in the variations of
the terms of exchange from one kind of organization to another. Wilson

1. A brilliant analysis of the manner in which substrata of opinion and attitude
articulate with factors of personality, on the one hand, and political institutions, on
the other, is provided by Robert E. Lane, *Political Ideology: Why the American
Common Man Believes What He Does* (New York: Free Press, 1962).

and Clark distinguished between material, solidary, and purposive organizations in terms of three different kinds of incentives that bring about three different kinds of commitment.[2] Etzioni's categories (coercive, utilitarian, and normative) overlap Wilson and Clark's and have much the same focus.[3] An organization has a fragile polity if its norms of exchange are weak and fundamentally nonbinding.

Second, constitutional norms specify the range of discretion and the decision responsibilities of officers, groups, and units. Rights and responsibilities are deeply embedded in different kinds of functional, territorial, and hierarchical units. The distinction between federated and corporate organization may be the broadest distinction in this regard, but even within corporate structures, questions of functional responsibility and autonomy and levels of centralization and decentralization may become basic constitutional parameters having great import for the polity's operation. It is clear that many crucial organizational changes in modern society involve constitutional norms regarding the rights and responsibilities of different groups within the organization. To cite only one widely known example, the range and rights of management as contrasted with unions involve the central constitutional norms of business corporations.

Third, constitutional norms are deeply embedded in an organization's relationship to the society of which it is a part. These norms involve such basic premises as: To whom is the organization responsible?—Under what conditions? The norms linking such an organization to society may undergo change during critical periods. For example, an organization's right to use business property for profit may be greatly modified in time of war. Furthermore, the norms linking an organization to the larger society may be partially or even fully unstated except during periods of crisis such as disasters.[4]

Finally, constitutional norms specify the foci of collective action—concerns falling inside or outside the zone of indifference of the organization and its subgroups. The foci of collective action include goals, target (clientele) groups, and technologies (means).

It should be clear that constitutional norms differ not only substantively from organization to organization, but also in their import and in-

2. Ibid.

3. Amitai Etzioni, *A Comparative Analysis of Complex Organizations* (New York: Free Press, 1961).

4. James D. Thompson and Robert W. Hawkes, "Disaster, Community Organization and Administrative Process," in *Man and Society in Disaster,* ed. George W. Baker and Dwight W. Chapman (New York: Basic Books, 1962), pp. 268–300.

tensity. Some organizations may change clientele groups or even goals with little consequence if clientele and goals are only tenuously associated. It should also be clear that a constitution is normative; polity, on the other hand, is the broad system of power, of which some parts may be nonlegitimate and even anticonstitutional. The latter situation usually represents a system of flux.

This discussion of the Chicago YMCA's polity utilizes two lines of analysis simultaneously. On the one hand, I will examine the development of the belief system surrounding the Association's scope, mission, and organization. On the other, I will describe the operating structures and positions of the institution as they legitimate discretion and distribute power through various offices and personnel. By interweaving beliefs (the substrata of opinion) and structure we should be able to observe the polity in operation.

KEY BELIEFS AND VALUES

The ideological commitments of the YMCA's Chicago professional staff have mirrored, in many respects, the general ideological commitments of secretaries discussed previously. The Chicago staff's attitudes toward the larger society and its perspectives on organizational policy have largely supported traditional conceptions of the YMCA's mission and constitution.

The basic staff approach has been that of "muscular Christianity." Staff members have been neither intellectual theorists nor missionaries determined to reform either individuals or the world. Nor have they been moralists, except by personal example. Overwhelmingly from middle- and lower-middle-class Protestant backgrounds, staff members have generally attached little importance to intellectual and ideological concerns. The *Reader's Digest* is typical of their leisure reading matter.[5] A phrase often used to describe a family in positive terms is "they're a good YMCA family"; that is, its members are "clean-cut" and "clean-living" and follow an athletic and unpretentious way of life.[6] At one time drinking or smoking in any degree would have been discouraged. Currently, however, only the older staff and their wives disapprove of smoking and moderate drinking.

Whether or not the secretaries have been politically liberal or con-

5. Emil Faubert, "Mr. YMCA Secretary," mimeographed (New York, n.d.).

6. Among over 250 professionals we could find only three cases of divorce, a substantially higher rate of marital stability than would be found in a random sample of middle-class Protestant Americans.

servative, in outward deportment they have been conservative and have rarely voiced allegiance to the Democratic party. Nor have they often expressed strong support for what are generally termed liberal social welfare policies. In the 1960 presidential election, for example, a straw vote revealed that only three of the Chicago general secretary's fifty cabinet members (the executive secretaries and Metropolitan office professional staff) planned to vote for Kennedy. Of those three, only one had openly avowed his support for Kennedy.

This brief picture of the staff's general perspectives is hardly more than a caricature; yet it highlights orientations that guide staff interpretation of, and reactions to, organizational structure. First, staff members' conception of the YMCA's Christian goals was not theological but rather activity-centered and "model"-centered. Most secretaries identified religion with morality and clean living. They conceived religious purposes as realized through good examples and healthy activities. Such a perspective had its outcome not in a missionary outlook (indeed, evangelizing for religious or social salvation lay outside the ken of most secretaries) but rather in an orientation toward a building-centered program and work with "acceptable" members of society.

In addition to this general orientation toward goals, the secretaries' perspectives on the organization are also relevant. At minimum there was general acceptance of the board of directors' dominance and control. Both background and training made it unlikely that the secretaries would follow any course of action other than accepting the general politics and persuasion of their boards. The board members generally represented success in the American style, and the secretaries honored them. Furthermore, their own backgrounds in Protestant evangelical denominations supported the Association's central constitutional norms of lay control and autonomy.

GOALS AND TARGET GROUPS

Over the decades these broad social, personal, and organizational perspectives have interacted with the changing economy and polity of the YMCA. As older programs such as Bible classes met clientele resistance, staff attitudes about their importance for implementing YMCA goals have changed. Similarly, with time, the relevant clientele groups have changed. As in any changing society, some persons change their attitudes to correspond with the directions in which the organization is moving, whereas others maintain their old positions and become increasingly alienated. The generational cycle is a major source of conflict within or-

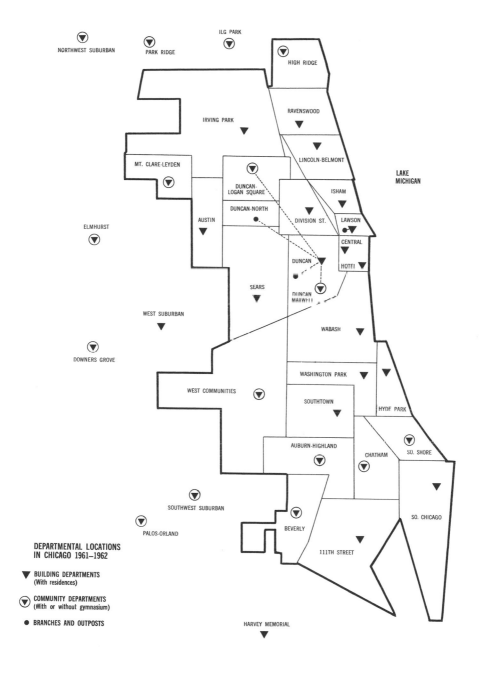

NORTHWEST SUBURBAN

PARK RIDGE

ILG PARK

HIGH RIDGE

RAVENSWOOD

IRVING PARK

MT. CLARE-LEYDEN

LINCOLN-BELMONT

LAKE MICHIGAN

DUNCAN-LOGAN SQUARE

ISHAM

DUNCAN-NORTH

ELMHURST

AUSTIN

DIVISION ST.

LAWSON

CENTRAL

DUNCAN

HOTEL

SEARS

DUNCAN MAXWELL

WEST SUBURBAN

DOWNERS GROVE

WABASH

WASHINGTON PARK

WEST COMMUNITIES

SOUTHTOWN

HYDE PARK

AUBURN-HIGHLAND

CHATHAM

SO. SHORE

SOUTHWEST SUBURBAN

PALOS-ORLAND

BEVERLY

SO. CHICAGO

111TH STREET

**DEPARTMENTAL LOCATIONS
IN CHICAGO 1961–1962**

▼ **BUILDING DEPARTMENTS**
(With residences)

⊛ **COMMUNITY DEPARTMENTS**
(With or without gymnasium)

● **BRANCHES AND OUTPOSTS**

HARVEY MEMORIAL

ganizations as well as in the larger society. For this analysis, however, the interest is less in this generational change than in the present concept of organizational goals and clientele groups. It is these conceptions which have provided a focus for collective action and a base for individual decisions. They represent evaluative norms for judging the utility of current programs and achievements.

An official statement of goals that is much used in the Chicago YMCA is as follows:

> The basic objective of the Young Men's Christian Association of Metropolitan Chicago is to aid in the development of Christian standards of living, conduct and life purposes in its members and constituency. In the attainment of this goal, the Association seeks to promote the physical, mental, and spiritual welfare of persons, and to emphasize reverence for God, responsibility for the common good, respect for personality and the application of the Golden Rule in human relationships.

Several aspects of this statement deserve emphasis. First, with typical YMCA breadth, it focuses on no specific clientele group, such as boys, young people, or adults. Furthermore, its aim is the broad, general one of enhancing the positive Christian virtues. Not limited to spreading Christianity through prayer or formal education, this statement is sufficiently broad to encompass any enhancing activity from typewriting courses (which enable persons to become more valuable employees) to work with youth gangs and delinquents. In using the terms *members* and *constituency,* the statement permits work with nonmembers. The statement does not indicate whether the means used by the organization should be preventive or rehabilitative. The very breadth of the statement permits a wide range of alternative interpretations for the organization's goals and mission.

What goal statements and clientele groups were the organization's professional staff likely to endorse? How did the staff interpret the organization's fundamental purposes? All full-time professional and senior nonprofessional staff (business managers and head desk clerks, for example) were asked to complete self-administered questionnaires.[7] The staff

7. Response rate was uniformly good. In all departments over 90 percent of staff completed questionnaires. The questionnaires were filled out in a group meeting with one of the project staff in attendance. The questionnaire was constructed before the political-economy framework was developed and contained large batteries of items dealing with issues in professionalization, perceptions of community problems, and

checked various statements regarding organizational goals. These statements were derived from an exploration of YMCA literature and from unstructured interviews. Staff members were asked to indicate those goals which they considered very important, slightly important, or not important for their particular departments. The percentage checking "very important" for the list of statements is given in table 11. Also presented are data on the staff's perceptions of their own *effectiveness* in each of the areas probed; these data indicate what staff members believed they were really accomplishing.

TABLE 11

GOALS FOR LOCAL DEPARTMENTS: RESPONSES OF LOCAL STAFF

Q.1: How *important* do you feel each of the following goals should be for your department?

Q.2: Regardless of how important you think each goal is, how *effective* do you think your department has been in pursuing these goals?

	"Very important" (Percent)	"Very effective" (Percent)
To serve as a community center which local groups can use and feel at ease in..............................	64	52
To develop people's special interests and skills (both physical and social)................................	83	56
To help develop character (a sense of individual worth and responsibility)...................................	97	42
To provide a place for people to develop friendships.....	69	61
To help solve community problems....................	44	17
To work for Christian ecumenism.....................	19	2
To bring people closer to Christianity.................	49	6

NOTE: Respondents included local departments only (N = 163). Personnel not in community departments (i.e., Metropolitan staff, YMCA Hotel staff, and members of the citywide Educational Department) were excluded.

The goal of character development clearly received almost complete consensus; for no other statement did as large a proportion of staff check the "very important" category. The statements regarding skill training, serving as a community center, and serving as a social center were also perceived by a majority of staff (over 60 percent) as very important goals. The two statements related directly to religious purposes received far fewer assents, as did those statements regarding the YMCA's function in solving community problems.

---

the like. Thus much of the data is irrelevant to the framework. Since the data were not collected specifically to test or amplify our framework, I have used them sparingly.

These percentages are amplified by an examination of staff views on organizational effectiveness. Few staff considered the YMCA very effective either in working for ecumenism or in bringing people closer to Christianity. Although many (49 percent) considered the latter goal important, only 6 percent believed it actually to be an area of great effectiveness. Only a small minority of staff viewed their departments as very effective in working on community problems.

Only 42 percent perceived the staff as very effective in developing character, although most believed this to be a very important goal. Finally a majority of staff considered their departments most effective in teaching skills and activities and in serving as a social and community center.

The broad pattern emerging from table 11 is as follows. Whereas a substantial number of staff still believe the organization's traditional religious goals to be important, few find the organization very effective in achieving this goal. Furthermore, few think that the organization is or should be effective in solving community problems; instead, most perceive the YMCA's role as that of a teacher of skills and as a community center. Although character development is the goal definition on which most staff agree, many are somewhat skeptical of their effectiveness in achieving such a goal. These self-perceptions reflect both the decline of long range membership involvement and psychological theories of personality development. The YMCA in these statements is not perceived as a missionary to the world but as a service center to individuals.

These perspectives on goals are amplified by examining the secretaries' preferences in clientele groups. Staff members were asked whether they believed their departments "definitely should," "preferably should," "may or may not," "preferably should not," or "definitely should not" serve various groups. They were also permitted to check "none in our area."

The YMCA's omnibus quality is reflected in these data (table 12). All ages above five, both sexes, and all class groups named were perceived by at least some staff as preferred clientele. Even atheists received acceptance by two-thirds of the professional staff. The only groups not accepted by a majority of staff were delinquent groups and preschool children. As the table indicates, even these groups did not receive outright rejection; instead, a substantial number of staff considered these discretionary (staff checked "may or may not") groups to be served.

The senior citizen and the preschool categories deserve special comment. These are the age groups for which, until recently, the YMCA had not organized any special programs. Yet these are age groups which have recently become target groups. Around the country, as well as in Chicago, YMCAs have begun to develop nursery schools. One Chicago department so involved—a suburban branch—was experiencing considerable difficulty building adequate community support. Similarly, there have been several experimental programs and conferences for senior citizens. Yet both of these groups fall outside the traditional clientele served by the YMCA.

TABLE 12

WHAT GROUPS SHOULD YOUR DEPARTMENT SERVE?—
LOCAL DEPARTMENT STAFF OPINION
(Percent)

	"Definitely should serve"	"Preferably should serve"	"May or may not serve"	"Preferably or definitely should not serve"	"None in our area"
High school youth.......	93	6	1	1	....
Grade school children....	91	7	2	1	....
Young men (18–30)......	87	9	2	2	....
Adult men (30–59).......	86	9	4	1	....
Catholics..............	79	15	6	0	....
Upper-income people (annual income over $8,000)..............	83	8	7	2	1
Jewish people..........	80	70	7	0	3
Lower-income people (annual income under $4,000)..............	73	16	6	3	3
Young women (18–30)....	79	10	6	4	2
Adult women (30–59).....	74	12	9	5	1
Negroes...............	62	16	3	2	17
Senior citizens (60 and over)..........	50	26	19	4	1
Atheists and agnostics....	50	17	21	10	1
Preschool children.......	31	14	31	24	1
Delinquent groups.......	27	19	34	12	9

NOTE: N = 163.

The opposition of many to including delinquents provides an excellent example of the YMCA's preventive focus, for a missionary perspective would clearly require their inclusion. It could be thought, since so many staff checked "may or may not" for delinquent groups, that the desire to avoid delinquents was not an expression of exclusion but a recognition that YMCA staff were not properly equipped to work with them. Likewise, the fact that only 44 percent thought that the YMCA should involve itself in work with community problems might not indicate total lack of interest in other than preventive and character development problems. Therefore, to pinpoint more precisely the degree of resistance to moving beyond traditional programs and clientele groups, the following question was posed:

> If you were on a committee considering new programs for your department, which of the following policies would you recommend?
> A. This department should aim more at "hard core" youth welfare problems like delinquency.
> B. It is okay for the department to deal with groups like delinquents, but they should be kept out of contact with other Y members.
> C. It is all right for the Metropolitan office to aim at some of the "hard core" problems, but our department should not get involved.
> D. The YMCA should concentrate on character-development programs with relatively well-adjusted individuals and leave "hard core" welfare problems to other agencies.

Table 13 presents the percentages of local department staff members choosing each alternative, as well as their perceptions of how other YMCA groups would view this question. Most local department staff clearly favor involvement with "hard core" problems; indeed, 59 percent (combined percentages for *A* and *B*) favor greater involvement. On the other hand, a sizable minority (26 percent) favor dealing only with the

TABLE 13

"HARD CORE" YOUTH WELFARE PROBLEMS: OPINIONS OF
LOCAL STAFF AND THEIR PERCEPTIONS OF OTHERS
(Percent)

	LOCAL STAFF'S OWN OPINION	LOCAL STAFF'S PERCEPTIONS OF		
		Boards	Executives	Metropolitan Staff
A. Aim more at these problems......	36	21	25	45
B. Keep them out of contact with other members................	23	30	31	17
C. Okay for Metropolitan office	14	21	23	20
D. Leave to other agencies..........	26	28	21	18

NOTE: N = 163.

relatively well-adjusted. Thus, although the Metropolitan Association's policy clearly supported such programs, considerable local resistance remained.

How do the local staff perceive other groups within the organization? In general, the staff perceived their own executives and boards of directors as being more likely than themselves to oppose greater attention to hard core youth welfare problems. The fact that the Metropolitan office actively promoted services related to these problems was readily apparent

TABLE 14

"HARD CORE" YOUTH WELFARE SERVICE: ATTITUDES OF
BOARDS, EXECUTIVE SECRETARIES,
AND METROPOLITAN STAFF
(Percent)

	Board Members (N = 280)[a]	Executive Secretaries (N = 35)	Metropolitan Staff[b] (N = 31)	Board Members' Perceptions of Board Members (N = 263)[c]
A. Aim more at these problems....	51	46	65	38
B. Keep them out of contact with other members.............	14	13	13	21
C. Okay for Metropolitan office...	7	11	16	12
D. Leave to other agencies........	28	30	6	30

[a] Nine did not answer.
[b] Metropolitan staff were asked what they believed the policy for the local departments should be.
[c] Twenty-six did not answer.

to staff. It should be noted that staff did not overwhelmingly believe that boards and executives want to isolate their departments from contact with these kinds of programs; they believed that the boards and executives were simply more cautious than they themselves were. The staff tended to believe that the executives and boards were more likely than they to want to avoid contact between the "hard core" and the regular clientele.

Since we had also administered questionnaires to the boards of thirteen local departments, to the executive secretaries themselves, and to the Metropolitan office staff, we were able to examine the actual distribution of opinion in these groups. These data are given in table 14.

The third column demonstrates the Metropolitan staff's strong concern with increased youth welfare programing. In this regard, they had supported the programing innovations introduced by Metropolitan leadership over the past few years. Possibly more interesting were the policy views of the boards. (Because the board sample overrepresents inner city boards, these distributions may not match that of local staff. Nevertheless, note the difference between boards' self-announced attitudes and their perceptions of their fellow board members' attitudes.) Quite opposite to staff expectations (table 13), board members said that they would like to see the YMCA become more involved in youth welfare programs. The table also demonstrates, however, that board members themselves are likely to perceive the majority viewpoint as more opposed to youth welfare policies than the board members' actual choices indicate—apparently a case of pluralistic ignorance.

The questionnaire alternative favoring "hard core" youth welfare policy gave, as an example, programs for delinquents. Since some areas included little delinquency, the results for both staff and board might only indicate that departments not facing delinquency in their areas voted against having programs for hard core youth welfare. In other words, larger proportions than the figures indicate might well favor welfare-type programs.

Certainly staff from outer city and suburban departments were less likely than staff and board from inner city departments to choose alternatives *A* and *B* on the welfare problem question: 51 percent of staff and 54 percent of boards from outer city and suburban departments favored alternatives *A* and *B,* whereas 65 percent of staff and 78 percent of boards from inner city and racially changing neighborhoods favored these alternatives. This greater emphasis on delinquency relates to a general orientation toward community problems. Responding to the goal statements presented in table 11, 49 percent of board and 52 percent of staff members from the inner city as contrasted with only 36 percent of board and 33 percent of staff members from the suburbs and outer city considered community problem solving an important goal for their departments. To a greater extent, then, suburban department staff and boards were satisfied with the YMCA's traditional posture toward community problems than were inner city staff and board members. If the Association existed mainly in suburban middle-class areas, there might be little pressure to move out of its traditional niche; as shown below (chaps. 8–11), however, its existence in working-class and lower-class areas forced both staff and boards to begin redefining the organizational niche.

To summarize briefly, the staff of the Chicago YMCA's local departments, like those of most Associations across the country, has increasingly defined the Association as a general service organization serving groups of all ages and religions. Even though the most preferred group remains youth, no serious resistance to either young children (above the age of five) or to adults exists. While the Chicago YMCA has increasingly involved itself in attempts to solve hard core youth welfare problems, the data indicate little consensus on this as a proper goal for the organization. However, this was an emerging concern for the Association. Because of changes in the society, on the other hand, the traditional goal of drawing people closer to Christianity had moved to a lower priority.

I have argued that goals and preferred clientele represent part of the polity's collective values. Indeed, any new programs had to be justified in terms of their conformity to the constitutional vow, that is, the YMCA "ought to be developing character," the YMCA "ought to be working with youth." There are, of course, other values which shape decisions and behavior, as well as choices of personnel programs and planning. The values discussed above, however, represent core values around which the others are arranged.

With the YMCA strictly hierarchical, with few decision centers influencing organizational directions, then an attempt to characterize organizational ideology and values beyond that of a small elite might be misplaced. Pluralistic organizations like the YMCA, with diffuse goals, however, require a broader sampling of the substratum of sentiment. Multiple power centers exist which influence the implementation of program. Furthermore, given the very breadth of goals and interpretations of them, each power center might well choose different interpretations and lines of action.

THE STRUCTURE OF THE POLITY

When the governing norms of an organization develop primarily by accretion, with little conflict or with conflict only over specific (though by no means unimportant) points of interpretation, the constitution of rights and duties has to be inferred not from official documents but rather from the actions of authoritative bodies. As is commonly known, often only the forms of legal offices are preserved, and even these elicit only ritual behavior with no commitment of emotion or value. This "play acting" holds as well (if not better) for the governments of large-scale organizations as for the governments of nations. Of course, the rituals may be linked to structures, practices, or contingent situations that do have meaning; thus attempts to abolish or change them may threaten other segments of the social system.

In the Chicago YMCA the clearest instance of such ritualistic behavior occurred in the formalistic functioning of the voting, or governing, members, who were officially charged with electing the board of managers. The voting members, who theoretically met once a year, consisted of 612 informed laymen nominated by the local departments and the board of managers. The voting members' official intent (as set forth in the by-laws) was as a constituency of informed members to elect the board of managers and to vote on other matters not delegated to the trustees or the board of managers. In actuality, the voting members never nominated or elected anyone: rather, they ratified, in a ritualized performance, the choice of a small nominating committee previously chosen by the board of managers. Metropolitan office staff members had begun to question this gap between official and actual function, with several suggesting that the annual meeting of the voting members should be solely for informing and involving influential laymen. The point of this example is simply that we must deal with the normative and actual rather than the official structure of power.

There is, however, yet another pitfall to be avoided: as much as possible in a study done at one point in time, we must avoid confusing the structure of power with the utilization of power based on the specific behavior of a particular person or group. We are not concerned with idiosyncratic definitions of roles and relationships but rather with the polity's traditions and secular trends.

As has been noted, the literature on large-scale organizations and voluntary associations utilizes two sets of terms to connote different polity structures: centralization-decentralization, and corporate-federated. The corporate-federated dimension refers to the relations of constituent units to the whole. In a federated organization several of the major constituent parts usually precede the founding of the overall organization, and these retain rights and jurisdictions over certain significant subunit processes and over parts of the total organizational process. For example, in a federated organization the appointment of executive personnel and the allocation of budgets may be done only with the advice or acquiescence of constituent units. Units within a federated organization usually have access to legal action against the total organization should these rights and jurisdictions be violated. Furthermore, in a federated organization the constituent part may have the right of withdrawal. With the exception of some industrial trade associations, of course, such an organizational type is more characteristic of voluntary associations than business organizations in the United States. Some European cartels do have a federated structure. The corporate form, on the other hand, "owns" its constituent units and, at least in law, can allocate resources at the discretion of the central decision maker.

The centralization-decentralization concept refers to the levels of decision making within a corporate form—even though, with reference to decision making, one would usually find a federated organization more decentralized than a corporate form. We speak of an organization as being more decentralized than another to the extent that a greater range of decisions is permitted at lower levels of the formal organization.

The YMCA at the national level, we have seen, has a federated structure. Since the Chicago Association has been legally a corporate structure, it would be tempting to analyze internal structure in terms of centralization-decentralization. To do so would be misleading, however, for no unitary chain of command has existed in which the levels of discretion of various positions could be ascertained. It is more useful to describe the structure in political metaphors. The Chicago Association had developed a dual power system eventuating in a pluralistic welter of decision centers that has encouraged intraorganizational bargaining. Figure 2 presents a schematic outline of the major groups and units and their relations. Here I have used such words as *appoints, concurs,* or *consults* to pinpoint official responsibilities. The interpretation of these words may vary, however. For instance, a local board might officially be expected to approve the appointment of an executive secretary but in some situations have no real options. Conflicts in the definitions of these responsibilities will be discussed below.

In examining the polity's structure I will review the decision functions, compositions, and interrelationships of each major group or individual within the polity at the time of my study: the board of trustees, the board of managers, boards of directors, the Metropolitan office staff, and the general secretary. Finally I will conclude by analyzing the role of the executive secretary and the principle of local autonomy.

Board of Trustees

The board of trustees consisted of twelve members appointed for life. They controlled all real estate and funds either used for further purchases of real estate or realized from real estate sales. This board was viewed as the Association's senior controlling group. With one exception all had had long experience with the YMCA. Drawn from among leading real estate, banking, and investment insurance firms, by charter the trustees had also to be drawn equally from the four denominations of the original

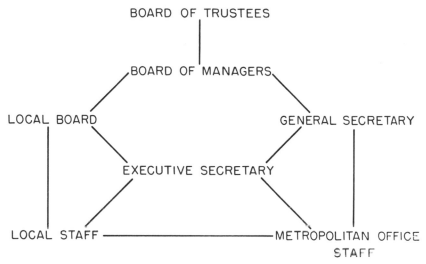

BOARD OF TRUSTEES

BOARD OF MANAGERS

LOCAL BOARD

GENERAL SECRETARY

EXECUTIVE SECRETARY

LOCAL STAFF ─────────────────── METROPOLITAN OFFICE STAFF

Board of trustees. All property is owned and controlled by the Metropolitan Association under the supervision of the board of trustees, a self-perpetuating body.

Board of managers. Operation of the Association is entrusted to the board of managers, also self-perpetuating.

Local board. In turn, the board of managers appoints local boards (thirty-seven in 1962) to oversee the operation of the local departments.

General secretary. The board of managers also appoints a general secretary, who has the responsibility of supervising the work of all staff of the Association.

Metropolitan office staff. The general secretary hires staff for coordinating and supervising a variety of Metropolitan functions, ranging from training to record keeping.

Executive secretary. An executive secretary is appointed to run each local department; he is hired in consultation between the general secretary and the local board.

Local staff. The executive secretary hires staff with the concurrence of the local board, and assigns staff responsibility for major areas of operation.

Fig. 2. A schematic outline of units and their responsibilities in the Chicago Association.

founders. Six of the twelve trustees in 1961 were listed in the *Social Register*. The trustees were formally responsible for the maintenance and preservation of the Association's essential properties and endowment funds. By the requirements of the corporate charter, the trustees met at least once a year; although special meetings could be called, they rarely met as often as quarterly. The trustees were required to approve all purchases or sales of land and facilities as well as all major building renovations or remodelings. Formally, then, they were in a position to hinder or promote specific directions of change; during the period of this study, however, they did not veto any recommendation made to them by the board of managers.

From this description it might appear that as an authoritative body the trustees were powerless. Although they did not initiate or veto specific actions by the board of managers, there were, however, general accounting policies that had emerged over the years and that were viewed as "policies of the trustees." These policies acted as a constraint on the Association's decisions and allocations. One of the most important of these was that each department's depreciation reserves (funds required to protect the investment of the total Association) were merged into the general investment pool; they were consequently not available to individual departments without specific grants of privilege and the board of trustees' approval. Since the general investment pool was also used to finance new buildings, depreciation reserves from local departments were actually subsidizing YMCA expansion into the suburbs. Over the years, this "trustees' policy" had placed outside the domain of the local departments certain funds which were not viewed as discretionary even by the Metropolitan office staff. It should be noted that the actual origin of this policy—the degree to which it was initiated by the trustees rather than by, perhaps, the general secretary—and of others like it is unknown. What is important is that this policy was a constraining force in decision making.

Although such policies acted as constraints on other groups in the organization, the trustees were not powerful or influential in the day-to-day operation of the Association. They were not consulted during the early stages of planning for expansion or for renovation, and, as a body, functioned more to legitimate decisions than to initiate or debate alternatives.

In part their legitimation of the managers' proposals could be expected, since key trustees (the president and three others) were also respected members of the board of managers. The president of the trustees was also the member of the board of managers most often involved in investigating and negotiating the alternatives to real estate purchases and utilization. In a real sense, then, the trustees were represented on the board of managers and the managers' decisions were quite naturally in terms acceptable to the trustees.

Board of Managers

The trustees' official bylaws delegated to the board of managers responsibility for the current operations of the Association, including the management and maintenance of facilities. In 1961 the board of managers had thirty-eight members, who had been recruited from three major sources. Some came to the board of managers after long service on local department boards or on subcommittees of the board. Those coming from local department boards had usually been officers of (and generous contributors to) their local departments. Only one of these was concurrently a local board chairman.

A second area for recruiting board members was provided by corporate and family connections. Several corporations, law firms, and families had enjoyed long connections with the YMCA, and it was informally expected that at least one senior member of certain firms would serve on the board of managers. The most prominent and longest standing of the corporate connections were those with Sears, Roebuck and Company and the Harris Trust and Savings Bank. The historic connection with Sears, Roebuck developed from two sources. First, one local YMCA department (actually named the Sears, Roebuck YMCA) was located directly across the street from the company's national headquarters on Chicago's West Side, and numerous Sears executives had been active members of its board of directors. These executives constituted an obvious potential base for recruitment to the Metropolitan board. Possibly more important, however, was the fact that Julius Rosenwald, a major builder of and stockholder in Sears and one of America's great philanthropists, had been an ardent supporter of the "colored" YMCA movement; Rosenwald guaranteed $25,000 to any community that could raise $75,000 within five years for the construction of Negro YMCAs.[8]

Likewise, some families had long historic connections with the Association. John V. Farwell had been one of the Chicago Association's original incorporators in 1861 and had donated large sums for its original

---

8. By 1920 twelve Negro departments had been built with Rosenwald funds (Hopkins, p. 458). Altogether, Rosenwald helped start twenty-eight Associations with gifts amounting to $637,000 (Dedmon, p. 184).

building. One of his grandnephews was a member of the board of trustees, and further family connections could be perceived in the future when the senior Farwell retired from the board.

A third source from which the board of managers drew members encompassed persons of high standing within the professional and business community. Metropolitan senior staff and board members intermittently sought support from the officers of large firms and from prominent professional men. This source was of special concern to senior staff, since the YMCA has always been in competition with other organizations for financial support, public and private legitimation, and management wisdom. Senior staff are always concerned to insure that the Metropolitan Association's board be a "power" board. They compared the prestige, reputation, and influence of their board members with those of other organizations and frequently discussed means by which more prestigious members might be attracted to the organization. (In 1961 20 percent of the board of managers were listed in the *Social Register*.)

The board of managers was officially responsible for formulating Association policy, for overseeing both operating programs and finances, and for appointing and guiding the general secretary. Because it was a large, cumbersome body (usually meeting as a whole only once a month), the board of managers delegated many of its functions to its committees. There was little debate or discussion during the board's monthly meetings (as is true of most such organizations) and the votes on most matters were pro forma.

There were several board committees responsible for reacting to the Metropolitan staff's proposals and suggestions and for choosing among alternative policies and programs. These committees included the personnel committee, the investment subcommittee, the program committee, the subcommittee on city-wide events, the detached worker committee, the marketing committee, subcommittees on the annual dinner and on the laymen's conference, and so on. Indeed, because of the emphasis on lay involvement and control, most major activities were accompanied by the structuring of a committee.

In terms of the scope of their mandate, three committees—the executive committee, the program committee and the committee on business operation—deserve special attention. The last two were the key permanent committees concerned with ongoing departmental operations. On the official level the mandate of the program committee involved encouraging new and creative programs and evaluating and approving departments' program plans. Because of the principle of local autonomy and the organization's enrollment economy, however, the program committee acted more as a general tool of discussion and suggestion than as a decision maker. Although it made periodic evaluations and conferred with the departments on one aspect or another of programs, except with regard to city-wide events it had no effective levers for control.

A key function of the business committee involved its approval each year of the department's budget plans and its examination each month of the departments' actual performance in terms of their individual income and expense goals. A second important function was the authority to approve departmental plans for renovation and expansion and for new facilities. In combination with staff it held a crucial control over the departments and could initiate proposals to reduce expenditures or warn departmental boards of impending problems. In some regards it represented the major focus of metropolitan control.

The executive committee, particularly in the persons of its officers and dominant members, was the most important. All proposals approved by the executive committee usually survived the full board. All major, Association-wide problems were considered by this committee. Several of its members were among the Association's best informed laymen, and in this respect they were often in a position to influence staff decisions as well as to shape independent judgments on matters.

The formal process for selecting executive committee members was quite vague. The president of the Association once remarked, "I don't know how a man gets on the executive committee, nor, for that matter, how he gets off." Although, for other committees, staff people and the board president would periodically suggest possible chairmen and members, and although the general committee structure was constantly being reviewed, the executive committee simply seemed to exist. In practice, the process was not that vague. With one exception each member could trace his joining the executive committee to either a board officership (president, vice-president, treasurer, or secretary) or a major committee chairmanship. The single exception had been a major donor to the Association (over several years he had given more than a quarter of a million dollars) with historic family connections. Once on the committee, members stayed on until they "resigned" through lack of attendance, resignation from the board of managers, or death.

Although the executive committee discussed all matters on the board's agenda as well as many other matters that could be handled informally (that is, without voting), these matters were not considered in the absence of senior staff consultation. The executive committee meetings were chaired by either the president or the vice-president, but between three and seven members of the senior staff usually attended. And even when a committee member presented a proposal or problem, he had usually been briefed by a staff member, and that staff member might be asked to amplify the proposal and answer questions. The *only* matter on which staff were not consulted was the salary of the general secretary and the choosing of his successor.

The executive committee, more than any other lay committee or group, constituted a power center within the organization. All proposals were funneled through it. Even proposals that were completely staff-generated were framed in terms acceptable to the board and the executive committee.

The board of managers' broad mandate for managing the Association's affairs had to be institutionalized through delegating day-to-day operating control, both of the Metropolitan Association and of the local departments. The YMCA's dual control system became important at this point. On the one hand the managers delegated their general supervisory functions to the departmental boards of directors, which were to carry out the Association's policies and promote the YMCA within their local areas. On the other hand, the board of managers appointed a general secretary with responsibility for supervising all staff and enforcing the general policy of the YMCA.

Whereas the principle of lay control was officially enshrined at the Metropolitan level, in the development of local departments two lines of control were established. Thus, formally, the local department executive had two masters, the local board and the general secretary; it was in the areas between these two authorities that problems could be debated, bargains struck, and postures adopted.

Local Boards of Directors

The boards of directors of local departments were a key element in the pluralistic nature of the YMCA's political system. Had these boards been conceived as essentially advisory in nature (as is true in some other organizations) their powers would have been considerably diminished. On the other hand, had they been closely linked to the board of managers, either as committees of the board or through a sharing of personnel, the distribution of power within the system would have been limited. In fact, the local boards enjoyed real power to make and to influence key decisions, and their relationship with the Metropolitan Association was such that they constituted separate centers of power.

The department boards were important elements of the Association's power system for several reasons. First, they were an important source of local funds and legitimation. Departmental board members not only contributed money themselves but were key fund raisers in local drives. Second, in terms of lay control, they were the employers of key professional staff; having received a recommendation of two or three candidates from the general secretary, a board had the right to hire an executive secretary for its department. Third, these boards approved the executive secretaries' salaries and were responsible for overseeing the budget and submitting a balanced one to the board of managers. When a board had consistently operated on a deficit budget, board members and staff alike felt that the board was doing an inadequate job; conversely, when a department was in the black, its board members took pride in that fact. The board's crucial role in hiring the executive and determining his salary, as well as in fund-raising, combined well with the high value placed on lay control. As a result the boards appeared to themselves and to others as the ultimate sources of authority in local affairs.

Although board members were conscious of the metropolitan context of local affairs, several factors contributed to a localistic orientation and a consequent centrifugal force in policy formulation. The most crucial of these factors were the process of recruiting board members, the lack of integrating mechanisms to unite board members with the Metropolitan board of managers, and the prevailing sense of local identification and local responsibility.

Officially, the members of local department boards were appointed by the board of managers. But just as the board of managers was in reality a self perpetuating group vis-à-vis the voting members, so also the local boards were self-perpetuating vis-à-vis the board of managers, which merely ratified the nominations of local nominating committees. These committees chose their nominees in consultation with the executive secretary and other members of the local board. New members were usually recruited among the businessmen and professionals who worked or lived in the community. The great majority of the more than one thousand local board members either lived or worked (many both lived and worked) within the areas served by their departments. Generally board members were drawn from outside the departmental area only when the departments were located in poor, heavily residential areas, or when they were very large departments encompassing a clientele broader than the local neighborhood. As a consequence of their local base, departmental boards as compared to the board of managers had a smaller pool of wealthy families and corporate executives upon which to draw. None of the boards had so much as 20 percent of their members listed in the *Social Register,* and twenty-seven departments had no members so listed.[9]

One should not infer, because board members were largely recruited within the local area and without consultations with the board of managers or the Metropolitan office staff, that the board of managers and its staff were uninterested in the quality or character of the local boards. Quite to the contrary, one board of managers committee actually discussed plans for "upgrading" the local boards, and an assistant general secretary had as part of his "portfolio" the development of training services and other devices for assisting local departments to develop better boards and raise the quality of recruitment. Nevertheless, individual recruitment was left to the local department.

There was a quite general agreement on certain characteristics for board members. They should have a commitment to the YMCA, a history of involvement, a proper "social and Christian motivation," and an ability to contribute money, program skills or knowledge, and stature. In the absence of all of these characteristics, some combination would do. And, as was true of their belief regarding new members, YMCA personnel often felt that commitment and knowledge would follow even though a man originally joined for superficial reasons. As a consequence, community stature and the ability to contribute funds held an important edge in many departments. Even with a broad consensus regarding the desirable characteristics of board members, it should be noted that specific instances of recruiting or of electing or removing officers might produce disagreements.

The independent selection and operation of boards might not have been the centrifugal force it was if the social and organizational experiences of board members with the board of managers had been such as to make them more aware of, and sympathetic with, the managers' policies. Although it would be easy to exaggerate such unawareness and lack of sympathy, the consensus that existed arose more from a "mechanical solidarity" of homogeneous expectations from the YMCA than from any "organic solidarity" of interdependent experience. Only a few board members served on city-wide committees, and the vast majority participated in only one city-wide function each year—the Association's annual

9. On the relation of the city's ecology to the recruitment of board members and to organizational effectiveness, see Mayer N. Zald, "Urban Differentiation, Boards of Directors and Organizational Effectiveness, *"American Journal of Sociology* 73 (1967): pp. 261–72.

dinner meeting. The presidents of the local departments were invited to attend the managers' meetings, but no more than three or four did so (and only one or two regularly). Furthermore, they were guests of the board of managers, not members of it.

Only recently (since 1959) has an annual laymen's conference been held which has devoted a day and a half to general discussion of the Association's problems. These meetings, attended by between one and two hundred board members and their wives, may have begun to contribute to a broader base of identification, but at best their effects have been slight.

By and large, boards had a narrow base of experience in the YMCA as such. Members worked for and identified with their local departments. Their committee and board experience involved only the operational needs of their own department within their community. Given this type of experience, board concern could be expected to transcend local departments only if the YMCA were still a social movement with broad evangelizing goals. Although a few board members still conceived the YMCA as an evangelizing organization, the vast majority saw the YMCA only in terms of their department and not as an onrushing movement of Christians.

To the extent that boards influenced policy, they represented a centrifugal pressure on the board of managers' policies. I shall argue later that the boards' existence as an independent power source within the organization, when combined with the YMCA's ideological posture, generally operated as a conservative pressure within the organization. What is more important for the moment, however, is that there were also centripetal pressures working for a homogeneity and uniformity of policy. The centripetal forces were represented by the other chain of command that developed under the board of managers, the general secretary, and his staff.

The Metropolitan Office

The Metropolitan office's professional staff, the executive secretary, and the local departments' professional staff were the major groups making recommendations to the board of managers and local boards of directors. It was they also who applied policy to specific situations and problems. Consequently, they could wield power in two directions. First, they were vital in shaping official policies at both metropolitan and local levels; these groups often affected not only the definition of issues but also, by their influence on the decision-making processes, the disposition of these issues. Second, as they implemented policies, they were in a position either to support or to sabotage accepted policies.

The historical development of the professionals' role in Chicago YMCA's Metropolitan office illustrates trends not only specific to the YMCA across the country, but also secular trends typical of professional roles in modern, large-scale organizations. If the YMCA secretaryship is conceived as having developed into a profession, then these trends have included an increased emphasis on formal education (rather than apprentice experience) for certification and an increased emphasis on the inclusion of social science courses in that education; whereas, initially, several courses in theology and the history of Christianity had been required, courses in group work, sociology, and psychology, as well as in the history and administration of the YMCA, have recently been considered more crucial.

More important for the organization of power and authority within the Association were the growth and changing definitions of the Metropolitan office staff's roles. These changing role definitions paralleled growing specializations in the larger society. As the Metropolitan office hired specialized personnel to generate programs and policies for specific areas, pressures arose for a uniformity of policy in carrying out the Association's business. Since the direction of this uniformity was shaped by the Metropolitan staff and board of managers' committees, the establishment of collective policies obviously had a centralizing effect. Furthermore, the increased level of expertise required and the dependence on these offices for coordinative activity resulted in an important decision-making role for "staff" (in the sense of staff-line) personnel.

At the time of this study the Metropolitan office employed at least thirty persons in responsible supervisory, auditing, and general staff functions, who represented the Metropolitan office's major managerial cadre. About twenty other staff above the stenographic level were on the Metropolitan payroll, but these were either not YMCA professionals, or were on special assignments to departments or only temporarily based in the Metropolitan office. Only fifteen years before, the Metropolitan office had been substantially smaller, and many staff portfolios now in existence (membership, personnel, public relations) were then handled on a catch-as-catch-can basis. Personnel policy, for example, had been determined by individual departments or, if considered centrally, had been treated haphazardly. The Metropolitan office's expansion occurred simultaneously with an extensive growth of the whole Association; many branches were either established or moved into new facilities during this period. The Metropolitan office program and administrative staff, however, appear to have grown more rapidly than the full-time professional staff of the total Association. One personnel office report showed a decline, from 1954 to 1963, of 18 percent in all full-time departmental staff, whereas the Metropolitan office staff increased by 33 percent during the same period.

Trends in the professional staff alone parallel these changes. Table 15 shows that from 1947 to 1963 local professional staff increased only 13 percent while Metropolitan professional staff grew 56 percent. Furthermore, the addition of the Detached Workers Program (street gang

TABLE 15

PROFESSIONAL STAFF: LOCAL DEPARTMENTS AND
METROPOLITAN OFFICE

	Local Department	Metropolitan Office	Total
1947.........	111	18	129
1957.........	138	23	161
1963.........	125	28	153

SOURCE: *Yearbook*s for appropriate years. These figures include only fully certified secretaries.

workers) to the Metropolitan office increased by sixteen the number of full-time personnel.

The Metropolitan office's professional personnel were formally considered a staff extension of the general secretary. Organized according to substantive specialties (business, architectural services, program services, insurance and maintenance, and public relations), none of the Metropolitan office's personnel supervised individual departments. Rather, all executives were directly responsible to the general secretary. Formally, the general secretary had thirty-seven executive secretaries responsible to him as well as nine assistant general secretaries. In formal terminology (which was rarely used) the executive secretaries were also assistant general secretaries, an indication of their formal equality with the Metropolitan office staff. In addition to the assistant general secretaries, there were other professional staff attached to the Metropolitan office. Some reported to the nine assistant general secretaries and were of no further concern to this study. The Detached Workers Program, the only direct service program so located, also operated directly from the Metropolitan office.

The Metropolitan office's assistant general secretaries were recruited from three main sources: the executive secretaries of departments, the executive secretaries and general secretaries of other Associations, and specialists recruited outside the YMCA. In Chicago such specialists included the assistant general secretary for personnel, the assistant general secretary for public relations, and the comptroller. In each case, the individual had originally been employed without strong YMCA identification and had first held a less important post. Two of the assistant general secretaries had been hired from Associations outside Chicago. One had been the general secretary in a city of about 75,000 population; the other had been the executive secretary in a small western community. The most important source of assistant general secretaries, however, was clearly the executive secretaries of Chicago departments. This source linked Metropolitan office personnel both with predecessors in that office (with whom sympathetic ties had usually been established) and with friends and colleagues in the local departments. Rather than encouraging factions, then, the network of positions and affiliations tended to create some real though loose ties of sympathy and orientation within the Association.

There was a formal equality among the nine assistant general secretaries in that the general secretary refused to make official distinctions among them or to promote one above the other in title. The salary scales and patterns of consultation with the general secretary and board of managers, however, as well as the pattern of consultation with departmental secretaries, indicated that in actual practice three or four (depending on the criteria used) of these secretaries did rank higher in the staff counsels. They were treated with deference by other assistants, were consulted oftener by the general secretary on crucial cases, and were generally considered part of the upper echelon. Included in this group were the comptroller, the assistant general secretary for operational services, and the assistant general secretary for program services. (The importance of these roles in the organization's political process will be considered in more detail below.)

The functions performed by the Metropolitan office varied widely. All had latent functions for the polity, however, and many, from the viewpoint of this study, were manifestly political. Four such sets of activities were (1) central services, (2) interdepartmental coordination and city-wide programing, (3) supervision, training, and control, and (4) program and facilities expansion.

Central services. Several functions were basically related to organizational economizing. For example, a self-insurance fund was maintained which permitted a much lower set of charges to the total Association than if each department had bought its own insurance. (Indeed, the fund's reserves had grown so large that consideration was being given to a further premium reduction which would release funds for other uses.) A central purchasing office established contracts with food suppliers, and prices were negotiated for building equipment, maintenance supplies, and program equipment. Advertising campaigns to publicize membership and program facilities were conducted through the Metropolitan office. A further function involved recruiting personnel from college much in the manner of corporations; the Metropolitan office utilized both college visits and a truncated training-tryout program.

These service functions were not without implications for the polity. Local departments, for example, could have negotiated their own insurance or hired their own architectural services or contractors, and in so doing they would have extended their network of relationships with board members and local businessmen. And certainly these were issues of occasional conflict. In one instance, a local department claimed that, negotiating alone, it could obtain better architectural drawings, at lower cost, for a planned renovation. In another instance, following a fire at a local department, a board member complained because his firm had not been asked to assist in securing the property against vandals and in later construction. Had the individual departments handled such matters, it would have increased their independence and decreased the Metropolitan office's resource and knowledge control.

Nevertheless, the performance of such functions in the Metropolitan office did not represent a fundamental lever of control or a tool for shaping the polity. These functions were generally handled in such a routine manner that only major changes brought the power relations into operation. Basically, the provision of such services through the Metropolitan office only represented previous decisions, made in the name of economy and efficiency, that had the broad effect of extending the range of duties systematically performed on the metropolitan level.

Interdepartmental coordination and city-wide programs. A second set of activities was the planning and coordination of city-wide and interdepartmental activities. These included athletic activities (such as football leagues for junior high school and senior elementary grades, swimming meets and track meets) and club and citizens' programs (such as the University of Good Government program for high schoolers). A related set of activities involved programing for board members and other lay committees.

Another set of interdepartmental activities involved the sharing of facilities. Departments that "owned" camps, for example, rented their property to others that did not; or owning departments might give non-owning ones a "cut" for signing campers for specified periods. One department might also arrange to use another's swimming pool. Although such activities were sometimes arranged directly between the parties involved, when the coordination involved several departments and required complicated scheduling, a city-wide committee would be convened consisting of members from the interested departments and from the Metropolitan office staff.

These committees had a dual effect on the polity. First, they increased communication and brought about a sharing of perspectives on the organization and program, effectively integrating the staff into an organization larger than the local department. Second, the policies adopted in such sharing programs could agree, disagree, or be neutral with respect to the Association's broad policies. Camping arrangements, for example, could mix youngsters from departments with either similar or dissimilar socioeconomic and ethnic backgrounds. The resolution of such possibilities could obviously further or hinder Association policy.

Supervision, training, and control. As the board of managers' central agent, the office staff's fundamental task was to review the performance of local department staff and to provide services for upgrading that performance. On the one hand, training courses or institutes were provided on such topics as fund raising and instruction in water safety. On the other, supervision was achieved through review of fiscal management, building maintenance, and general departmental performance. These could be broken down into such areas as cafeteria management, membership enrollment, varieties of program activity, and so on.

Given the political economy of the YMCA, it was easier to achieve effective supervision of the departments' financial affairs than of program affairs. The central point, however, is that the existence and effectiveness of the Metropolitan office's review of performance was a crucial centripetal element in the organization. When linked with various enforcement mechanisms, these mechanisms formed the crux of political control.

Program and facilities expansion. The Metropolitan office staff funneled to the board of managers all proposals for renovation, for expansion of facilities, and for possible new departments and new programs. New program ideas might arise within a local department, in YMCAs or other organizations within or outside the Chicago area, within the Metropolitan office, or even within the federal government. Unless the idea could be easily implemented, however, subsidy funds might be necessary to underwrite initial expenses; such funds often had to be generated through the board of managers, which necessitated Metropolitan staff clearance of the proposal.

Similarly, proposals for new departments usually required the support of the board of managers. Often initial local support for a new department would be stimulated by the assignment of a secretary to a storefront operation in the target area. Sometimes a secretary might be so assigned even without local support. A decision to construct a new building also involved the Metropolitan staff, which was responsible for assessing the plan's feasibility and (possibly) assigning staff to assist in local fund raising.

It was in these supervision and control activities, on the one hand, and expansion and development activities, on the other, that the Metropolitan office exercised its strongest power. For it was through the processes of supervision and program facilitation that the office could most affect local operations.

Since a local department's board of directors was officially responsible for hiring its executive secretary and determining his salary, and since the executive secretary, in turn, hired his own staff, it might be thought that the Metropolitan office staff possessed few mechanisms for gaining compliance with its goals. It might be thought that they were dependent solely upon the pure logic of their programs. Several mechanisms, or sanctions, were available to the Metropolitan office staff, however, and these were used to achieve at least some degree of sensitivity to their wishes. One of the most important of these was the fact that the Metropolitan office controlled the referral system within the total Association. The opening of a professional position somewhere within the organization normally prompted the Metropolitan office to recommend likely candidates. This was true for positions within the Chicago Association as well as in other cities. Within the city the executive secretary's mobility depended absolutely upon the Metropolitan office. The mobility route normally involved promotion from smaller YMCAs to larger ones, and it was a general practice for boards to confer with the Metropolitan office regarding salary raises for the executive. Both of these factors provided obvious levers to increase the secretary's agreeableness.

Of possibly equal importance was the Metropolitan office's control over deficit financing, matching funds, and subsidy funds. An executive's ability to operate his department satisfactorily might depend on his ability to convince the Metropolitan office staff of his needs, and this in turn might depend upon his previous degree of compliance with Metropolitan office directives. I shall return to this topic in discussing the consequences of the political economy.

In addition to outlining the major functions of the Metropolitan office I might also indicate some of the mechanisms used to formulate policy recommendations and gain consensus. As we have seen, the Metropolitan office was essentially an extension of the general secretary. As the Association grew and as specialized functions multiplied, it became more and more difficult for him to maintain close contact with all staff. One solution to this difficulty was the creation of the general secretary's cabinet. Beginning in the 1930s as a formal meeting of all Chicago Association professional staff, the cabinet slowly developed into an elite body consisting of all assistant general secretaries (executive secretaries and division heads from the Metropolitan office) and a few of the lower-level Metropolitan professionals. This group met once a month and within itself served more for information transmission than for policy debate. The cabinet, however, was gradually structured into subcommittees which considered and made recommendations on issues ranging from membership policy to financial problems. These committees were usually chaired by one of the more highly respected executives and had as staff secretary a member of the Metropolitan staff. A fairly wide consensus was generally developed on the issues considered by these committees.

Furthermore, as a younger personnel generation matured knowing nothing other than a large, central Metropolitan office, the general perception of its legitimate authority was bound to increase. Nevertheless, to some of the older executives the Metropolitan office staff were interlopers restricting their autonomy.

The Executive Secretary and Local Autonomy

I have described the dual authority system as developing from the delegation of local operating authority to departmental boards of directors, on the one hand, and, on the other, from staff supervision by the general secretary. The Metropolitan office clearly went beyond staff supervision, for it overviewed the total operation of the local department.

Given the dual system, the potential for conflict seemed substantial, and yet in practice it was not very high. The explanation for this apparent contradiction must be sought in the role of the executive and the principle of local autonomy.

The executive secretary was to some degree caught between the Metropolitan office and the local board. Disagreements on policy direction raised the possibility of conflict and role strain (or, for that matter, role neutralization). Several features of the YMCA's organization facilitated his adaptation, however. First, his prime responsibility was by definition to the local department. Most of his work hours were spent interacting with his local staff and board. As long as his budget was balanced, he would incur neither great wrath nor great pressure from the Metropolitan office. Second, the Chicago YMCA's ideology, adopted from the national Association, strongly supported the principle of local autonomy. Since the YMCA's goals were often perceived in terms of serving the needs of the local community, it was natural to asume that a secretary's first duty was to define these needs and plan to meet them. The principle of local autonomy also operated to bolster board power, producing another centrifugal force within the Metropolitan Association. Even if the executive had manipulated a passive board, its proclaimed actions or orientations could be used to justify his independence from the Metropolitan office. The principle of autonomy also implied that in choosing programs or personnel the choice was a matter for local decision. In such a situation, the Metropolitan office could frequently only suggest direction; decisions lay with the local department.

The principle of local autonomy was a basic constitutional principle. Not that it was rigidly adhered to: instead, like states' rights, it represented a rallying point and a norm against which change was often measured. The analogy to states' rights should not be overdrawn. First, the principle of local autonomy was applied more pervasively in the YMCA than the principle of states' rights in the United States. States' rights has usually been a cover issue for a more specific (often racial) conflict. Second, strife within the Association over the principle was much more covert than overt. Nevertheless, the transformation of the organization to be described (in Part III) will involve an account of an attack on the norm.

5

The Money Economy

Among other changes the YMCA's historical transformation from evangelism to general services contributed to a fundamental realignment in its funding sources, in its incentive offerings to members and personnel, and in its internal division of labor and central productive tasks. Some of the changes in central productive tasks that equally affected the Chicago Association as well as others have been discussed earlier. But we need to show quite specifically the interpenetration of the polity with the funding sources and economic problems of local departments, for the political principle of local autonomy was tied to the basic economy.

A sociological description of an organization's money economy must accomplish several fundamental tasks. It must first describe the organization's exchange network with clientele and funders. What income sources are available? Are they so concentrated as to issue in extreme dependence on one or two buyers or dispersers? Is the organization operating in a competitive context? Is it oligopolistic? Does the organization hold either a monopoly or monopsony? Is it limited to one or two products, or does it have numerous products and markets? What is the relationship of the organizational economy to fluctuations in the business cycle? To fluctuations in raw material prices? Furthermore, and most important for any study of organizational change, what are the long-range "industry" trends for growth or decline?

When studying any organization which depends on some funds sources apart from its clientele (buyers), the sociologist must examine the norms and rules that have developed in either public legislative committees or in relationship to major donors.

A sociological study of organizational economy must also describe and analyze the internal decision rules for allocating facilities—men, money, and tools. Since the theory of the firm ignores the internal structure of organization, economists have largely bypassed this problem. Only those

112

like Joel Dean[1] (who focused on internal prices charged by multiproduct and decentralized firms) have considered this an important problem for economic analysis. Unfortunately, there is no sociology of accounting rules. The economist and accountant generally want internal prices to operate as gauges of unit efficiency. Similarly, they want cost allocated in a "true" form so as to mirror actual expenditures. Both cost accounting techniques and competitive bidding are designed to assure efficiency. In a sense, both suggest a given type of political goal—efficiency. Of course, accounting and budgeting systems may serve other goals besides efficiency. They may be designed to preserve capital, to expose choices to collective and centralized scrutiny, and the like.[2]

The resolution of cost allocation has long-range implications for organizational growth and change. Consider an industrial firm's allocation of research and development costs. If the organization's research and development work is closely determined by demands or budgets approved by the operating departments, the organization may not allocate funds for "pie in the sky" projects. Yet from the organization's long-range viewpoint, such projects may be necessary. Or consider an organization with two options: to buy services from an outside corporation at a lower price than its own internal division will offer or buy its goods from its internal division, whose price includes research and development costs. Since such costs might result in a future payoff, the corporation's long-range advantage might well be to buy the more expensive, internal product.

As the analysis moves away from efficiency criteria (usually short-range in concept), the whole area of cost allocation and the nature of decision rules becomes grist for political economics. What difference does it make to a firm and to an organization's internal power system if the research and development unit receives a flat sum yearly rather than having to submit a separate budget for each project? How are overhead costs allocated among units (if they are allocated at all)? How are internal loans and capital investments treated? Which areas of budget making

1. "Decentralization and Intra-Company Pricing," *Harvard Business Review* 33 (1955): 65–74. See also William J. Baumol, *Business Behavior, Value, and Growth* (New York: Macmillan Co., 1959). Baumol argues that oligopolistic firms hold a sales-maximization goal subject to a minimum-profit constraint, rather than a profit-maximization goal. His explanation, which could be termed a political-economy interpretation, is based on managerial incentive, maintenance of morale, and the firm's position in the marketplace (see chaps. 6 and 7).

2. Aaron Wildavsky, "The Political Economy of Efficiency," *The Public Interest* 8 (1967): 30–48.

and expenditure are automated? Which are systematically reviewed? By whom? It would be feckless at this point to attempt a more theoretical and systematic approach to accounting systems. Suffice it to state that internal rules can be conservative or radical; they can inhibit or encourage the mobilization of organizational power; and they can fortify or hinder ongoing power arrangements.

The Chicago YMCA was funded by a network of clients and benefactors, with complex organizational relations. In part it operated as a business, attempting to sell services for a profit which was intended to subsidize core programs. Core programs, while generating some of their own support, rarely broke even. And not only were business profits used to subsidize programs, the YMCA operated, at least in part, as a charitable institution: it received yearly donations from board members, funds from an annual campaign and a substantial amount from the Community Fund Red Feather Drive. Capital funds were generated through random (though cultivated) bequests and endowments, as well as through separate capital fund drives.

Were all funds received by the Association entered in a central ledger and disbursed according to a central decision maker, both the description and the analysis of the YMCA's economy would be simplified. Each department, however, had its own annual budget and its own endowment funds (though the latter were managed by the Metropolitan office). Furthermore, over the years some departments had made "deals" with the board of managers and the general secretary which had resulted in different accounting rules for specific cases. We must, then, not only examine the income sources of departments but also explain how these are treated and interpreted by staff and boards to affect departmental economies.

SOURCES OF INCOME

Local departments received funds from four major sources: business or "club" income, membership and program income, contributions, and Metropolitan subsidies.

Business Income

The New York YMCA's first major building devoted its first floors to shops in order to generate an income subsidy for programs. Soon afterward, however, YMCAs throughout the country began to realize that a source of income directly consonant with their goal of serving single young men was available. The first dormitories met a real need, for in the burgeoning cities the supply of rental units was limited and the less expensive hotels were usually located in zones of transition (areas with "tempting pleasures"). Dormitories would thus not only provide funds but would also "save" young men from sinful temptations. The first building constructed according to the Chicago YMCA's specifications included a men's dormitory.

At the time of my study nineteen of Chicago's local departments had residences. If occupany rates were maintained, the residences represented a source of subsidy for the rest of the program. In general, residences were initially built with endowment capital from the Metropolitan Association. As such they represented an investment of the board of trustees, and income from the residences (after deduction by the department of costs and a 10 percent management fee) went to the Metropolitan Association. Thus a residence contributed income for program directly to a department only if through capital drives or special arrangements, the board of directors was able to purchase the residence part of their plant from the Metropolitan Association.

Most of the residences have been sound investments for the Association. Many older buildings have been depreciated over time and even with low charges to users give a return on investment of over 20 percent each year. Residences built more recently, if they maintain relatively full occupancy, generally earn no less than 5 to 8 percent a year.

The gross profit from residences (not the rate of return) is determined by three variables: cost of operation, daily and weekly room charges, and occupancy rate. The occupancy rate is a source of difficulty during economic recessions and when a residence's surrounding area shifts from white to Negro. (This aspect is discussed in greater detail in chapter 7.) The YMCA always attempts to price its rooms well below the general market of "comparable" rooms. Still, as in many businesses, there is no exact means for measuring what the market can bear. Daily room prices ranged from $2.00 to $8.00, depending on the residence's newness, its location, and clientele demand. In one instance a YMCA raised its base price from $2.75 to $3.00 a day, substantially improving its profits without affecting its occupancy rate.

Membership Fees and Program Income

The YMCA considers itself an association of members, and membership fees represent a substantial part of its income. These are usually geared to a certain range of activities. For example, a youth membership of $12.00 a year in a middle-income neighborhood provided free access to the swimming pool and gym and membership in one of the clubs, but it did not include scuba-diving instructions, or other special classes. Each type of membership was geared to the services offered and the clientele's ability to pay.

A general principle for establishing fees was that all adult programs should be self-sustaining. Thus membership in the Businessmen's Club could range from $100 to $250 a year, depending on the elegance of the facilities. Cost analysis, however, was rarely done for specific programs, and many executives believed that the adult programs were actually subsidized by other aspects of the economy. Apart from membership fees, many specific classes and programs made direct charges. Since some Roman Catholic officials continued to consider the YMCA a Protestant religious organization, they discouraged Catholics from taking out general memberships. Thus when a department was located in a largely Catholic area, a larger proportion of fees would be specific to program.

For some of the small departments the focus on adolescent club programs may make the membership concept an actuality; in most cases, however, the YMCA offered a diverse set of programs and activities, and ties to members were of short duration. For example, youth memberships in only eleven departments had a median length greater than one year. Most memberships were actually formed around such specific activities as athletic programs, classes, and other direct services.

Contribution Income

An important source of contribution income was the Community Fund. As in many cities, Chicago's Red Feather Drive takes place at work; individual agencies, however, are also allowed to solicit their "families." The YMCA, for example, was permitted to solicit funds from board members and others who had held memberships or who stood in some other relationship to the Association. Therefore, annual fund drives, sometimes consuming vast amounts of staff and lay time, were waged.

As one of the oldest and largest members of the Community Fund, the YMCA received one of the largest annual appropriations (over $500,000 annually). Among the youth agencies, it was exceeded only by the Boy Scouts. This money was given to the total Association, earmarked for local departments, with the bulk going to departments in poorer neighborhoods. Suburban departments participated separately in their suburban Chests.

Metropolitan Subsidies

From its investment income, the profits of its hotel and laundry operation, the Metropolitan board of managers' fund-raising campaign, and its fees for services to the departments (such as auditing and architecture), the Metropolitan office was able to contribute to the current operations of local departments, and it did so through deficit loans and special program subsidies.

If a department's budget showed a deficit (planned or unplanned), that department could request a loan at 4 percent interest. This loan was carried on the books from year to year, as were the interest charges. Second, if the department or the Metropolitan office wished to run an experimental or innovative program (such as a new kind of club or class), an outright subsidy could be arranged. Often such subsidies were given with the explicit understanding that once the program became self-supporting the department would finance the full operation alone.

What are the implications for goal setting of receiving income from these different sources? As a general rule, to attempt to maximize any of these sources had different consequences for goal setting and organizational priorities. Increasing income from the membership program and business operations, of course, depended upon satisfying the customer. Creating programs based on customer desire resulted in the enrollment economy discussed earlier, and income was determined by number of members rather than by hierarchical decisions of necessary service offerings.

Increasing contributions and endowments depended at least partially on projecting an image of need. It also depended on the interpersonal network of boards and staff surrounding the local department. To a certain extent, increasing both contributions from the Community Fund and Metropolitan program subsidies depended on satisfying professional criteria and an image of program vitality which could not be met with membership fees alone. Thus the different income bases are associated with variation in the relative influence of groups in setting priorities and programs. It is certainly clear that departments received different proportions of income from the four major sources. Indeed, four major department types can be distinguished in terms of their size and the major funding basis of their economies: the small program department, the larger program department, the mixed business and program department, and the large business department.

Fifteen departments were of the small program type and had no income from business features. Most of their income came from program and membership fees, contributions, and Metropolitan loans. Two of the smaller program departments were, in fact, "outposts" (young departments founded with subsidies from the board of managers in order to determine whether local community and neighborhood interest could be generated). Two of the small program departments were formally branches of larger departments, but their income and expense accounts were separately kept and their subsidies (at least in part) were drawn from the Metropolitan office. Sometimes operating from store fronts, these departments were considered experimental and could be dropped if no strong support developed. A department was "dispensable" until it had initiated its own major, fund-raising drive. The smallest program departments had annual expenses of under $50,000.

The larger and more permanent of this first type were located in YMCA buildings, although without a full array of services. Lacking dormitories and cafeterias, they sometimes had only a meeting room, a small gymnasium (convertible to an auditorium), and some office space. Located predominantly in residential neighborhoods and smaller suburbs, the small program departments were in the paradoxical position of being more dependent on contributions than the larger departments, yet (in general) having both a smaller base from which to solicit funds as well as a less powerful and prestigious board of directors whose members could themselves both contribute and raise funds. Their annual expenses ranged from $60,000 to $90,000.

Three departments could be considered large program departments. These, like the smaller ones, had no business features but were much larger in plant size, staff size, and annual budget.

These larger program departments had full physical facilities including handball courts, Business Men's Clubs, gymnasiums and swimming pools, and many meeting rooms, and all were located in suburban communities. Although housed in large buildings, they were not necessarily all "healthy" operations, for one was always on loan and forced to retrench while another was a thriving operation.

There were fifteen mixed departments. Although the smaller of these overlapped with the larger program departments in size, all were larger than the small program departments. Located near nucleated shopping centers in either larger suburban areas or industrial sections of the city, the mixed departments included residences ranging in size from 200 to 400 rooms. At the same time, program features remained a substantial part of their operations. With one exception these YMCAs were among the older departments. Only one had been built since World War II, as contrasted with eight of the small program departments. Like some of the smaller program departments, they were sometimes located in changing neighborhoods. But by contrast they had both the board strength and the income possibilities in their residences with which to weather the transition.

Finally there were two departments that were fundamentally hotels. One had much more program activity than the other primarily because it operated a boys' outpost but also because its residential population was less transient. These were two of the three largest departments. The third was a branch devoted to educational activities for the city, and until 1945 it included an accredited four-year college (what was to become Roosevelt University). After 1945 the Central branch had offered vocational and avocational courses; in recent years, however, it had started an accredited high school program and eventually it added a junior college. The high school was used particularly for students having difficulty in the public school system.

The departmental economies that have been described shape the activities of each department, and the skill distributions and perspectives of staff. Furthermore, size of department, health of the department, and the programing of each department are related to the general perspectives about the YMCA that staff and board members hold and to careers in the organization.

METROPOLITAN ACCOUNTING AND DEPARTMENTAL ECONOMICS

In part each department operated as an autonomous agency, courting "customers" and contributors and competing with other agencies and enterprises for dollars. The economics of the local departments, however, much like divisions of a decentralized corporation, were also tied into the accounting and funding processes of the Metropolitan Association, and the economic health of the departments reflected these procedures.

Although the local departments might maintain bank accounts under their own names, and the executive secretary might often allocate large amounts of money at his own discretion, the local boards and executive secretaries were legally, at best, agents of the Metropolitan Association. All property and endowments for all departments were owned by the Association. As will be shown, however, the organization's constitution with regard to property differed from the legal status of the property.

Two major kinds of accounting systems must be distinguished: the annual income and expense accounts, and endowment funds accounts. The expense accounts included depreciation reserves on the board of managers' residence investments, profit and loss reserves, maintenance reserves, and interest on loans from the board of managers, as well as actual operating expenses (salaries, utilities, supplies, and so on). The income accounts reflected all sources of income: cafeteria and business income, membership and program fees, contributions, and interest and dividends from endowment funds.

The endowment fund accounting system was designed for two purposes. On the one hand, it segregated each major donation, recording the income from it and the specific use of that income. On the other, the total endowment pool was open for investment by the board of managers with the intent of preserving or increasing the Association's productive funds.

Although legally the endowment belonged to the Association, most donors related to the Association through specific departments and programs, and to encourage their giving, the Association in effect committed itself to use the interest from endowment funds for the department or purpose to which the donor related. Furthermore, overall capital gains in the investment portfolio were distributed proportionately to each of the endowment funds.

What were the justifications for the accounting system, and what were some of its consequences for the organization's political economy? The basic justification for the annual budget system, with its strict emphasis on balanced budgets, was that it constituted good business practice. By conceiving each department as an autonomous unit with equal relevance to Association goals, the budget process gave to the board of managers and the general secretary a consistent standard with which to determine when a branch was not performing adequately. If a deficit was foreseen, a department had to cut costs. The basic criterion for expansion or construction of service thus became the local department's ability to finance itself. Community Fund monies, of course, were distributed partly with regard to conceptions of community needs; nevertheless, Metropolitan office decisions were influenced by a department's ability to balance its budget. At the end of each year deficit loans could be used to balance the budget, but the interest charges would contribute to future deficits.

The basic policies were justified in terms of good management. When asked about the policy, Chicago staff would argue that many city Associations not adhering to such a policy had frittered away their endowments on losing operations and had been unable even to maintain their facilities properly, let alone to expand as Chicago had. In short, the budget policy promoted maintenance and growth, regardless of the relationship of maintenance and growth either to need or to the YMCA's abstract goals. They also were a logical extension of the principle of local autonomy and were consistent with the general ethos of the YMCA. Not only were the departments to be autonomous in program operation, but in fiscal self-responsibility as well. Such budget policies fitted in with the businesslike stance of the board of managers.

The policies with respect to endowment fund accounting and use seemed obviously just to most members of the organization. First of all, they gave a benefactor a sense of pride and involvement in his donation. Because gifts were placed in a separate account, each retained the benefactor's name and purposes. The consequences of this policy were striking, affecting local department economies and the Association's internal polity. Some departments possessed a financial base that permitted them to weather recessions and neighborhood demographic changes far better than other departments. Thus the departments with large endowments rarely became dependent on the Association for loans. Indeed, in at least one extreme case, a department was able to play an independent role relative to the Metropolitan office and even developed a subpolity among other departments in the city.

The largest endowment was held by the Joseph S. Duncan Department. Duncan, a wealthy factory owner on the West Side, had first become interested in the YMCA in the 1920s, when some vandals broke windows in his factory. Over the years, he and his family gave several millions of dollars to the YMCA, and by 1962 the Duncan YMCA "owned" 34 percent of the Association's total income-producing funds. (The Metropolitan office, by contrast, owned only 21 percent of the general fund.) As the inner city departments underwent change, the board of managers found it increasingly hard to support them. One solution was to have the wealthy Duncan department assist in subsidizing them. Without giving Duncan full authority over them, four departments were placed in a relationship to it. The two larger and older of these continued to maintain direct relationships with the Metropolitan Association; their executives were considered equals with other executives, continued as part of the general secretary's cabinet, and were perceived as full-scale executive secretaries. The two smaller departments, however, became more immediately dependent upon Duncan for both staff supervision and administrative services. Furthermore, their executives were not part of the general secretary's cabinet. All four departments received income subsidies from Duncan, forming an association within the Metropolitan Association. Many people perceived the Duncan board (already noted for its great independence, largely bolstered by its financial position) as one of the more powerful forces in the Association.

Endowment fund accounting procedures not only increased the power of some departments but also resulted in a situation which found poor departments continually struggling to pay interest on loans granted from endowment funds (Duncan's and others). In a sense, then, while the accounting rules for both income and expense as well as endowment funds made good business sense, they contributed to a situation in which the rich departments became richer and the poor, poorer.

The Metropolitan accounting rules constituted an internal set of constraints on the local departments' economies. The income sources themselves (the contributions, business features, membership, and program income discussed earlier) constituted an external link between the departmental economies and the communities within which they existed. We can now try to see what effect these internal and external constraints had upon the economic health of departments.

THE ECONOMIC HEALTH OF DEPARTMENTS

In terms of their fiscal state from 1959 to 1962, the departments fell into four broad categories: *expanding, balanced-stable, balanced-marginal,* and *unstable-deficit.*

The expanding department was one which, because of endowment, type of community, geographic location within the community, and the role played by the YMCA within the community, produced a surplus of income. Operating without a deficit, though possibly receiving Community Fund money for some programs, these were departments in which income had continued to grow or had stabilized at a rate substantially high enough for the department to consider expanding facilities and programs (and thus producing even greater income). They had been considering capital fund drives and had begun to negotiate with the Metropolitan office for matching funds. Between four and seven departments fitted this category (a range rather than an absolute number is given since some departments potentially belonged in this category even though they were not operating in the specific manner described). Expanding departments located in the inner city were characterized either by a large endowment or massive business features (that is, the department was chiefly a hotel). Expanding departments in the suburbs or outer city were located on heavy traffic routes and had built extensive community identification.

The balanced-stable department had, over the last few years, maintained a fairly even level of income and expenditure without being forced to curtail staff or program to balance its budget; the prospect for such a department was healthy stability. Although changing community and economic conditions might affect these departments, current operations allowed them to operate a full, balanced program. The twelve to fifteen departments in this category were mostly located in stable neighborhoods or neighborhoods which had undergone a demographic change several years previously.

The balanced-marginal department carried on a precarious existence. Having incurred deficits for several years, it typically had reduced its staff and was overworking the remainder. A balanced income-expense ratio had been almost achieved (yearly deficits, at least, were small); on the other hand, the facility was generally underutilized. Some of these departments might be considered balanced-stable, but they were peculiarly vulnerable to economic recessions and usually made less impact on their communities than an economically more secure operation might make. A few years earlier, several of these departments might have been classified as unstable-deficit operations; at the time of this study, however, a fairly stable level of operation had been achieved.

Departments dependent on membership fees and contributions were extremely susceptible to this condition since they lacked the extra subsidy of residence income (although not all of the balanced marginal departments were so lacking). Inner city departments were also likely to be in this category (although again, not all balanced-marginal departments were located in the inner city). An important factor in determining a department's success was its location. Several were located away from the mainstream of their communities. At least one was almost hidden. Others were geographically very close to competing agencies. (Unfortunately for its success as a welfare organization, the YMCA had in the past sometimes been more concerned with the price of land and obtaining gifts of land than with nearness to markets or proximity to competing agencies.) Since the YMCA is a mass service organization, such factors may be critical to a department's success. Between ten and fourteen departments fell into this category.

Finally, the unstable-deficit departments had, year after year, incurred deficit loans from the Metropolitan Association. They might or might not have had good programing, but departmental conditions had issued either in great income fluctuations or uncontrollable expenditures. They were most likely to be located in changing communities, and several departments now classified as balanced-marginal had once fallen into this category. During the time of this study, three departments, at most, could be so classified, and of these, only one was continuously in that position; moreover, in 1963 even that department had balanced its income and expenditure.

In examining the relative economic health of departments, one can discern the effects both of Metropolitan decisions and of the quality of executive and board leadership. Some departments were poorly located, but often it was difficult to allocate responsibility for a department's malfunctioning. Indeed, in one of these cases a department's location and structure were frankly experimental. The Metropolitan YMCA had assisted in funding a suburban department equipped with an outdoor swimming pool and hockey rink. It gradually became clear that the pool and hockey rink could not provide adequate income for sound operation. The degree of inadequacy was easily demonstrated. Visiting the department late on a winter evening, one might find the executive secretary (a man paid over $10,000 a year in 1961) sweeping off the hockey rink. In other departments it was clear that executives were incompetent to handle certain aspects of their work. More important than assigning responsibility for economic ill health, however, is noting its consequences. At least one-third of the departments operated as either balanced-marginal or unstable-deficit operations, and in these operations program staff were cut to the minimum. The plants were utilized, but only with great effort by staff and wide dependence on less expensive (and less qualified) part-time staff and volunteers.

CONCLUSION

Various aspects of the Association's economy as described above, on the one hand, helped maintain the organization's broad goals and polity and, on the other, directly affected role relations and goal attainment.

First, the Association's broad service goals were reinforced by the funding sources that had been developed to implement and define goals. And the process operated reciprocally also. Whereas a newly founded department might decide to focus on a more narrowly defined target group or set of programs, an older department would find such a refocusing perilous, for part of its sustaining income would immediately be withdrawn. Only with massive subsidies could departments refocus. Historically, the diversified economy was created to pursue certain broad goals, but it in turn became a set of constraints holding and committing the organization to those very goals.

Secondly, the dependence of departments on their boards for direct contributions and for fund-raising efforts reinforced the board members' official position within the polity and contributed to organizational pluralism. As long as the executive secretaries, the board of managers, and the Metropolitan staff perceived the boards as an important source of funds, organizational ideology regarding the role of laymen and the importance of boards in policy making was certain to be supported. Deference to board ideas—real or imagined—would be maintained.

Given the diversified economy and the broad service goals of the organization, tension was created between two aspects of the YMCA's fundamental constitution. Because of its historic Christian attachments the YMCA has always searched out areas of "need." It could not turn away from welfare and rehabilitational problems, but because of its diverse, building-centered program and its ethos of businesslike efficiency it has often turned away from areas of need which could not be met within its framework. Even the budget rules and treatment of endowment funds have had this effect, intended or not. Aside from the distribution of Community Fund money, the YMCA stressed self-financing, not income redistribution to meet need.

The diversified economy and budget-making procedures also had consequences for role relations between executives and the Metropolitan office staff. These are discussed in more detail below. It suffices here to note that the relative independence of the executive secretary was related to the economic health of his department. An executive in a balanced-stable or expanding department conferred with the Metropolitan office staff at his own discretion. Some never conferred; others conferred only for reassurance; whereas still others made a practice of using the board of managers and the Metropolitan office as a resource base. These last perceived consultation as a mechanism for tapping a source of useful knowledge and experience.

The executives in balanced-marginal or deficit operations, however, had no such leeway. Staff members from the Metropolitan office found reasons to confer with them, and conjoint plans were made to reduce deficits. The Metropolitan office staff watched such departments closely. Inevitably, then, these executives and departments were more dependent upon the Metropolitan office staff and had fewer options in their programs, personnel, and facilities. Furthermore, the boards of these departments were less likely to exert an independent role in policy making.

6

Consequences of the Political Economy: Executive Roles and Departmental Programs

The links between the diverse bases of the Chicago Association's enrollment economy and the Association's broad service goals, the strong local identification and centripetal pressures, and the multiple power centers have had a pervasive influence on the Association's internal processes, its ability to implement policy, and its external relations. In order to demonstrate the very substantial impact of the Association's political economy on other aspects of its social system, we shall explore the "operator syndrome" of executive secretaries, the modes of program supervision and innovation, and the factional alliances within the organization.

CAREER LINES AND THE OPERATOR SYNDROME

Central to the analysis of any social system is an examination of key roles and their relationship to the roles of others. It is certainly clear that one key role within the YMCA is that of the executive secretary. Not only is the executive secretary the chief administrative officer of his department, he is frequently the key person in mobilizing local support, in initiating programs, in negotiating with the Metropolitan office, and in formulating local policies. How he carries out his role is a function of his personality and training, as well as of the demands made upon him.

One of the theses emerging from this study was that the Chicago Association's political economy produced an "operator syndrome." That is, the career model traditionally pictured for the executive seemed to be that of the head of a smooth, efficient operation, regardless of program quality or innovation. Within the context of the pluralistic political economy of the Association and its budget rules, the "operator" was permitted

126

great independence and autonomy. Because of the polity's pluralism "operators" might choose strategies that resembled a kind of coalition or political alliance; only the more articulate and effective executives, however, could play the game. Some executives good at forming coalitions were not operators: because of organizational dependencies they could not be as freewheeling as the "operators."

Executive secretaries were recruited from among junior-level professional personnel. Although in years past executives had sometimes been recruited from outside the Chicago Association, in recent years promotions had followed either Metropolitan office or local department service. The latter was the more common route. A typical career followed this pattern: Whether recruited from George Williams College or elsewhere, the new secretary first filled a program position such as general youth program secretary or physical program secretary. A few immediately entered business or administrative roles, but those doing so had usually been hired directly from business. Until 1940 a secretary might have planned his career around one specific program (witness the old saying "Boys' work for life"). In the general YMCA movement, however, the secretary has increasingly become a supervisor of part-time and other personnel, and specific program attachments have declined.

Unlike occupations requiring substantial technical training, YMCA work requires fairly general skills. Although some secretaries had chosen YMCA careers as early as high school, many others were hired after first trying careers in business or teaching. Particularly in Chicago, with George Williams College in the vicinity, prospective secretaries could work toward certification while simultaneously holding full-time jobs.

Regardless of a person's point of entry into YMCA work, the desire for increased prestige or autonomy or higher salary pointed toward an executive position. Although it was possible to move from a program position in a small department to one in a larger operation, or to be promoted from assistant program secretary to program secretary, the number of options within program work was limited. No department had more than ten or eleven professional positions (including food service manager, but excluding head housekeeper, building maintenance superintendent, etc.), and most operated with between three and seven secretaries. Inevitably, then, and early in a secretary's employment, career mobility virtually required becoming an executive.

Usually a secretary's first executive position was within one of the smaller, program-oriented departments. Having once become an executive secretary, however, his further mobility required promotion to a larger department. During the period of this study there were six moves from program to executive positions and eight from the executive secretaryship of a smaller to a larger department, but there were no shifts from larger to smaller departments. Positions became available when men retired, accepted staff positions in the Metropolitan office, became executives of larger departments, became general secretaries in other communities, or (in one case) were fired. During the period of this study, only one executive moved into a program position, and that was located in another city.

Movement into the Metropolitan office staff was potentially, but not necessarily, a promotion. Two of the four executives shifted to the Metropolitan staff were moved after long periods of perceived mismanagement (although they performed adequately in their more limited Metropolitan roles). Only one of the others was clearly a promotion. Furthermore, since several Metropolitan staff roles had developed only during the last decade and had gradually shifted in definition, the desirability of roles below that of assistant general secretary was ambiguous.

The Association's salary scales were also linked to the size of operations; the executives of the three or four largest departments were on a par with the key staff members in the Metropolitan office immediately under the general secretary. Thus in terms of visibility, mobility route, and salary, the executives of larger departments provided potential models for other secretaries.

The larger departments' political economies were precisely such as to encourage an operator syndrome. The executives who were essentially efficient managers, balancing a complex business and having good relations with their boards, were actually referred to by other executives as "good operators." They had an independent and managerial perspective, as opposed to a need-oriented point of view. The operator syndrome was a function of the local autonomy principle operating in conjunction with the complex enrollment economy and a technology (means for achieving character development) that was difficult to supervise. The executives who manifested the operator syndrome most clearly had devised a style of relating to their boards and to the Metropolitan office which effectively freed them from organizational pressure.

The operator syndrome was an option available only to the executive whose departmental economy was relatively strong, regardless of its program vitality. If an economy was strong, encompassing a balanced or expanding resource base and profitable residence and cafeteria operations, a department's board of directors was likely to be satisfied with executive performance, and the Metropolitan office had no way of sanctioning him. The operator had great latitude for action and gave an appearance of great competence.

It is surprising that the Association had never developed systematic criteria for evaluating performance beyond the balance sheet. Nevertheless, several features of the Association's organization contributed to the development and prevalence of the syndrome. It was related to the principle of local autonomy in that as long as a department was operating efficiently, the Metropolitan office had no lever for intrusion into its affairs. Whereas its role in coordinating interdepartmental activities, supervising city-wide programs, and sponsoring training institutes was clear, the Metropolitan office made no attempt to provide systematic supervision of local program. This was true at least in part because of the difficulty of measuring program quality beyond counts of the number of clients. The combination of this factor with various intricate aspects of the executive's role—financial management, community relations, board development, and staff supervision—issued in the operator syndrome as a mechanism for juggling a complex set of demands with relatively little strain. (Such a syndrome, of course, can only occur in an organization whose basic mission is so diffuse that efficiency can be substituted for professional technique or vital program achievements.)

The importance of the operator syndrome lay chiefly in its function as a model for the younger executive secretaries. The better of the senior executive secretaries had prestige and were respected by their juniors to the extent that their style matched that of the operator syndrome. Thus they encouraged development of the syndrome in others and reinforced the tradition.

An example will illustrate the importance attached to the syndrome. The Metropolitan office invited one of the senior operators, known as an excellent fund raiser, to conduct a training course in fund-raising techniques. All departments were invited to send their professional staff. Although such training programs were often undersubscribed, for this course twice the expected number (about forty) actually enrolled, necessitating a second section of the course.

Secretaries utilizing this style varied among themselves. Some were somnolent, and the success of their departments was a function of little work and lots of environmental luck. Some, however, were quite vigorous. In an extreme form of the syndrome an operator might even ignore the Metropolitan office. Senior staff told of a recently retired executive who had operated an essentially balanced, stable department within a nucleated commercial and industrial center and who always refused to see any Metropolitan official except the general secretary in his local office. Senior staff members claimed to have been "thrown out" when they visited him at his department. This story is important partly because it illustrates so well the local executive's power and autonomy but also because of its potential mythical and symbolic quality. Not all operators maintained such an independent stance. They conferred frequently with their boards and with the Metropolitan office and were active in planning new projects. Nevertheless, the "operator" label applied; their primary concern was smoothness of operation, and they did not test the basic stability of their complex economies with risky outreach programs or untested innovations.

That the operator syndrome, an executive style mirroring that of the manager or owner of a medium- to small-sized business, could ever develop at all reflects the historic evolution of YMCA goals and economy both in Chicago and throughout the United States. The syndrome was also related, however, to fundamental difficulties in program supervision.

PROGRAM EVALUATION AND SUPERVISION

Aside from its historic linkage to Protestantism, at the heart of the local autonomy principle was the belief that each department and its board were best able to establish local program needs (demands). Whereas fiscal control was maintained by requiring balanced annual budgets, which were supervised by the board of managers and reinforced by dependency on the board of managers for deficit support, no such control or review procedure was attempted over program offerings. These had their centrifugal aspects—in their great variety, in the measurement of demand for them, in their effectiveness, in their sources or origins, and in the skill or competence required to carry them out. Such aspects of program (the economic productive tasks of the organization) affected the legitimacy of Metropolitan supervision, the effectiveness of alternative forms of supervision, and the coalition styles used by the Metropolitan office to introduce program innovations.

Although centrifugal forces predominated in program evaluation, there were centripetal forces also. Membership statistics were available on an annual and semiannual basis. These were broken down by sex and age as well as by membership classification (full privilege, limited privilege, etc.). Thus membership trends could be examined by Metropolitan staff. Furthermore, it was common knowledge which departments had vital program staffs and which did not; almost everyone knew which executive secretaries were "getting by" on their residences and cafeterias and which were making a fairly substantial impact on their communities. As one member of the board of managers put it, "You can tell a good YMCA if it is noisy, crowded, and just a little dirty." Although such a criterion is not technically elegant, it is pragmatically sound. Why, then, could a more adequate supervisory program not be established? I have already suggested the effect of the local autonomy principle, but several aspects of the YMCA's distinctive "program mix" must also be noted.

Diversity of Clientele-Based Program

To an outsider most YMCAs seem alike. Like chain department stores operating both old and new branches, the departments of the Chicago Association appear to differ more in architecture than in program (the product offered to the customer). The outsider's image consists of "gym and swim," cafeteria and residence, and camps for kids. But the outsider is wrong.[1] First, any given department maintains a wide range of programs. As has been noted, a few of the smaller departments concentrate on youth programs; yet even these programs may differ widely in their emphasis on various age groups and on recreation versus "character-building clubs," structured versus unstructured activity, building-centered versus community-centered activities, and character-development versus remedial and rehabilitation programs.[2] The larger departments are heavily adult-centered, but these also present a bewildering array of programs: "learning for living" classes, social and recreational groups, CORE *and* Kiwanis meetings, executive clubs for service and social purposes, Businessmen's Clubs, and adult recreation leagues. Each department tailors its program and staff to its facilities and to the perceived demands of its local community. One community department has a thriving teen-age club program while another, competing with high school and church activities, has difficulty getting teen-agers inside the door. This,

1. He would be wrong about department store chains, too; each unit of chains emphasizing products with different styles and fashions adapts lines to clientele preferences.

2. Character-building clubs as contrasted with recreation groups place more emphasis on educational programs, service to others, and on growth of self-awareness. Remedial and rehabilitational programs work with people with specific or general disabilities or deviances.

then, is the first pressure for localized program planning and control. The executive and his staff are on the scene and can constantly adjust their product mix in terms of facilities, needs, and demand as they interact with boards, other laymen, community leaders, and members. Therefore, Metropolitan office staff generally did not attempt to determine the program mix for local departments.

Information and Resource Control

Other organizations depend on local staff to determine product mix, yet still maintain control over the range and content of programs through centralized decisions on which product lines to permit. By centralizing development of new products and providing resources for modifying facilities and organization to handle different lines, the central office of many organizations is able to design effectively the template for branches. To the extent that local departments required capital financing for some major program modification (expanding the Businessmen's Club or building a roller rink), the Metropolitan staff might play an important consultative role in local program decisions. When capital expenditures were not necessary, however, the Metropolitan program staff's role was less crucial, for the departments' broad program repertory was not a Chicago Association product but was rather part of the total YMCA movement's stock in trade. Information regarding various programs was available through manuals, previous staff experience, training programs, area and national conferences, and publications of the Association of Secretaries. Clearly, new products and skills were not developed primarily within the Chicago Association.

Legitimacy of Supervision

Not only were the local staff generally independent of the Metropolitan office for their techniques and programs, the general programing of Chicago departments caused difficulties in supervising program operation and in establishing an adequate, workable supervisory or consulting relationship.

In a professional and collegial context, legitimacy of supervision requires three conditions. (1) There must be visible, agreed-upon standards of performance. (2) The supervisor must be able to communicate these standards and demonstrate more adequate modes of performance. (3) As a consequence of these two prior conditions, the subordinate must accept the validity, or legitimacy of the consultant's (supervisor's) knowledge.

With the more technical, impersonal, skill-based activities, such competence was most readily demonstrated; a Metropolitan staff person with special skills could easily demonstrate them and train local staff. For example, skills in teaching specific sports (such as swimming) were fairly widely recognized. For skills involving interpersonal relationships, however (such as a style of relating to teen-agers, of supervising volunteers, or of developing boards), the criteria were vague and supervision was difficult. The tasks did not lend themselves to precise technological specification.

Since the theoretical or technical base of many programs was hard to demonstrate, it was consequently difficult to legitimate the Metropolitan staff's status. To paraphrase one executive secretary, "There isn't much the Metropolitan program staff can teach my men; they already know how to run a camp or athletic program as well as anyone downtown." Even though experience might single one staff member out as especially effective in interpersonal relations (in managing club programs, for example), he might experience difficulty in communicating this skill to others. Such skills were not impossible to teach, but it was difficult to do so within short time periods.

That in fact local department staff did not legitimate an active program supervision role for the Metropolitan office can be seen from the contrasts provided in table 16. Staff clearly recognized that the Metropolitan office did indeed influence business and fiscal policies much more than program. Not only did they recognize that influence, they also appear to have accepted the legitimacy of Metropolitan influence on business matters.

This table is also interesting as it relates to the principle of local autonomy. Consider the fact that roughly two-thirds of the staff saw no necessity for the *owning* Association to be involved in either program planning or financial administration!

PROMOTING PROGRAM INNOVATION

The absence of legitimacy for Metropolitan involvement in program planning combined with the legitimation of local autonomy created a dilemma for the Metropolitan office in working with local staff on program planning. Formally, the Metropolitan program staff's task was to supervise local program staff; however, they had no legitimated mechanisms for doing so.

When Metropolitan program personnel were coordinating city-wide events, the role ambiguity vanished, since a standard set of organizing procedures had developed. Again, in setting up athletic leagues or in establishing training institutes, a similar routinization existed. In the supervision of club programs or the encouragement of overall program development, however, no such standards existed.

Several consequences resulted from this ambiguity. First, no systematic pattern existed for evaluating or overviewing program. At one point,

TABLE 16

LOCAL STAFF PERCEPTIONS OF METROPOLITAN STAFF'S ACTUAL AND LEGITIMATE
INFLUENCE ON FINANCIAL AND PROGRAM AFFAIRS
(Percent)

	Agree *or* Strongly agree	Disagree *or* Strongly disagree	Don't know
Actual influence: On the whole the Metropolitan office staff has a great deal of influence—			
(1) over the way financial and business matters are handled in this department;.....	51	39	10
(2) over program planning for this department................................	18	76	6

	Preferably should *or* Definitely should	May *or* May not	Preferably should not *or* Definitely should not
Legitimate influence: Ideally, do you feel the Metropolitan office staff should—			
(1) have a great deal of influence over the way financial and business matters are handled in the department?...........	38	36	26
(2) have a great deal of influence over program planning for the department?	26	46	28

NOTE: For the questions on financial and business matters, N = 162 (one did not answer); on program planning, 163.

a committee of the board of managers, including staff personnel, spent several months visiting and conferring with the program committees and staff members of several departments, particularly community departments. This kind of review procedure had not been done before, however, and it had no institutionalized role in the Association.

During the period of this study, the activities of the Metropolitan program secretaries were in a constant state of flux, more so than was true for any other part of the Metropolitan office. At one point, two of the Metropolitan office's program secretaries were operating as a team of "friendly visitors," spending a day or two in each of several local departments, observing program and conferring with local staff. Yet the secretaries dropped this visiting program, complaining that local staff "didn't know what to do with us." At another point the program staff was focusing on a single age group.

Whether or not the assistant general secretary for program recognized the political economic basis for his staff's difficulties, he had essentially shaped his role to avoid local supervision, focusing instead on program innovation. Both he and the general secretary were committed to promoting the organization's dynamic nature, and this required recognizing needs and innovating program. How did they do it?

The Initiation and Diffusion of Program Innovation

A discussion of specific program innovations and their diffusion must consider two categories: programs that blended with previous concepts of goals, clientele groups, and funding sources, and programs that did not. The former were largely noncontroversial. The second, which generally represented wide departures from previous clientele, goals, or funding, often required considerable debate and manipulation. In the noncontroversial category were such ventures as new adult education classes such as "scientific relaxation" and new ways of staffing traditional programs such as the Indian Guides or Tri-Y or Hi-Y clubs. The controversial category has included the federal poverty program, detached worker programs with delinquent gangs, and departments directed totally to one age group or type of program.

Noncontroversial program innovation did not involve changes in polity or polity definition; so accounting for their initiation and diffusion requires primarily an examination of the Association's internal economic processes as they relate to innovation. (Controversial program innovations, which generally *did* involve polity changes, are discussed in part 3.)

Innovative ideas might originate inside or outside the Chicago YMCA. Such ideas might be new activities to supplement ongoing programs or new ways of organizing old programs. Two examples will be discussed: (1) the introduction of a new physical education course in "scientific relaxation," and (2) a concerted effort to revitalize the Hi-Y (male) and Tri-Y (female) teen-age club programs.

Scientific relaxation was a technique, developed by a prominent professor at George Williams College, which utilized a set of physical and mental procedures to enable a person consciously to relieve tension. Beginning with explanations and demonstrations regarding the functioning of the central nervous system, the instructor gradually imparted the techniques of relaxation to his pupils. The major consumers for the course were expected to be male adults who, owing to personality characteristics or job-induced tension, showed signs of an inability to relax, such as irritability, difficulty in sleeping, loss of weight, and nervous speech patterns. The professor enjoyed an international reputation for innovation in the field of physical education. Many successful cases of dramatic improvement could be cited. The YMCA's difficulties lay in training instructors, developing the market, and evaluating the program's potential growth.

In 1961 the Metropolitan office first initiated a training course to which each executive secretary was told to send either the local physical director or one of his assistants. The courses not only trained personnel in the techniques of teaching scientific relaxation but included techniques for recruitment and advertisement as well. Simultaneously, an attempt was made to assess the market. During the trial phase, no more than five departments (two of which already had large physical education programs for men and Businessmen's Clubs), initiated courses. Within two years only two women instructors were still teaching the courses, and by 1967 only one department had a fully operative program.

The method used to spread the program and the reasons for its lack of success are instructive for understanding program innovation processes. The Metropolitan office's role was purely that of a facilitator. It provided the *opportunity* for departments to learn the techniques, and because of the general secretary's strong interest the training sessions were well attended. Lacking a well-cultivated market demand, systematic follow-up, and subsidy incentives from the Metropolitan office, however, the program did not spread widely.

This instance illustrates both the necessity for generating demand and the dependence of innovation on support from the local executive and professional staff. Since the training program had essentially been imposed on the physical directors and since there was little unsolicited demand, they saw no reason to promote the program.[3]

3. Scientific relaxation was incorporated as part of George Williams College's training program. In 1967, one of the women instructors who had maintained an interest in it reported that young physical directors just out of the College were beginning

Scientific relaxation was, at best, a marginal innovation in adult programing. More fundamental was an attempt to rebuild the teen-age club program. In this case, the experimental innovation in staffing a core organizational program (which was strongly supported by the Metropolitan office) was a resounding success. Yet no department, on its own, picked up the program!

If any population was viewed as a key target group, it was teen-agers. Since the development of youth work in the early 1900s, YMCA workers had transformed the phrase *young men* into *youth*. Teen-agers represented the pliable adolescent, a type of individual in whom the YMCA could still effect character development. The Freudian revolution, of course, had somewhat damaged belief in the adolescent's mutability; nevertheless, youth were still the key group: because teen-agers interacted most intensively with each other and with staff for the longest periods of time, the teen-age club program was basic to character development. Unlike any of the special skills programs, it had goals (service, learning about the world, understanding one's own role in it), that seemed unusually conducive to character development. Nationwide, however, the teen-age club program was in difficulty. As noted in chapter 2, teen-agers had become a declining part of the YMCA's total membership.

Several difficulties were immediately evident. First, it was easier to involve girls than boys. In some departments the girls' groups outnumbered the boys' as much as five or ten to one. The absence of boys' groups hampered total growth, however, for one of this program's attractions for girls was activity with the boys' clubs. Second, the clubs needed supervision and systematic counseling if they were to cohere for any length of time. Because so many staff roles required multiple duties, however, it seemed impossible to obtain adequate supervision.

After consulting research personnel from the National Council and other persons interested in adolescent development, the program committee of the board of managers recommended an experiment in which a staff person would be attached to a department and given sole responsibility for club development. The traditional Hi-Y–Tri-Y program would be followed except that a new girls' club would be started only when a new boys' club could also be started. Furthermore, the staff members would develop techniques for training club advisors and recruiting mem-

---

to promote the program in YMCAs around the country. This example indicates how change in programing could emerge through changing socialization of professionals.

bers. The experiment was conducted in a suburban department whose program had been particularly anemic and whose physical plant was creating a large economic drain on the Association.

By all accounts the program was a success. Within a year and a half, thirteen clubs were operating where before there had been only four; the clubs were active and the sex ratio was equalized. Steps had been taken to develop training courses. Yet no other department picked up the program or rearranged staff personnel to attempt the same strategy. Why?

The executive secretaries were aware of the successful experiment, but in reality it did not make good sense for them to set up the same program within their own departments. First, whereas the Metropolitan office would subsidize an experiment, it would not offer to subsidize a specific operating program. And although in time such a program could become financially rewarding, initially it would require heavy subsidy. Since most departments already considered themselves understaffed, the necessary realignment would have created an intolerable strain. Clearly the Association's economy and role structure hindered the success of this program although it was quite in line with the YMCA's basic conceptions. The experiment, accordingly, was allowed to die.

Two further points in connection with this example are worth making. First, in an organization with greater central control, a decision to develop a teen-age club program throughout the Association could have been given broad general support, including provision for initial financing.[4] Second, the innovation did not actually die, for program personnel continued to seek ways to improve the teen-age club program. Two years later, with massive support from the Metropolitan office, a consolidated suburban department focused all its resources on club program development, with considerable success. Clearly the Association's staff had retained its interest in this central target group; the difficulty lay in transforming this concern into organizational reality.

Innovation and Coalition Formation

This discussion can now be related to an earlier discussion of the relationship of political economy to executive style. There it was noted that one style in particular, that of the coalition manager (unlike the "operator"), represented an adaptation to the fact that, though local autonomy was possible, the local executive was able to gain both support for inno-

4. Of course, this observation does not advocate centralization but merely describes one of its probable consequences.

vation and help in meeting the problems of a changing environment from the Metropolitan staff. As contrasted with the operator syndrome, the executive choosing a coalition style was more likely to confer with and seek to exploit the resources and program goals of the Metropolitan office.

An examination of the history of the Metropolitan office's relationship to the departments reveals many particularistic decisions. During the 1930s, for example, one department was allowed to treat all residence profit as a return on its own endowment, even though the residence had been financed from the general endowment fund. In another instance a department had been allowed to treat its "front desk" expense as part of residence upkeep, rather than as a general department expense (thus shifting administrative cost from the department to the board of managers). Other cases seemed to indicate that the general secretary acted more leniently toward troubled departments located in areas to which he himself in some way had been attached. Since many of these particular istic decisions were known to exist, and since it was clear that individual lines or relationships could be developed, an executive secretary had alternative modes available for relating to the Metropolitan office. Most important, his mode of relating affected his access to resources.

Although particularistic relationships might depend on friendship or other historical factors, it was clear that during the period of this study an executive's easiest route to establishing such a line or relationship was to show interest in the problems either of the poor or of delinquents, or to evidence a sensitive, outreaching stance in handling strains from the racial transition of neighborhoods. Subsidy requests from secretaries who both manifested liberal attitudes and programs in these areas and maintained close contact with the general secretary and other key Metropolitan staff were likely to receive the most cordial reception. In several cases, the executive secretaries maintained close contact by writing long, detailed memoranda to the general secretary, summarizing departmental problems and plans. Even without such reports, however, the executive could build a link simply by imaginative programing and by involving the Metropolitan staff in program planning.

The coalition style manifested itself best in four executive secretaries. Others conferred regularly with the Metropolitan staff but made no special attempt to advance key Metropolitan programs or interests. Still others obtained program subsidies on a one-shot basis. One suburban executive, for instance, collaborated with the Metropolitan office in subsidizing a special staff member to develop the Indian Guides, a father-son program of joint activities involving Indian ritual. In this case, however, no continuing relationship developed. The executive was perceived as one of the more independently minded, and neither special promotion nor special consideration was likely to become a factor in the relationship.

Metropolitan staff were aware that the coalition style might bring charges of favoritism against them. But since they had goals of their own and since they were unable to generate system-wide incentives or authority for innovation, the coalition style was almost a necessary result.

Other strategies or role styles also developed within this political economy. For instance, some resisted Metropolitan pressures for change by arguing that their boards would not tolerate the change or were resisting a new direction. Given the dual structure of the polity, such a strategy permitted the executive to insulate himself from the Metropolitan office. Since the Metropolitan staff controlled promotions, however, the strategy eventually had negative consequences for career mobility.

7

Crucial Policies and Their Implementation

At the highest organizational levels, attempts are made to rationalize decision criteria and to establish general rules and procedures to guide decisions and alternative lines of action for an entire organization. Almost any organizational policy can be analyzed, both in its genesis and its substance, in terms of its relationship to political economy. The fact, for instance, that some labor unions have national pension plans, whereas others prefer regional or local ones, or the fact that one group is well protected by a pension plan, whereas others are not, clearly reflects both the structure of the polity and the economic power and positions of the parties involved. Within the YMCA it would be feasible to examine any general rule and its implementation in these terms. Purchasing policies, budget policies, and other practices reflect Association goals, its power structure, and its economy.

From the viewpoint of the organization's ongoing adaptation, however, two aspects of policy are crucial: the rules or policies relating to the geographic expansion and contraction of services and those determining clientele and the manner in which clients within geographic areas will be served. More specifically, I want to consider how the political economy affects policies on establishing new departments and how it relates to serving Negroes of various ages and statuses.

EXPANSION POLICY: THE EQUATION OF COMMUNITY NEED WITH COMMUNITY SUPPORT

When and where is a new department to be established? When and where is a department to construct a new building? When are facilities to be remodeled or expanded? These questions, which relate to large capital commitments, are among the most basic that any organization must answer. One major avenue for organizational change and growth is the acquisition of new facilities serving new groups or areas. Capital commitments are even more important for the long-range shaping of an organization such as the YMCA than for other organizations because such commitments are not easily withdrawn. Unlike businesses, the YMCA rarely cuts its losses in unprofitable commitments by selling the facilities involved. To use Selznick's terms, a department has an institutional value; it becomes an end in itself. Thus, if we can discern and explain the criteria for expansion, we will at least partially understand the Association's mode of adaptation to the community.

The Chicago Association was basically committed to expanding YMCA services within the metropolitan area rather than simply maintaining or upgrading existent services. The board of managers and Metropolitan staff were in favor of upgrading quality, but such a consideration was not central when they considered various uses for endowment funds. In part the expansion orientation issued from the recognition that expansion attracted new resources and investments in YMCA facilities from outside the Association.

Given an expansionist orientation, what criteria were involved? First, no investment could be made which would become a permanent drain on the endowment funds and the board of managers. If a grant was made for a new facility, the department involved was expected to "stand on its own feet." Second, and related to the first, a department's ability to support itself was indicated by the degree of its community support: How organized were the department's lay supporters, and how willing and able were they to conduct fund-raising drives?

Several aspects of the Association's expansion policy should be discussed. First, the criteria for establishing a department (that is, an identifiable YMCA organization within a specific geographic area) differed from those for building a new facility. The former might occur as a professional response to perception of community need, but the latter required firm community support. Second, the broad character development goals established few priorities concerning groups to be served or areas of the city most in need of YMCA services. Consequently, support was most often sought from (and expansion generally occurred in) traditional areas with traditional groups. Third, historic organizational myths and postures surrounded the expansion policies. Therefore, at the Association's highest levels, there was little attempt to consider alternative strategies, long-range consequences, or broadly comprehensive plans for development.

Ideologically, the founding of a new department and the development of its facilities were viewed as the responsibility of committed laymen. In its archetypal form, the pattern was as follows. First, a group of laymen, former YMCA members and presumably good Protestant church members, living in a neighborhood or suburb without a YMCA, would gradually realize that their neighborhood "needed" a YMCA. After much discussion among themselves and others, a few laymen would approach the general secretary for Metropolitan support in locating a staff person to do the "leg work" of initiating a program. Once underway, a ground swell of local support and enthusiasm for the program generally produced a conviction that the department needed a building. With the advice and consent of the Metropolitan board of managers, a fund drive would be initiated, with the board matching funds fifty-fifty. Community support would be overwhelming, and shortly the new facility, in sparkling modern architecture, would be available for use.

Several features of this myth should be noted, especially the emphasis on lay and local initiation. The board of managers and the professional staff were perceived (ideally) as responding to an initiative from outside the organization and not as centrally directing the initiation of expansion. Second, "need" constituted a state of affairs defined by local laymen. Again, there was no general means for either assessing need or comparing alternative needs. Third, the ideology stressed the importance of local, interested, community-minded laymen. An area lacking such laymen was, from this perspective, excluded from the possible expansion sites.

Although this myth was widespread, there was no concerted attempt to change the myth into reality or to require decisions to conform to the myth; in fact, several instances of departure from these perspectives will be noted below. The myth did serve, however, to reinforce traditional modes of organizational decision making.

How were departments actually initiated, and when did they construct buildings? The process did, on occasion, follow the ideological model. Laymen approached the Metropolitan staff for support and a staff member would be assigned and a building program initiated. Even these cases, however, showed important variations. In one dramatic instance, the proposal for establishing a department in a rapidly expanding suburban area was followed by a counterproposal, signed by approximately 150 community leaders and agency executives, which asked that the YMCA *not* initiate such a program. The petition asserted that the area already included a sufficiency of similar agencies and that another could not be funded. Nevertheless, backed by its initial core of interested laymen, the Metropolitan office proceeded. Under the leadership of a particularly effective secretary—a bluff, piano-playing, former football player who was active in the American Legion and other civic organizations—they first established a wide-ranging youth program, gradually developed community acceptance, and finally erected one of the largest departmental buildings of the postwar era. In this instance, the departures from the model consisted in a substantial body of community opposition and the Metropolitan office's response to this—namely, to depart from its usual definition of community need or support.

In other instances, programs were established without any real evidence of community interest. A staff member placed in an "outpost" of an already established department would attempt both to build a program and to garner lay support. Adequate programing alone was insufficient, for if community support was not forthcoming, it was unlikely, in the post–World War II era, that a building would be constructed.

Community support, for all intents and purposes, meant active laymen willing to contribute money. There are indeed instances in both the early and the later history of the organization in which a department's only support was a philanthropist's willingness to erect a department in a given location. Three examples illustrate. In 1910 the owner of a department store chain offered to finance a YMCA building on the edge of a shopping center. The surrounding area was largely Roman Catholic (at that time an especially unpromising support base). Nevertheless, the department was built and a vigorous program established.

Again, in the mid-1950s the Association established a program department on the edge of a large, rapidly growing suburban area and industrial park. No building plans were anticipated until the Association was given some land at a busy highway intersection. This suburban area had been judged especially inhospitable to community-wide agencies. One national fund-raising firm had even said in a letter that the community was hopeless for fund raising, arguing that the area was riven by ethnic cleavages. There was little community identification, and business people took little interest. Nonetheless, even though the department's program was shaky and even though a nearby suburb housed a second shaky department, a fund-raising campaign was launched. The Metropolitan office detailed a senior assistant general secretary to devote himself to the campaign.

His technique, as he described it, was to build elite interest before asking for money. He enlisted the chief executives of the larger companies for an advisory board and then printed their pictures in a full-page advertisement in the suburban newspaper. The necessary funds were in fact raised, and eventually a new, $3,000,000 department was built. According to this secretary, support for the YMCA issued also in increased community identification. For instance, where previously only the assistant auditor of a firm might have been designated to head a Community Chest drive, now in some of the corporations vice-presidents were often so assigned.[1]

The third instance occurred in 1963, when the wealthy owner of a plumbing company offered the YMCA $400,000 to finance a teen-age facility in his suburb. The YMCA lost no time accepting the opportunity.

These three are, of course, extreme instances of the underlying decision process which arises when an expansionist orientation is combined with the YMCA's political economy. By the Association's definition, any community had "needs" which a department could meet. In the second instance cited above, the new YMCA was perceived as meeting not only the needs of the suburban residents but also those of the executives of the companies in the industrial park, in supplying training for their employees. Since goals and needs were so loosely defined, the YMCA was well placed to respond to outside initiatives, whether from philanthropists or other local leaders. The very looseness of expansion goals, however, worked against the establishment of priorities. Wherever initiatives or opportunities arose, the YMCA might accept the challenge. But the reverse should also be noted: in the absence of priorities, areas lacking leadership interest in the YMCA or philanthropic backing were neglected. Aside from a new department in a Negro neighborhood which was supported by the leaders of an old South Side department, not a single new department was built in the inner city area during the postwar period. Some inner city outposts were begun, but given its dependence on either local or philanthropic interests, the Association's political economy almost inevitably drew it to the suburbs in the postwar era.

That this effect was a function of political economy and not simply of the organization's economy can be shown by contrasting it with another youth agency devoted to working-class services. The chief executive of this organization asserted that inner city expansion was always planned from the central headquarters. Although the organization had to scramble for funds, it had always sought support for facilities primarily in those areas which contained its chief targets, working-class youth.

1. Norton Long has noted that even if a community elite is not functioning, agency professionals must create one. "Local Community as an Ecology of Games," *American Journal of Sociology* 64 (November 1958): 251–61.

RACE RELATIONS AND THE YMCA

No organization involved with interpersonal relations in the web of a metropolitan area can avoid decisions and policies related to social differences in general, and race and ethnicity in particular. Who shall be served? Under what conditions? Who shall be employed? In what positions? These questions have confronted all organizational decision makers in our urban areas. Whether the organization is a neighborhood grocery store or a large manufacturing corporation, the matching of product line, plant, and store location to potential clientele and the selection and promotion of personnel involve social differentiation.

Although most urban organizations must make decisions (or at least follow implicit policies) on matters related to ethnicity, for many organizations decisions and their implementation may bear a closer relation to economic concerns than to fundamental polity definition. The YMCA's historic attachments, however—first to evangelical Protestantism and later to the social gospel and liberal trends in theology—inevitably made the selection of clientele crucial to the essence of its organizational identity.

Although the YMCA's involvement with women, with Roman Catholics, and with Jews has continued to constitute a marginal area of dispute, the fundamental policy to serve them has long been established. Occasionally, a Jewish board member has indicated his discomfort regarding the Christian prayer used at the beginning of a board meeting. Or again, he might pursue certain policies with unusual caution precisely because he is Jewish. And occasionally a Catholic priest has chastised a parishioner for serving on a YMCA board. Within itself, however, the Chicago YMCA, having long since taken the basic steps to incorporate women, Catholics, and Jews, was at peace on these issues. The full incorporation of Negroes into the YMCA posed greater difficulties. The pressures for complete incorporation had risen markedly since World War II, but important sources of resistance had emerged within the polity, and incorporation was intimately linked to the economic and membership difficulties of many local departments.

Some departments were totally Negro in staff, boards, and membership composition, and had been so historically. Others were completely integrated. Still others, however, were at best only partially integrated. As Chicago's Negro population increased and dispersed and as the civil rights movement grew more intense, departments serving border areas and departments that had only partially incorporated Negroes found themselves facing economic and political quandaries.

The board of managers' formal written policy was explicit and unequivocal (though probably not widely known). In 1944 the board had passed a resolution clearly stating its position of total openness, of complete racial, religious, and ethnic incorporation. But this position must be viewed in terms of the YMCA's historic posture, both at the national level and in Chicago. Within that context, and given the structure of the local polity, we can understand the less than perfect implementation of the policy which actually existed.

Historically, city departments have generally avoided controversial issues. At times, to be sure, the student associations (abetted by missionary-spirited staff members) were deeply involved in the controversial issues of the day. And occasionally a national staff member or local secretary became personally involved in divisive issues. Yet unlike the Young Women's Christian Association, which has long been explicitly involved in controversial social issues,[2] or the Protestant ministry which, while often conservative, has still included built-in pockets of protest,[3] the Chicago Association focused on program offerings rather than on contributing to the debate of public issues.

Moreover, the Association's connection to business interests, to the railroads, and to the middle class has often given it a conservative image. This image was bolstered during New Deal days because the Chicago business elite were among the most anti-Roosevelt in the country.

The Chicago YMCA's historic relationship to Chicago Negroes presented a rather mixed appearance. On the one hand, Julius Rosenwald had early endowed a Chicago YMCA for Negroes (as he had done elsewhere in the country). The historic pattern had not focused on integration, however, and integration as a broad issue developed rapidly only after World War II. Simultaneously, the YMCA became involved in a public dispute with Roosevelt University—which had been a part of the Chicago YMCA. In partial justification of Roosevelt University's separation from the YMCA, the university's president, Edward Sparling, claimed that the Association had pressured the school to discriminate against various ethnic and racial groups and had objected to his open-door policy. The board of managers rejected this as nonsense and attributed Sparling's dismissal to his usurpation of authority in senior

2. Galen Fisher, p. 183. The Young Women's Christian Association, for example, has strongly supported the United Nations and racial integration. At least one southern state considers the YWCA persona non grata.

3. Philip E. Hammond and Robert E. Mitchell, "Segmentation of Radicalism: The Case of the Protestant Minister," *American Journal of Sociology* 71 (September 1965): 133–43.

administrative appointments.[4] Whichever position was closer to fact, the Association's public image with respect to race was certainly not above suspicion.

Given this historic background, the 1944 policy statement just cited was neither visible nor especially consonant with the YMCA's actual position and reputation either outside or inside the organization. Many secretaries had never heard of the policy, and it was only very late in my study that the 1944 statement came to light.

During the period of this study and the decade preceding it, external pressures and internal logic were pressing the board of managers and the Metropolitan office to hold the 1944 policy up to view as both necessary and appropriate and to implement it vigorously. Yet neither of these actions were taken (a situation emphasized by the fact that the policy statement itself gathered dust in the files). Thus the board of managers' policy and the general secretaries' intentions with respect to that policy could only be demonstrated through specific actions. The general posture of the board of managers and the general secretary favored integration, but this was not a burning issue for them. And since the board and the secretary were committed to working out problems at the local level, the Metropolitan office was likely to involve itself in local issues only when the interests of the entire Association were threatened either through bad public relations or legal action.

The crucial question then is: How did local departments adapt to the presence and pressure of Negroes in their communities? Two departments responded by gerrymandering their boundaries. These two were located near the outer edge of the city. In terms of the areas that the Metropolitan office had expected these departments to serve, both had Negro enclaves (dating back at least to public housing projects initiated during World War II). Both departments avoided any program or advertisement of activities which the Negroes in the area could interpret as indicating that the departments were open to them.

Other departments offered less resistance. The timing of integration in local departments followed roughly the same sequence. The first program area to be fully integrated was usually the youth program. Once a YMCA began to accept Negro youths into membership, the only bar became the membership fee. In some cases this could represent a substantial barrier. In one changing neighborhood, for example, the department, serving a middle- and upper-middle-class white clientele, charged twenty-five dollars a year for membership. After several years of resisting even the board

4. Dedmon, pp. 280–93.

of managers' gentle pressure, the department finally began accepting Negroes into membership, although after two years only eighteen had been admitted, the high fees discouraging many potential Negro applicants.[5] Once membership barriers had been broken, however, the department was opened up for other kinds of programs. Soon volunteer tutoring programs were underway in the building and, at a later time, programs connected with the war on poverty were located there.

This pattern of admitting Negroes first into the youth program was quite clear, and by the end of the major fieldwork for this study (1963), only one department serving a partially Negro area still systematically excluded them from youth programs.

It was much more difficult to integrate the adult programs. Adult programs, residences, and the Businessmen's Clubs, in that order, were usually the last programs to be integrated. Indeed, the period of this study was marked by continually recurring difficulties, since numerous departments maintained some segregated facilities To a large extent, if the adult program served people who worked rather than lived in an area, little attempt to shift programs would occur: the department would continue to cater to the white businessmen working in the area. Although most departments gradually incorporated Negroes into their adult program, the residences and the Businessmen's Clubs both continued to create difficulties long after a department's youth program had been completely integrated. Indeed in some departments a crazy-quilt pattern developed consisting of an integrated youth program, Negro professional staff members, a residence with a hidden quota program, and a lily-white Businessmen's Club.

When a neighborhood began to change its racial composition, the department's board and staff were likely to do some informal soul searching regarding the department's relationship to the newcomers. This soul searching involved the board and staff members' commitments to their neighborhood and departments, as well as their conceptions of the YMCA's purposes. At this stage the board and staff were usually all Caucasian. Even after Negroes had been accepted in youth programs and partially accepted in the residences, board and staff would attempt to protect the residences from full Negro occupancy. They were often concerned with a "tipping point" (the point at which a predominance of Negroes would cause whites to leave the residence, eventuating in an all-Negro residence). Most board members did not want an all-Negro de-

5. The decision to lower fees radically is related to a basic shift in the economy of a local department; this is discussed in chapter 10.

partment, and even when the youth programs stabilized as integrated operations, both boards and staff feared that a totally Negro residence would affect the composition of the rest of the department's program, which might subsequently be perceived as largely for Negroes. As neighborhoods changed, however, the number of whites wanting to live in the residence dwindled.

In all cases of quota maintenance, the residences came to be run uneconomically because the quota restriction resulted in unfilled capacity. (Since a shortage of Negro housing and a high rate of Negro transiency were facts of urban life, department residences located in largely Negro neighborhoods were always utilized to full capacity.) The quota systems were maintained by turning away Negroes who wanted a room only for a night or two and by careful informal screening to determine the most desirable permanent residents.

In general, then, board and staff, committed to the department as it had developed and to the community as it had previously existed, attempted to slow the pace of integration; they generally permitted at least partial integration of youth program but held back on the residence for some time, resulting in uneconomic utilization of the facility.

The most determined holdouts, however, were the Businessmen's Clubs. Located in all the larger departments and several of the smaller ones, these were the YMCA's version of the private athletic club. They charged fees upward from $100 a year as well as an initiation fee. Aside from access to a department's general athletic facilities—weight-lifting room, handball court, gymnasium, and swimming pool—the Businessmen's Club had private locker rooms, sometimes a masseur, steam baths, and card rooms. In some of them a small dining room separated from the main cafeteria was also provided. Board members were often active users of the club. The Businessmen's Clubs represented a high-status group for the department, as well as a relatively solidified and powerful group with direct representation of their interests on the board of directors. The almost total segregation of Businessmen's Clubs produced some embarrassing moments. In one department, for instance, a Negro member of the board of directors wanted to join the club and resigned from the board when he was not permitted to do so. In the department located in the same building as the Metropolitan office a Negro member of the Metropolitan staff was refused access. Even though several members of the club resigned in protest, a few days later the club was desegregated on orders from the professional staff. In this case the professional staff were willing to move rapidly and vigorously, regardless of the consequences.

How can we explain this crazy-quilt pattern and the Metropolitan office's response to specific instances of segregation? At the local level, the necessity for managing membership sentiments in an enrollment economy led staff and boards alike to be most willing to integrate those groups or categories of people (such as youth programs) whose white members would protest least. At the Metropolitan level, the concern to maintain local boards and the principle of local autonomy resulted in an ambivalent posture which eventuated in action only when broader implications demanded it.[6]

The difficulty of managing membership sentiments in an enrollment economy is simply that if the organization antagonizes its members, they can resign. The more powerful the members (either through their financial contributions or their direct organizational access to the board), the less likely it is that the organization will attempt to move against their interests. By and large, parents did not protest the integration of the youth programs. Youth memberships might decrease, but as often as not this was not due to a protest withdrawal of members from department programs but to the fact that as more Negroes moved into the area, the whites moved out. Youth membership declined because the department often did not react fast enough to incorporate Negroes by lowering fees and by publicizing its openness.

With respect to the residences and the Businessmen's Clubs, however, board members and staff felt constrained by the attitudes of salient groups. In some cases the staff members themselves opposed integration. In one department, which maintained a completely integrated residence, the Metropolitan staff believed that the staff director of the Businessmen's Club was responsible for mobilizing resistance to its integration. Yet in the view of the Metropolitan office no action could be taken until he retired (at least, not without "stirring up a hornet's nest"), for he was highly regarded by the members.

The board of managers acted strongly only when their own interests were at stake. In one such case a member of the board of managers' executive committee believed that a local department was jeopardizing the total Association by refusing to accept a Negro who resided outside the department's area (that is, the department was claiming that it could not accept him because he lived outside its boundaries). The board member wanted the department ordered to accept this person into member-

6. It should be noted that the more centralized organization for working-class youth discussed earlier had also on occasion yielded to pressures from local residents. In the most blatant case, a branch located in the same block as a fully integrated elementary school totally excluded Negroes because residents from the immediate all-white neighborhood threatened to withdraw their children.

ship. The other committee members, however, sided with the local department saying, in effect, "They have worked to build a community department, and we have to go slow." On the other hand, when a Negro complained that he was refused a haircut from a barber shop located in a local department's building and threatened a legal suit, the barber was ordered to cut his hair. When the barber refused, his lease was terminated. A legal suit would have embarrassed the Association's posture of general concern for the Negro community and would have issued in internal conflict and dissent. Most integration situations, however, posed problems only for specific departments and thus lacked a general organizational audience. With its multiplicity of other commitments and concerns, the board of managers and the general office staff did not require complete conformity to the 1944 policy statement. Full implementation would have required either an incident affecting the entire organization or a major change in the leadership's value constellation.

I have concentrated on resistance to integration, but such a concentration is one-sided. One department with a crusading staff leadership received an award from the city's Human Relations Commission for its effectiveness in integrating Negroes and helping to stabilize a changing middle-class residential area. Another department, after an initial period of resistance, was transformed into an enthusiastic center for working with and changing the community. The point is, of course, that a crazy-quilt pattern could exist on both sides of the integration question precisely because of the Association's diverse political economy.

A comparison of the Association's expansion policy with that relating to racial integration produces an important contrast. The policy of requiring local initiative and funding for expansion was one that allowed the organization to grow by assimilating new elements and resources. It was a policy of capital expansion at the periphery. In many ways this expansion resembled the process of capital formation as it occurs in a laissez-faire economy as opposed to a hierarchical, centralized state. (The existence of matching grants, to be sure, weakens the analogy.) Although the policy lacked priority standards, the lack would not be perceived by most YMCA members as a major weakness precisely because the organization's goals were so broad. On the other hand, the policy relating to the incorporation of Negroes into previously white departments was ambivalent and conservative. It was an organization-maintaining policy that allowed the Association to retain board and business commitments and simultaneously to preserve local autonomy. At the same time, for specific cases, the ambivalent policy enforcement resulted in occasional external threats.

ALTERNATIVES FOREGONE: POLITICAL ECONOMY AND EXTERNAL LINKAGES

Just as policies and related aspects of social organization emerge from and in turn shape political economy, so also the external linkages and niche of an organization interrelate with its political economy. Some of these linkages (ties to the business community and to the Protestant denominations) have already been discussed briefly.[7] The preventative versus rehabilitative orientation and breadth of program goals reflect linkages to clientele, types of potential personnel, and other inputs from the environment. These goals, programs, and clientele, which serve to define niche, were closely tied to crucial policies. Nowhere is that truth more evident than in the discussion of YMCA expansion policy, for it is clear that this policy, which operated to encourage suburban departments, was continually reaffirming the Association's diffuse-program, general-service niche.

One approach to the question of niche taking would be to ask what alternative niches the YMCA might have filled, but this approach, if carried too far, would be both feckless and boring. It would be feckless because the historical options are simply too numerous. It would be boring because the options would only be the reverse or converse of the present organizations. Nevertheless, in closing this chapter and preparing to discuss organizational transformation in the next, I want to mention a few of the alternatives foregone. These concern program, clientele, and political and organizational ties.

As YMCAs in America and in Chicago developed, it became clear that their forte lay in mass and group programs designed to "serve" rather than "change." Thus the organization has generally foregone options that would involve it in rehabilitation—either of groups or of individuals—and in foregoing such options, it has also lost the economic base that such programs might bring. In particular it has foregone an image of fulfilling crucial needs, whether of Christian ethics or religion. It was striking to note the frequency with which YMCA people, when asked to discuss the Association's Christian emphasis, described its overseas missionary work —that is, its support of YMCAs in other countries. A sense of mission is, after all, difficult to maintain when one is teaching swimming to middle-class children. The absence of a social mission image also deprived the

7. These linkages are informal rather than formal. Although in earlier times (1844–1930) specific denominational ties may have strongly constrained board members' actions because of their commitment to denominational doctrine, by the 1960s linkages to Protestant denominations were vague and implied only a general identification.

Association of contact with professionals and laymen who were more committed to social problems or to helping people with more extreme needs than the YMCA seemed to be serving. Some laymen and staff perceived the YMCA's program as exemplifying the Christian way of life— as *being* Christian. But it was not easy to convince others of the special Christian virtues of the organization.

The historic linkage to the Protestant business community also exacted its costs. In particular, though located in a largely Democratic city with the country's most powerful Democratic political organization, the YMCA sat on the sidelines. Only two members of the board of managers had active political careers and both had been candidates on the Republican ticket. No alderman served on local department boards. Although some Democratic judges had had connections to the Association, at the time of this study no direct ties existed. This political vacuum was no small matter. Other youth-serving organizations maintaining such linkages were able to use them to gain resources. Indeed, the free use of an old police station or firehouse could have provided means for establishing a new branch. Similarly, the organization's ties to both the private and the public social welfare community were extremely weak; the YMCA simply had not appeared interested in venturing outside its own building-centered program. When a member of the Public Housing Authority's staff was asked why the YMCA was not involved in operating community programs (as was a comparable youth-serving organization), the answer was simply that the Association did not seem to be interested and always raised too many problems. Whether the staff member was right or wrong, the alternative foregone was the free use (actually for "rent" of a dollar a year) of $500,000 buildings located in several of the larger housing projects.

The same difficulty had existed historically in the YMCA's relation to the Community Fund. Although one of the larger benefactors of the Red Feather Drive, YMCA staff perceived themselves as benefiting from inertial tradition (and not the most welcome tradition, in the eyes of Red Feather personnel).

In each of these alternatives foregone, the YMCA, as it developed, had rejected (though not on an explicit basis) an option for altering its selection and definition of niche. In the process of transformation, described in the next section, some of these alternatives foregone would become alternatives chosen.

Part III
Transforming a Traditional Organization

Introduction to Part III

There are four main criteria for evaluating theory: its precision of prediction, its internal coherence, the breadth or range of its application, and its ability to explore new facets of the real world. In other words, does the theoretical scheme or conceptual stance lead to precise prediction? Does it solve problems or explain previous theories? Does it open up new areas of investigation? Does it point to new interpretations of phenomena that have hitherto seemed trivial and so remained unanalyzed?

I make no claims here for precise prediction. Furthermore, although I believe the framework can be demonstrated to be internally consistent, I am not attempting to explicate its coherence in any detail. (Such an explication would necessitate a more abstract presentation of concepts, definitions, and assumptions than I present here.) But I believe I can demonstrate the usefulness of this framework for illuminating facets of organizational life and for exploring a broad range of organizational phenomena. Most specifically, I think it will be clear that a distinctive value of the political-economy approach lies in its illumination of the process of organizational change.

Technological, ideological, and social changes in the larger society impinge on the niches of complex organizations and on both the internal structure and conceptions of goals and function held by organizational members. Externally, social change affects the wants and demands of potential customers or clients, potential employees, financial supporters, and the number and strength of competing and cooperating organizations. Internally, social change in the larger society affects the self-definition of niche, of alternative modes of organization, and indeed of legitimate goals.

The earlier analysis was largely static, in that I attempted to describe the basic structure of the political economy as it existed in the late 1950s and early 1960s. The YMCA of Metropolitan Chicago, however, was involved—before, during, and after this study—in a series of organizational changes. These changes were, in part, adaptations to change in the megalopolis and in American society, in part adaptations to the growth of the YMCA itself, and in part adaptation initiated to satisfy the personal and organizational values of key leaders. In all cases the external societal changes were filtered through the Association's political economy either through changing sources of funds, clientele demands, or the values and ideologies of persons in power centers. The changes initiated included not only radical innovation leading to a partial redefinition of polity and economy but also changes designed mainly to reinforce or preserve the traditional political economy.

These changes in the Chicago YMCA's political economy were not compelled by inexorable, deterministic forces requiring it to adapt or face disaster. Rather, moral choices and values regarding what the YMCA *ought* to be, operating in conjunction with social pressures and opportunities, explain the directions of change. The resulting political economy was not a total reshaping of niche and structure; instead, new and sometimes conflicting elements were grafted onto the older structure. Policies, personnel, and power relations were changed to accommodate the new conceptions of function. Simultaneously, much of the traditional political economy was maintained; these changes represented a revitalization of organizational mission as well as a partial redefinition of niche.

8

The Beginnings of Change

Enmeshed within value-laden commitments, ideologies, and sentiments, the YMCA found that its easiest course was clearly to stick to well-beaten paths as it instituted change. And local Associations around the country have indeed followed the middle class to the suburbs, broadened the age groups they serve, and modernized their physical plants. Family membership and programs like the Indian Guides typify innovations which caused excitement among YMCA staff and were watched with great interest. Yet such changes could occur without appealing to new groups, for they involved only minor changes in niche or political economy.

Deeper changes, involving a radical shift in niche and related political economy, could occur only where there had already been considerable change in an Association's immediate societal environment. In Chicago, demographic changes and population growth had affected the demand for services and the relevance of local programs to the areas served. Furthermore, changes in managerial concepts and definitions of social problems, emerging from the larger society but also occurring in Chicago, were beginning to penetrate the Metropolitan YMCA.

POPULATION COMPOSITION

Changing population composition within department neighborhoods evoked specific responses from the YMCA and constituted a backdrop for the YMCA's increasing concern with the adequacy of its services to the lower-class Negro population. Chicago's population changes during the postwar decade paralleled those of other large northern cities. During the decade 1950–60, population in the standard metropolitan statistical area grew from approximately 5,178,000 to 6,221,000. The white population of the area grew 14 percent and the nonwhite population 66 percent. In the city of Chicago, white population declined 14 percent while

159

the nonwhite population increased 64 percent.[1] The rapidly growing inner city Negro population brought about an increasing spread of Negroes on the South and West sides and a much smaller spread on the North Side of Chicago. Of special interest to this research was the *perception* of population changes and its consequences for Metropolitan staff. Changes in perceived demand, affected partly by the actual shifts in population and partly by the climate for racial problem definition, began to affect evaluation of program by YMCA staff and boards.

Suburban Departments

Ten suburban departments had been created since World War II, some located in older suburbs and satellite cities that had never formed independent YMCAs and others in new tract areas lacking both old commercial and industrial centers and residential construction. In all these instances, integration and service to Negroes were of marginal concern. Neither the local departments nor the Metropolitan office perceived existing or impending problems.

Outer Ring Departments

Five departments had existed on the outer ring for over forty years. Four were building departments with residences, whereas one, located in a mixed Catholic-Protestant area, was a community department. Of these five, three faced impending racial change. Their areas already included Negro enclaves, and some of the Metropolitan staff considered change inevitable—even though, in two cases, the local board and staff resisted incorporating Negroes into programs.

Inner City Departments

The remaining nineteen departments were in the inner city. (As elsewhere, this figure excludes three that lacked a neighborhood base.) Three departments built since World War II were located in predominantly white and middle-class areas. One area was mixed Protestant-Jewish; another had already changed from largely Catholic and Protestant to a mixture of Catholic, Protestant, and Jewish middle class; it was, however, increasingly including Negro and white working-class members. The third was a predominantly Catholic, upper-working-class and lower-middle-class area (median family income in 1960, $7,712). The

1. D. J. Bogue and D. P. Dandekar, *Population Trends and Prospects for the Chicago–Northwestern Indiana Consolidated Metropolitan Area: 1960–1990* (Chicago: Population Research and Training Center of the University of Chicago, 1962), pp. 3–4.

department located in the second of these three areas had strongly resisted serving Negroes, but, under Metropolitan office pressure, had begun to change in the late 1950s and early 1960s.

Although many of the remaining sixteen departments were neighborhood-based and served predominantly working-class white and Negro neighborhoods, nearly all of them were in communities with a changing ethnic, class, or racial base. Three of these had been fairly stable, two continuously serving working-class white communities and one serving a working-class Negro community. (One of these three had resisted incorporating Negroes only by ignoring their presence in the area.) The other thirteen had undergone varying ethnic, racial, and class changes, generally serving more of the working class and more Negroes, Mexicans, or Puerto Ricans. One of these had previously catered to middle-class Negroes and had shifted to working-class Negroes, but the typical pattern emphasized a shift in the percentage of an area's Negroes served.

A survey of all thirty-four neighborhood departments revealed that at least a third had confronted massive changes in the population composition of their areas. Stated another way, in the early 1960s, less than a third of the departments that had been in existence ten years previously were confronting the same population composition that they had in the early 1950s.

Another way to view population composition and its impact is to examine the 1961–62 distribution of whites and nonwhites in the areas served in the nonresident membership of departments. Data relevant to this question are presented in table 17.

A lower proportion of whites in the membership than in the area usually indicates that the whites live farther from the department than nonwhites (that is, the actual service area is smaller than the geographic area formally designated by the Association, and the whites live in the more distant parts of this area). A large, white adult membership in a geographic area which is largely nonwhite usually indicates that the department is located in a commercial and industrial center and draws its adult members primarily from those who live outside the service area. These data indicate that twelve of the thirty-four departments included substantial proportions (over 10 percent) of Negroes in their youth populations.

Given, first, the number of departments with substantial proportions of Negroes and, second, the typicality of population change, the YMCA had to develop modes of adaptation. Earlier I noted that many departments besides those in the inner city had difficulty balancing their bud-

TABLE 17

The Racial Picture: Whites in Service Areas versus White Membership
(Percent)

Department[a]	Whites in Service Areas	White Youth Members	White Adult Members
Park Ridge............	99.9	99	100
Mount Clare-Leyden....	99.9	100	100
West Communities......	99.9	100	100
Austin................	99.8	100	100
Elmhurst..............	99.8	100	100
Northwest Suburban....	99.8	100	100
Irving Park............	99.8	100	100
Duncan-Logan Square...	99.7	97	98
Duncan-North.........	99.6	99	98
Downers Grove........	99.6	100	100
High Ridge............	99.3	99	99
Ilg Park..............	99.3	100	100
West Suburban.........	98.7	100	100
Division..............	98.2	68	83
Southwest Suburban....	98.1	100	100
Palos-Orland..........	97.4	100	100
South Chicago........	97.3	85	75
Beverly..............	97.1	100	100
Lincoln-Belmont.......	97.0	97	99
Ravenswood..........	96.9	94	97
South Shore..........	91.6	100	100
Harvey...............	89.3	89	94
Auburn Highland.......	88.4	93	99
Isham Memorial.......	84.6	32	64
111th Street...........	82.2	99	99
Lawson..............	63.8	26	97
Duncan-Maxwell.......	63.0	0	18
Duncan..............	57.1	37	71
Hyde Park............	48.6	58	90
Southtown............	48.0	8	49
Sears, Roebuck	46.4	0	75
Chatham..............	37.8	31	73
Wabash Avenue........	10.1	0	4
Washington Park.......	.8	0	0

SOURCES: Service area percentages (as of 1960) are from Charles Kamen and Mayer Zald, "Selected Characteristics of the Residents of Service Areas of the Local Departments of the Metropolitan Chicago Young Men's Christian Association," mimeographed (Chicago: YMCA of Metropolitan Chicago, 1964). Membership figures as of 1962 are from Mayer N. Zald and Patricia Jenkins, "Membership Survey: Summary Report," mimeographed (Chicago: YMCA of Metropolitan Chicago, 1963).

NOTE: Excluded are the Hotel, Central, and Duncan-Medical departments.

[a] Ranked by percentage of whites in service area.

gets. It was apparent to both staff and board members, however, that racial change brought economic problems and that the inner city departments had to be supported by both Community Fund appropriations and by loans from the board of managers, if they were not radically to curtail program.

MANAGERIAL CONCEPTS AND DEFINITION OF SOCIAL PROBLEMS

After World War II, changes occurring in the larger society's system of belief affected the decision premises and operating style of the Association's executive core. Two rough categories can be perceived: changes in managerial concepts and changes in society's perspectives on its social problems and on the YMCA's relevance to such problems. Although the former can be seen as distinct from the latter, both have affected the ideological and decision-making context in which changes in political economy occurred.

Managerial Concepts

Obviously many aspects of managerial attitudes, concepts, and ideology affected the YMCA. Three that related specifically to polity definitions and processes were the increased use of outside consultants, management by "goal setting," and broader use of small group discussion techniques.

First, the Association began to seek expert, outside consultation and advice on specific problems. Computer companies and the Association's accountants cooperated in the mechanization of records (at the time of this study mechanization had been most fully applied to salaries and membership counting). Indeed, this study itself grew out of a belief in the importance of outside "objective" studies.

Second, the organization began to manage by "goal setting." An outgrowth of the decentralization process in major industrial and merchandizing concerns, goal setting by executives has become integral to the process of personnel appraisal. Industrial goals are usually set for individual "profit centers" even if nowhere else; but even within profit centers or on broad corporate bases, goals related to performance, long-range planning, and the like have increasingly become part of the rhetoric of management and of the actual personnel appraisal process.

In the Chicago YMCA the goal-setting process was incorporated into Metropolitan office management and the board of managers through a process of setting both annual and long-range goals. Although some goals were quite specific (examining and reporting on the feasibility of placing vending machines in local departments, or raising X thousand dollars in contributions), others were more general ("reexamining total structure and function"—the present study was conducted under this mandate). The goals were set by board committees and implemented by staff in conjunction with the board. These procedures provided one mechanism for raising alternatives and focusing problems. Although the process could easily be subverted into window dressing, it was effective in readying the Association for a broader assessment of alternatives than had been possible under the older management style.

Goal-setting techniques could also have been employed to evaluate the executive secretaries' performance; indeed, the executives' broad autonomy was tailor-made for systematic goal-setting procedures. Yet at the time of this study, no such application had been made. Instead, an evaluation or appraisal form was used which asked questions of both key laymen and Metropolitan staff regarding the adequancy of executive and local staff performance. The questions probed not specific accomplishments, but general abilities (Did he confer well with laymen? Was he a good administrator? etc.). The appraisals, which occurred every three years after a staff member's first year in a job, constituted a backstop in the evaluation procedure and were not used for program or administrative planning.

Third, like many other organizations, the Chicago YMCA had accepted the challenge of the group discussion and sensitivity training, provided by groups such as the National Training Laboratories. Indeed, the YMCA represented fertile soil for such techniques, because they are based on concepts of participant democracy and of information sharing and openness that blend well with the Christian leadership emphases of the YMCA's historic ideology. Several key staff members had attended training laboratories specifically arranged for YMCA personnel. Chicago's personnel director joined the staff of the Midwest Training Laboratories; and YMCA internal training meetings were increasingly dominated by group discussion and feedback techniques. At the annual staff retreat, a nationally known T-group trainer began serving as an annual consultant.

Although the general secretary did not himself participate in such activities, he encouraged his staff to do so. His legitimation of this activity was crucial, because only thereby could staff participation have been financed by the Chicago Association. (A few general secretaries from other cities resisted the use of group discussion techniques and, indeed, debate over its relevance took place on the national level.) Such group devices served several functions. First, they provided a forum for discussing difficulties specific to given organizational structures and policies. Second, they aided in locating sources of resistance to new policies or organizational changes. Finally, they contributed to a perception of participation in policy formation even when the executive core were choosing among issues raised by staff to create their own organizational agenda.

These internal innovations emerged from concepts of management process then current in the larger society. Other innovations had a narrower focus but also revealed the YMCA's concern to keep pace with larger trends. The board of managers, for example, developed a "marketing committee" to suggest ways of packaging and presenting programs, to assess needs or "demand," and to evaluate the scope and effectiveness of new programs. The committee's lay personnel included the head of an advertising agency and a department store's corporate vice-president in charge of marketing. The committee's very title flies in the face of traditional views of the YMCA (and of welfare organizations generally), and yet it makes explicit the voluntary enrollment character of most YMCA programs.

The management ideology and innovations discussed above, while not representing fundamental transformations of the organization, obviously had implications for the YMCA's economy and polity. These new techniques *could* have been used to reaffirm traditional character. Instead, however, they became linked with environmental redefinitions of organizational goals.

Awareness of Social Problems

More important than changes in managerial ideology, changes in the perception of social problems and in the related ideology affecting the YMCA's goals and polity also took place. These included perceptions of suburbanization and changes in megalopolis, the growth of the civil rights movement and the changing status of Negroes, and, finally, changes in the attitudes of businessmen (especially corporate leaders) toward Chicago's Democratic machine and (more broadly) toward liberal social welfare policy. First, the decade of the 1950s saw a broad and increasing concern over the fate of the city develop. During this decade questions began to emerge regarding the relation of suburbs to the city, the growth of Negro slums, urban renewal, superhighway development, and the preservation of the central business district. These were issues which, though arising earlier, became crucial after the close of the Korean War and increased in intensity during the latter half of the 1950s and early

1960s. The mere fact that such issues were considered crucial in the larger society is no indication that they shaped the Association's alternatives and definitions; yet they certainly were part of the matrix for staff and lay perceptions.

The changes in megalopolis were, of course, related to the influx of Negroes into the central city. Some of the actual demographic facts as they affected the Chicago YMCA have been presented, but the ideological battle over civil rights was a key issue requiring much soul searching on the part of some YMCA boards and staff. This soul searching, as was noted in the preceding chapter, was not unrelated to Negroes' increased willingness to assert their rights to equal service.

The last major ideological change that must be noted was the relationship of local influential businessmen to the Democratic party. The late fifties saw a growing awareness that Richard Daley was providing "good government," hospitable to business interests. *Fortune* published a paean to Chicago and Mayor Daley, and leading businessmen supported his reelection in 1959 and again in 1963.[2] It became clear, as prominent board members were increasingly identified with liberal causes, that this change of perspectives was affecting the board of managers. At one point the head of the Illinois Public Aid Commission, also the president of a Chicago department store firm, was a member of the board of managers. A former Community Chest executive, he was well known in liberal circles and had been considered as a Democratic senatorial candidate. Other board members had been identified with urban renewal and other civic projects. Although the board's cast was overwhelmingly conservative and Republican, strong anti–New Deal sentiments of the earlier period had clearly begun to recede, and the appearance of monolithic conservatism had altered.

These changes in perception of social problems and in attitude toward the perception of the Negro's status, as well as the managerial changes discussed earlier, formed the context within which major organizational transformation took place.

THE BEGINNINGS OF NICHE CHANGE

The study of organizational history is marked by the stories of hundreds of organizations that went out of existence by failure to adapt to social change. Other organizations have survived and retained their iden-

---

2. William Bowen, "Chicago: They Didn't Have to Burn It Down after All," *Fortune*, January 1965, pp. 142–61. Mayor Daley's good relations with the business elite were maintained at least until the Democratic party convention of 1968.

tity, while losing vitality and strength. Still others have radically altered their niche as well as their organizational identity. Here we are concerned with the beginnings of massive and radical (though partial) redefinitions of the niche and identity of the Chicago YMCA. The change was massive because it eventually issued a new economy totaling almost 50 percent of the 1961 budget and a sizable increase in professional staff. It was radical because the organization developed new definitions of operational goals and of clients to be served, as well as a new set of relations with both local and federal governmental agencies. Yet the change was only partial because many old lines of endeavor remained intact. The new political economy was grafted onto the old, affecting it both marginally and at the center of its constitutional norms. The change involved the organization in service to delinquents and school dropouts and in imaginative programs for employing the unemployed in self-help jobs. It brought the Association into contact with new sources of personnel outside its traditional base. It brought about a redefinition of relations between the staff and lay people and between the Association and both national philanthropic foundations and the federal government. Marginally, it also issued in redefinitions of the Metropolitan office's role as it related to local departments.

Before describing the changes, I will first dispose of three simple, deterministic interpretations that might be advanced: the societal, the economic, and the political. The first would argue that, as the larger society changes, organizations within it must change. As society has changed, status relations between Negroes and whites have changed, and as attempts have been made to resolve problems of poverty and delinquency, there must also effect organizational change. Such an interpretation would be true in the long run, provided the total society changed (by definition it would *have* to be true). Nevertheless, it is an exceedingly gross interpretation that does not permit explanation of which organizations will change first and (since not all change) which will change at all. Furthermore, it ignores the *process* of change.

The economic interpretation would be somewhat more efficient than the societal. In brief, it would hold that, as an area's population changed, the organization's economy would be put under stress. Particularly within the Chicago YMCA, with its heavy concentration of Negro and inner city locations, the stress would have had to be met by innovations resulting in new sources of funds. This argument is more appealing than the previous one because it implies a mechanism—economic pressure—to trigger organizational change. The explanation is naive, however, and not very informative. It cannot explain why other organizations (the YWCA, for instance) with fewer inner city commitments had earlier adopted "advanced" positions on racial matters. It also provides no means for discerning which of the many alternatives facing the organization could also have been chosen. Indeed, for two reasons, this explanation is ultimately false: it ignores organizational structure and processes as a set of intervening processes explaining change, and it ignores the basic economic health of the whole Chicago Association as compared with other large metropolitan Associations—in its membership growth rate, its sizable endowment figures, and its deficit-free operation. (The inner city departments may have posed problems, but these certainly never constituted a crisis.) It may be that the Chicago YMCA's large commitments of fixed, inner city resources (buildings) made it more responsive to the need for change than other city Associations lacking such large commitments; yet the directions of change finally chosen were not inevitable, and a simple economic determinant provides no mechanism for explaining the selection of one alternative above another.

Finally, the political explanation has the potential to interpret changes in goals, in the constitution of power, and in the values of key decision makers. The selection of a general secretary who favored the "program line" (described in the next chapter) was certainly not unimportant to the directions of change; yet only with knowledge of the simultaneous development of central fund sources could the particular directions of change have been perceived. I will argue, then, that both political and economic processes must be considered if directions of change are to be understood.

Leadership Sources

At least as late as 1954, the Chicago YMCA gave no indications that it would shortly become involved in a radical redefinition of its niche, and that it would begin moving in a different direction from that of most other Associations. Immediately after World War II, the Association began to expand rapidly. Between 1945 and 1954 nine new departments were founded, two in white, working-class and lower-middle-class areas, one in a Negro neighborhood, and six in suburbs. Once a department had been named and located in an area, it was likely (assuming it could develop financial backing) eventually to have its own building. Indeed, by 1961, ten of the fourteen departments established between 1940 and 1959 had erected buildings. Of the ten new buildings, nine were in the outer ring and suburbs and one (backed by Negro professional and business leadership) was located in a Negro neighborhood.

Although during the 1930s one inner city department located in a Polish-Catholic neighborhood had employed a street worker in the Shaw-McKay community-organization style, that program had died out. With the great move to the suburbs and without any indication of inner city vitality, it seemed unlikely that the Association would undertake any more such organizationally adventurous programs.

In 1954 a new general secretary was appointed (his predecessor had served for fifteen years). In a 1961 interview, the general secretary recalled that, at the time he took office, he had two major concerns: to raise the level of the Metropolitan office's concern with program (as contrasted with finances) and to bring more "warmth" to the office. The assistant general secretary for program services (appointed at the same time on the general secretary's recommendation) noted that, when he took office, he and the general secretary had both wanted to "do something" about the inner city. He felt that he had perceived a growing recognition within the Association that, in terms of both program and finance, its inner city program was not functioning adequately. With respect to finances, only one or two inner city departments had adequate economic leadership and an adequate fund-raising base either through contributions or membership fees. With respect to program, the two men recognized that fees were often too high for the poor neighborhoods and that lower, more flexible fee structures had to be developed. Furthermore, they recognized that the program was totally inadequate for reaching adolescents; the departments were notably isolated from street-corner youth and gangs.

In part the remembrance of things past works to rationalize later actions, but it is a matter of record that these two men had come from "program" backgrounds and were strongly committed to innovation and development. The question immediately arises: How were these men selected? Why did the Association's board of managers choose two men with such program commitments? Was the board aware of the impending multiplicity of inner city problems? Was there a strong consensus that the Association *had* to increase its inner city activity and that, consequently, a different type of leadership was required?

Succession processes are obviously key political events within organizations; succession may occur in an almost routine and traditional manner or it may be subjected to great debate and represent organizational crises and choices. In this instance, chance factors in the succession process cannot be overlooked. Historically, Chicago has chosen its general secretary from among its own senior personnel. As the country's largest Association, it has been nationally perceived as a training ground for other general secretaries, and other city Associations have often drawn from it when recruiting replacements for their own general secretaries. In Chicago, as in many large city Associations, the role of the general secretary was usually defined as administrator and fund raiser rather than as goal setter or innovator; the latter tasks were delegated to local personnel. The two previous general secretaries had been recruited from among the Association's senior business personnel.

The new secretary, Lloyd McClow, had served in the Metropolitan office since 1945, working in personnel and general administration; he had not been the senior staff person and had not been the heir apparent. Earlier annual reports list another assistant general secretary ahead of McClow in a nonalphabetic list. Furthermore, staff asserted that this second man had been the logical successor to Frank Hathaway, the former general secretary. In 1949, however, at the age of fifty-one, this assistant general secretary and comptroller had died. The following year McClow had been listed as the associate general secretary, a rank above the other senior staff members. There is no evidnce from either staff or board comments that McClow was the heir apparent before that time; indeed there is some evidence from their comments that, as a "replacement," he had been somewhat insecure in the office.

Later it will become apparent that the personal characteristics of key leaders are important to the transformation of the Chicago Association. It may seem that I place considerable explanatory weight on the accident of death, but would anyone deny the relevance of death and succession to the political analysis of regimes? Only the most deterministic approaches would slight such events. YMCAs all over the United States were to a greater or lesser extent buffeted by demographic change, the civil rights movement and the opportunities provided by the War on Poverty. That the Chicago Association led in that engagement was due to its central political leadership. Although McClow's succession was partly a result of chance, many members of the board of managers supported his accession. Simultaneously with his succession, the board of managers elected a new president, a man with long experience in program evaluation (he had been chairman of the board's program committee and had served on state and national program committees). In this respect, the growing awareness of inner city needs and internal organizational processes affected McClow's election.

At the time of his accession, McClow was not confronting an organization in crisis. First, while some departments showed deficits, the general economy was strong and expanding. The annual reports through 1954 evidence no great concern but rather indicate a continually expanding capital and expense base. Second, there was no evidence that the search for a successor was defined in any than the traditional terms. As far as can be discerned, no debates had occurred over either goals and directions or the appropriateness of the existing organizational niche. McClow had had considerable YMCA experience and had earlier been executive secretary of two of the largest departments. That he had strong program interests appears not to have been merely incidental to his selection, but it was not decisive either. Finally, McClow's program experience and interest followed the conventional YMCA model. His experience had been partly in working-class areas, but he had not reshaped his departments' traditional services or the groups served. There was clearly little to indicate that his regime would see a massive redefinition of goals and an internal polity change.

Nor was the selection of a new assistant general secretary for program services indicative of these new directions. In McClow's words, "I selected him because he had good program ideas and drive. Many program men don't have the drive." The new assistant general secretary had been the executive secretary of a highly successful, satellite-city department before coming to the Metropolitan office.

McClow's first two years were marked by a growing awareness that the Association faced inner city difficulties. A later document implies that, in 1955, the Association consciously decided to remain in the inner city and to involve the board of managers in a continuous, concentrated support program for inner city departments.[3] (The board began raising money for an inner city fund to back up this commitment.) This contrasts with the usual assumption that board support was to be intermittent and problem-specific. Whether or not a *single* strategic decision was made, however, a general policy of commitment was clearly beginning to form.

Although attention to the inner city clearly became more noticeable during McClow's tenure, it should not be thought that staff members alone had an interest in the inner city. One member of the board of managers commented that he had first heard the proposal for a specific inner city program from another board member (a highly respected minister

---

3. The document was a 1958 proposal to the Ford Foundation requesting support for the Youth Gangs Project.

of long standing on the board). Indeed, one of the most committed and widely experienced board members claimed that the board members were growing aware of the city's new problems simultaneously with the staff and quickly perceived the YMCA's mission in the inner city. Furthermore, other staff members noted that the decision to become involved with inner city problems was made in the mid-1950s, roughly at the same time that Sears, Roebuck (a major YMCA supporter) decided to keep its headquarters on the West Side of Chicago; the president of the board of managers from 1957 to 1959 was also the president of Sears, Roebuck and Co. Such factors as these resulted in growing board concern about inner city planning.[4]

The board's initial approach was limited to financing inner city departments and developing new programs. There was no explicit awareness or special attention to changes in the Association's polity which might issue from these new programs and financing approaches. Staff, however, rapidly became aware that funds were easier to raise when a specific program, such as the inner city fund, was the focus of contributor attention. The idea of an inner city fund contained a missionary thrust that a request for general contributions lacked.

Program Sources: The Youth Gangs Pilot Project

In 1956, the first radically different program, the Youth Gangs Pilot Project, was initiated with one street worker. (The program was later called the Detached Worker Program.) Three of the initial operating assumptions underlying this program were especially relevant to later developments. First, the Association admitted (indeed, argued) that a building-centered approach was inadequate to reach delinquents and gangs. Thus the traditional means for reaching clients (advertising and then waiting for clients to walk in) was supplanted by a systematic attempt to reach out. Second, and equally important in its polity implications, the program was specifically designed to reach gangs and members of gangs; by contrast with its usual preventive approach, the Association was actively attempting to reach a "malfunctioning" group of youth. Finally, the first worker hired was assigned to the Metropolitan office

---

4. Even the light emphasis on economic factors I have suggested may be too much. On reading this chapter one important board member of long standing felt that I had overemphasized economic factors. He stressed Christian values and organizational ethos as the determining factors. American scholars must guard against the tendency to interpret political conflicts and choices as essentially economic problems. See Peter F. Drucker, "On the 'Economic Basis' of American Politics," *The Public Interest* 10 (Winter 1968): 30–42.

rather than to a local department. The Metropolitan office, long only a service and coordinative agent for the departments, was now directly conducting programs.

The reasons for quartering the detached worker in the Metropolitan office were varied. First, as a pilot project of the Metropolitan office, the program could be better supervised if it were lodged there. Second, examination of similar programs in other cities had revealed that many were plagued by staff cooptation into local department work. Since the role was new and ambiguous, it seemed sensible to insure that it not be incorporated into the more clear-cut work of the local departments. Third, there was some recognition that local departments would resist introduction of the detached worker and his clients into the local department (some departments, however, would have cooperated, and so this last reason is not compelling). Whatever the mixed bag of reasons, locating the detached worker in the Metropolitan office was to have important consequences for the Association's overall structure.

The program grew from one staff member in 1956 to three in 1957 and eight in 1958. By 1958 it included a director, his assistant, one secretary, and five fieldworkers. In 1958 also, the board of managers committed themselves to a five-year program, replacing the previous year-by-year approach. They also began a funding program which included support, granted in 1959, from the Ford Foundation and a research grant from the National Institutes of Mental Health. By this point the project consisted of twelve fieldworkers and an annual budget of about $140,000 (excluding research funds of about $50,000 a year for three years). As the program developed, it included not only street gang work but also employment opportunities, special counseling, and training.

The effects of this program in the Association's transformation were many, the least important of which was the amount of money expended ($140,000 a year represented less than 1 percent of the total Association's expenses). More important for the emerging political economy than the shape and financial size of the program were the new personnel models, organizational relationships, and perspectives engendered by the program.

New personnel models. Early in the development of the Detached Worker Program, it became clear that traditional YMCA personnel were irrelevant to the program's tasks. Success required the detached worker to possess the characteristics of an indigenous leader—a social background, language, and presentation of self which was similar to that of the group he was attempting to reach. Thus, into the ranks of clean-cut

YMCA workers were introduced "cool cats," "secular cynics," and the like. The program's director, with a master's degree from the University of Chicago, had a long history of involvement with liberal Democratic politics and had worked in the sheriff's office. The fieldworkers, while possessing college backgrounds, were predominantly the products of urban ghettoes. Furthermore, they were often cynical about religion, and some had had earlier clashes with the police and other authorities. These men were not isolated from the rest of the organization; on the contrary, they became highly visible, received larger salaries than many professionals who had served the Association for several years, and they had access to program automobiles to increase their mobility. Clearly, this program was highly favored, and a new model of YMCA worker was being introduced.

Organizational relationships. The Detached Worker Program changed old relationships and opened up new ones with philanthropic foundations, community welfare and coordinating agencies, local government and politicians, social scientists, and fund-granting bodies of the federal government.

1. Philanthropic Foundations. The Chicago Association had previously received funds from local philanthropic foundations for specific programs. Indeed, one foundation, based on a fortune made by a local department store chain, had historic connections with one local department, and the executive director of the foundation was one of the more active members of the board of managers. (At a later time, this connection produced an organizational dilemma. The foundation made it clear that if this department supported an urban renewal plan for the area— which might hurt a branch store in the neighborhood—it would not be able to give further support to that department. The departmental staff and the Metropolitan office, nevertheless, favored involvement in the urban renewal plans.) The Association, however, had never marketed any program with major national foundations. The Detached Worker Program, was the first: it was funded partially by the Ford Foundation. Its director was later employed by the Ford Foundation, and still later became an upper-echelon member of the War on Poverty. A continuing series of consultations began in which the YMCA worked with both national and local foundations.

2. Connections with Community Welfare Agencies. The Association's involvement in programs like this, combined with the actively innovating role of several inner city departments, began to change the YMCA's image in welfare and community fund-raising circles. As one of the oldest

and largest members of the Community Fund, the YMCA's annual "take" among agencies serving youth was second only to that of the Boy Scouts. Nevertheless, the Association's executives and senior laymen still felt that the Welfare Council and Community Fund staff held a relatively negative view of the YMCA as a traditional, somewhat old-fashioned, organization.

Beginning with their accession in 1954, the general secretary and the assistant general secretary for program services began to participate in the Welfare Council's Hard-to-Reach Youth Project. Further, the assistant general secretary for program services began to participate more frequently in monthly luncheon meetings with the directors of Chicago's major youth-serving organizations.

When the YMCA launched a massive centennial fund-raising drive in 1958, the Association, despite the fact that citywide fund-raising drives were usually allowed to seek only capital funds, obtained permission from the Community Fund to request operating funds for the Detached Worker Program. The centennial fund drive of $7,000,000 was an innovation within the traditional political economy which had generally raised money from individual contributors. Many board members felt the YMCA could not raise the amount requested and that it was foolish to undertake the drive, but the general secretary argued that the Association would never again have an opportunity like the centennial. The board did manage to scale down the original staff goal, which was considerably more than $7,000,000. The drive was successfully conducted and permitted expansion of the traditional economy as well as the development of new programs. (In this case the successful venture also gave staff and board members confidence that the YMCA could present itself to relevant publics more vigorously than before.) By 1963, staff and informed laymen believed that a fundamental change in perspective on the YMCA had occurred. For instance, staff of the Welfare Council helped promote YMCA special projects and the Community Fund used movies of inner city YMCA programs as a public relations and fund-raising device. Although it would be difficult to prove the attitude change was matched with larger proportionate allocations, certainly greater receptivity to the Association had developed.

3. Local Government and Politics. The Detached Worker Program immediately affected the Association's relationship to both governmental bodies and politicians. The YMCA, we have seen, had traditionally maintained a hands-off relationship with politicians and had established few relations with civil servants or other bureaucratic functionaries.

Some statistics are illuminating. Our survey of staff attitudes had asked, "How often have you had contact with police or governmental personnel?" Seven percent of local staff reported frequent (i.e., "nearly every day" and "once or twice a week") contact with police or other personnel. Contrast this with figures for another youth-serving agency in which 23 percent reported weekly or daily contact with such personnel. Clearly the YMCA staff had relatively little police contact.

Members of the Detached Worker Program, however, held meetings with police captains and juvenile officers in all sections of the city, and a fairly cooperative relationship developed. Furthermore, as inner city involvement grew, senior staff recognized that the good auspices of the mayor would be useful. Thus, even before the War on Poverty was begun, the mayor had been invited to speak at an annual banquet and on a later occasion he appeared at a local department banquet. Such involvement with the mayor met resistance from board members, although much less resistance than staff had anticipated. The gains were enormous, or so staff believed. At one point, when a grant had been held up in Washington, staff believed that the funds were finally released only after a telephone call from the mayor. As the War on Poverty and its attendant programs got underway, the YMCA became even more deeply involved with local government and political forces.

4. Relations with Social Scientists and Federal Agencies. The Detached Worker Program was initially conceived and developed in consultation with social scientists. As the pilot year proceeded, the need for systematic research and evaluation emerged. At all stages social science perspectives had permeated the project even though specific research findings were not particularly germane. By the close of 1958, in consultation with sociologists at the University of Chicago, a research project had been developed and an application made to the National Institute of Mental Health. Although the research was funded to the university, the project had several consequences for the YMCA. First, senior staff began to learn the procedures for applying to federal agencies and working with them. Second, the research grant provided funds for four fieldworkers—a direct program gain. Third, the contact with social scientists was important in providing a different perspective.

New Perspectives

The contacts with other agencies, with the federal government, with political figures, and with social scientists were helpful in destroying traditional perspectives in the YMCA. These contacts contributed to a process, already operative in the larger society, whereby traditional procedures and client groups could be questioned or, at minimum, re-examined. Analyses of boards and community structures began to show a social science rather than the older "Christian virtue" flavor. Funds from federal sources were found to be as good as others, and perhaps better. Furthermore, traditional concepts of community and individual need were destroyed. The older models of leadership and character training through wholesome activities made little sense in work with youth whose problems were where to sleep at night or how to find a job. One staff member pointed out that there were even certain specific benefits to federal program money: large individual contributors had to be cultivated continually whereas federal grants were more specific.

By 1962, then, the cumulative effects of changes in the demographic composition of the city, in the society's definition of social problems and in management concepts had begun to make inroads upon the Association's traditional political economy. New sources of funds were being tapped and new program conceptions were being introduced at the polity's highest levels.

The new perspectives did not fully permeate the organization, however, nor was the Detached Worker Program accepted throughout the organization. Furthermore, this program, while exciting, was small. Sources of resistance, the remodeling of the internal polity, and the enlargement of the Association's inner city role should now be examined.

9

The Politics of Choosing a Successor

By 1963 the Detached Worker Program was fairly well established and it was widely recognized within the Association that it constituted a first-class fund-raising and public relations device (potential middle-class contributors were particularly impressed with the stories told by the workers themselves as they explained the program, and contributors seemed more willing to support this kind of program than swimming classes or other, more traditional, programs). Further, strong lay support for this type of program had been generated at the Metropolitan level, in selected departments, and within relevant external publics.

In many ways, however, the traditional political economy remained unaffected. Executive secretaries continued to use their boards of directors as the central authority for their departments. (Even if, informally, the executives ignored local board's directives.) The principle of local autonomy and the Metropolitan office's minimal role in local affairs still seemed to hold. This situation changed with the advent of both the War on Poverty and a new general secretary. The new general secretary actively promoted a changed balance of professional-lay relations. In conjunction with the War on Poverty, his selection issued in a more powerful Metropolitan center with a clearer set of priorities for both inner city and suburban areas. An examination of the political process by which this secretary was chosen is crucial for understanding the further development and change of the Association's political economy.

SUCCESSION AND ORGANIZATIONS

The less routine an organization is in its internal processes and the less stable its relationship to its environment, the more important, potentially, is the process by which its leaders are chosen. Stated somewhat differently, the more either polity or niche fluctuate, the greater are the potential effects of a change in leadership. Earlier I argued that the choice of

178

McClow as general secretary occurred before the pressures for redefinition and change had become fully apparent. Obviously the YMCA was changing at that earlier time, but as far as can be known, the direction of goals was not a central concern. The criterion for the choice of successor at that time was apparently simply individual competence rather than ability or inclination to effect change. The choice of McClow's successor, however, was obviously perceived as having substantial implications for later directions; this particular choice, therefore, will be discussed in some detail, and the process involved will be treated as essentially political.[1]

Organizations' succession processes vary according to the organization's basic constitution. It is probably true, for example, that federated organizations with multiple power centers are less likely to develop "crown prince systems" than are more bureaucratic organizations.[2] Furthermore, the relative size and power of a bureaucratic staff determine both the manpower pool and the importance of choices from within a central office's staff. Such aspects of executive office as length of tenure, review processes, and the like reflect constitutional norms regarding the executive's relation to the constituency.

Not only is the structure of the succession process dependent upon the organization's constitution but successors' relevant characteristics are linked to basic goal concepts and organizational need. Since large-scale organizations, unlike nations, usually have voluntary membership and relatively specific goals, it is often assumed that members of such organizations are all working for a common good. At the formal level, recognition is not given to the diverse interests of groups nor are ideologies crystallized into recognized, competing political philosophies. Therefore differences in members' perspectives do not result in the formation of openly competing groups nor in the institutionalization of political conflict. As a general proposition, the more corporate an organization's polity, the less open and crystallized will be the political conflicts within it; political processes will be subterranean. When a successor must be appointed, however, both sectional interests and allegiances stemming from latent role identities can be expected to influence the outcome.

1. The choice process has been treated in greater detail in my article, "Who Shall Rule: A Political Analysis of Succession in a Large Welfare Organization," *Pacific Sociological Review* 8 (Spring 1965): 52–60.

2. J. David Edelstein, "An Organizational Theory of Union Democracy," *American Sociological Review* 32 (1967): 19–31.

Political analysis of succession processes within large-scale organizations is difficult for several reasons. Most important, the assumption of goal consensus and the episodic character of succession make it appear an almost apolitical process—a change in power holding without politics. Since one defining feature of large-scale organizations is relatively specific goals, the choice of a successor often appears to involve only criteria of effectiveness and not political processes, mandates, and skill for political competence.[3] Effectiveness is defined as finding the proper man for a particular task rather than as finding a person who can balance an organization's competing forces and groups and redefine their ends.

The episodic character of succession processes also may cause one to ignore their essentially political character. Where succession choices occur regularly, the observer has an opportunity to relate the major features of the process to underlying structural features. When an organizational chief executive is chosen only occasionally, however, it is difficult to separate the idiosyncratic from the structural: it is difficult to determine what derives from particular personalities operating at a particular moment and what derives from underlying political forces.

Furthermore, even though a formal electoral machinery may exist, succession in organizations lacking explicit competitive processes or representation of interests is determined, like other major decisions, by an inner circle that is consulted on most major decisions. The legal election procedure generally produces "unanimous" choices, and underlying power struggles remain invisible. The final vote of the boards of directors provides no clue to the reality of the process. Only if the succession process becomes repetitive and competitive do the formal procedures and criteria begin to reflect political structure.

Regardless of investigative difficulties, however, the actual process of choosing a successor reflects an organization's political realities. At mini-

3. Indeed, most of the literature on succession processes in organizations emphasizes its impact on leadership effectiveness and on the general topic of leadership style. See Oscar Grusky, "Managerial Succession and Organizational Effectiveness," *American Journal of Sociology* 64 (July 1963): 21–31; Oscar Grusky, "Role Conflict in Organization: A Study of Prison Camp Officials," *Administrative Science Quarterly* 3 (March 1959): 463–67; and R. H. Guest, *Organizational Change* (Homewood, Ill.: Dorsey Press, 1962).

Some of the literature examines the organizational determinants of selection processes. See Oscar Grusky, "Corporate Size, Bureaucratization and Managerial Succession," *American Journal of Sociology* 67 (November 1961): 261–69; and Richard O. Carlson, "Succession and Performance Among School Superintendents," *Administrative Science Quarterly* 6 (September 1961): 210–27.

mum, this choice must reflect an organization's power balance. For example, given family ownership of a corporation, management's choice of a successor must receive the family's approval. Or again, unless minor interests are strong enough to wage a proxy fight, a corporation board chairman or president can largely control the election of his own successor. In fact, a whole line of successors may be controlled, and over a number of decades.

The process of choosing a successor not only reflects an organization's balance of power but also provides an opportunity for general examination of goals and policy, for succession processes produce mandates. At this point in time an organization may choose to reexamine goals and directions and attempt to link this reexamination to the selection of its new chief officer. Moreover, the reexamination may itself produce shifts in an organization's goals and in the distribution of power among staff groups and the board of directors.

To analyze the political aspects of succession, one must first consider the mechanisms of choice (that is, the set of procedures used to make decisions) and the participants in the decision—their influence, organization, and orientation. One must also examine the characteristics of the potential successors, especially their orientations, affiliations, and distinctive competencies. Before examining the succession material itself, however, I should restate three aspects of the Chicago YMCA's operation which bear directly on the succession process. These are its broadly stated goals, its emphasis on lay control, and its emphasis on preventive programs.

Broadly Stated Goals

The YMCA's broadly stated goals permit debate regarding the organization's focal concerns. Unlike some organizations in which relatively clear measures of effectiveness can be linked with consensually agreed upon goals, the YMCA's different interests may argue for different goals. In a sense, historically speaking, the organization's traditions slowly establish these goals. Nonetheless, it is easy to demonstrate by a detailed examination of the Association that crucial choice points did involve goal choices. Furthermore—and most important to this argument—these choice points have been closely related to the selection of successors. Thus, for example, the Chicago Association's history records that, during the 1880s, the chief executive resigned when new board members supported a less evangelistic, more recreation-oriented program.

Emphasis on Preventive Programs

As noted earlier, the YMCA has typically served the relatively well adjusted members of the society. Since organizational goals have focused on character development rather than on rehabilitation or reclamation, and since membership fees have been an important financial resource, the organization's alternatives have been restricted both by its goals and by its resource base to a more middle-class constituency than most service and welfare organizations. This link with the adjusted middle class has constituted a serious constraint as the organization has attempted to survive in an environment increasingly composed of the unadjusted working class. The organization was prohibited by capital investments, as well as the humanitarian goals of board and staff, from relocating its departments. Further, unlike Protestant churches, the YMCA clientele was composed essentially of individual, short-term members, and it was thus relatively easy for the Association to shift from its traditional target group. The YMCA was clearly committed by numerous factors to remaining in the inner city.

Given this commitment, the organization was thus forced to seek means for sustaining itself, and the succession process became a crucial aspect of this search.

Lay Control

Again, as noted earlier, the YMCA has maintained a historic emphasis on the importance of its board. This ideology resulted in part from the Association's lack of an esoteric knowledge base, but it was also partially the result of its Protestant origins. Although professional staff clearly controlled the information and definitions of specific situations, the boards nevertheless continued to exercise considerable control. Indeed, board interests and positions sometimes produced actions directly opposite to those desired by the professionals. Furthermore, particularly in the selection of a new general secretary, the board's prerogative was very clearly stated.

I might summarize the two aspects of the Association that had the most crucial effect on the choice of a successor. First, although in most organizations there is debate between traditionalists and progressives, in the YMCA (as in other welfare or service organizations with broadly defined missions), the debate affects more than simply choice of means; it affects basic goal definitions as well. In this particular situation key choices regarding the organization's relationship to the inner city were involved, especially the questions of selecting later directions and of maintaining traditional bases or adapting to changing communities. Secondly, the emphasis on lay control implied that, if the professionals were to affect the choice of a successor, they must do so largely through indirect and informal means. They must maximize their potential by choosing among and acting upon the available alternatives before the actual time of selection (as by creating a "crown prince") or by manipulating the selection process itself. Unlike the situation existing in business corporations, the chief executive formally had little direct influence on the selection of his successor. Thus, if the lay people involved were particularly interested in any one candidate, their weight would overrule that of the professional. Only if their interest was small or if they were divided, could the professionals' choices be influential.

THE CHOOSING OF A SUCCESSOR

In the general secretary's view, his successor should be chosen a year and a half before his scheduled retirement. He had originally wanted the choice made about six months in advance. One of the main candidates for his job, however, had recently been interviewed for the same post in another city, and since the general secretary tended to favor this candidate, he wanted the decision made before the candidate seriously considered leaving Chicago.

The general secretary, having never promoted any of the assistant general secretaries to associate general secretary, had never had a second in command. The president of the board of managers, in conjunction with the general secretary, decided to nominate a second in command with the explicit expectation that the latter's service would constitute a training period for the general secretary's job. The president of the board of managers, again in consultation with the general secretary, agreed to have an enlarged executive committee of the board begin consideration of requirements for the position. This enlarged committee would then make a recommendation to the full board.

The Main Contenders

As I have noted, the Chicago YMCA has historically chosen its chief executive from among its own personnel. A total of seven candidates were suggested by various members of the enlarged executive committee, but only three were seriously considered, and one of these was a "dark horse" candidate (i.e., he possessed the necessary qualifications but was likely to be selected only if a runoff were required). All three candidates had served many years with the Chicago Association. All were among the Association's four or five highest paid staff, and all had long central office experience (central office service in a responsible position was in reality a prerequisite for serious candidacy). As assistant general secretaries in the Metropolitan office the three were coequal with a larger group of about ten staff members, but in terms of informal rankings and responsibilities, Mr. Maddy and Mr. Leaf clearly held the greatest responsibility and were the most likely candidates. Mr. Dunkel,[4] the dark horse, was the oldest of the three, only five or six years short of retirement. He was vigorous, however, and it was not his age but rather his somewhat lesser role in the organization that weakened his candidacy. This analysis will center on factors working for and against the two main candidates.

Maddy, the business candidate. Maddy had spent his entire adult life working for the Chicago YMCA, largely in administrative positions, and during the past ten years had been the organization's chief business officer. Distinguished-looking and fifty-five years of age, he was initially the leading contender for several reasons. First, he had followed McClow through several positions within the Association. And although McClow had not appointed him associate general secretary, there nonetheless existed a general belief that he was, in fact, the number two man. (The author also expected Maddy to be chosen.)

Second, in his role as chief business officer, Maddy had enjoyed a long association with many of the more "substantial men," as McClow called them, on the board of managers—powerful bankers, investment brokers, and other very conservative members of the board. Two years earlier, one of these men had told Maddy that, at the appropriate time, he would support him for the top post, thereby disposing Maddy to reject a position in another city. Given the importance of informal influence patterns in a noncompetitive board, and given the episodic character of succession choice, the influence of these men seemed to be dominant.

Third, and less tangibly, Maddy represented a traditional perspective within the organization. Though not overtly opposing McClow's innovations over the past decade, staff members saw him as supporting the traditional approach to sound management, upholding the Association's preventive goals and the middle-class orientations. Given the Chicago Association's historic emphasis on sound management practice, Maddy seemed the logical choice.

4. The names Leaf, Maddy, and Dunkel are fictitious.

Leaf, the program innovator. Ten years younger than Maddy, Leaf had worked for the YMCA since leaving the armed services. Whereas Maddy had spent his lifetime with the Chicago Association, Leaf had had prior experience as a recreation man in the public parks system and had also been strongly influenced by his training in the Air Force command school. With McClow's strong support, Leaf, as the Association's chief program officer, had initiated several departures from traditional procedure, including the services to delinquents discussed earlier. He did not, however, neglect the Association's traditional programs and had encouraged such programs as the Hi-Y–Tri-Y staff innovation mentioned earlier.

Leaf strongly identified with social welfare and liberal points of view. Whereas Maddy and other executive-level personnel might have the *Wall Street Journal* or *Fortune* on their desks, Leaf was more likely to have the latest report on the Aid to Dependent Children program. Leaf was outspoken in his relations with other staff and with board members. Whereas Maddy had associated with the more substantial businessmen on the board, Leaf had gravitated toward the younger board members, men who had been invited to serve on the board precisely because of their ability to work on new programs.

Leaf supporters did not appear to be in control of the board, and Leaf, by his own statement, did not consider himself seriously in the running for the position. He had begun to explore other opportunities. At this point an important member of the executive committee (he had been president of the board of managers when McClow took office) told Leaf that the matter of McClow's successor had never been discussed and that the position was wide open.

The Process of Election

When discussing the choice of a second in command, both McClow and the board president agreed in preferring a person who, like McClow, would continue the emphasis on innovation. Since the president generally played a mediating role on the board of managers, however, McClow felt a responsibility to support or push the president into a more assertive role. Both men agreed on a process that would allow a full discussion of the directions the board wanted the Association to take as well as a full analysis of the candidates. This process had not been used for previous successions; rather, the chief professional had directly advised the inner group, which made most major decisions. Since McClow strongly favored lay control, he did not use direct means for shaping their decisions and in this instance resisted their attempts to get him to name his own choice.

The process first required the enlarged executive committee to hold two or three meetings to discuss the Association's goals and future directions. As a basis for discussion, the president asked McClow to formulate a list of areas in which the organization needed strengthening. These areas favored neither candidate since both financial and program considerations were included. McClow attended one meeting in order to present his views on the Association's needs for the next decade. The executive committee then drew up a list of seven candidates and agreed to interview the top three. Each was given a half-hour interview for which he was asked to prepare beforehand his views on (1) the Chicago YMCA's future, (2) its competition from other organizations in qualifying for and earning public support, and (3) its capacity to expand its services in fields vital to the needs of the city. After these interviews the committee met again to debate the candidates' merits. Again it should be stressed that these discussion areas formally favored neither candidate.

The election process worked against Maddy in several ways. First, it broke up the expectation pattern in which Maddy appeared the likely successor. The longer the debate, the more possible an alternative appeared. Second, it exposed Leaf to a group of men with whom he had had little previous contact. At least two of the board's more important members consciously withheld judgment until they had had more contact with Leaf. Third, in any systematic discussion of program and directions of change, Leaf would quite naturally emerge as the more far-sighted and forward-looking, for he was the more articulate of the two and the posing of questions revealed his articulation. (Members of the executive committee later mentioned that Maddy never answered the questions, discussing instead his own background in the organization.) One top staff member expressed the belief that the longer discussion continued, the better were Leaf's chances; an immediate decision, however, would clearly favor Maddy.

As the debate proceeded and Leaf was increasingly seriously considered, one of the older and more traditional (and formerly very influential) board members interjected a set of previously unmentioned considerations, namely, that Leaf was unfit as an administrator. The committee called in McClow to comment on these charges. McClow was astounded, for he did not believe that this board member possessed sufficiently detailed information on the Association to make such assertions. (McClow attributed the opposition to this member's association with people outside the board of managers and to McClow's predecessor, who, through an involved process, had come to oppose Leaf; the predecessor had retained an office in the building.) McClow presented to the executive committee evidence from the annual ratings of executive personnel which disproved the charges. Furthermore, when asked directly by an important board member (a substantial contributor to the organization) for his opinion, McClow used the opportunity to support Leaf. The committee then voted to nominate Leaf.

Throughout the discussion, the president did not take an assertive role, serving more as a discussion leader than as a prime mover. He did, however, utilize his power as chairman of the executive committee. At the executive committee's last meeting before announcing its nomination to the full board, the board member who had questioned Leaf's administrative abilities tried to reopen the question. The president asserted his prerogatives strongly, arguing that the process had been fair and that all relevant considerations had been discussed; thus further debate was prevented.

BOARD COMPOSITION, EXECUTIVE ROLE, AND SOCIAL PROCESS

Thus far we have considered only the process of selection and not the elements and combinations of power which contributed to Leaf's election. In retrospect, two points are crucial: (1) the board was not monolithic and reactionary in its ideological and social orientations, and it had supported welfare innovation when the members' direct interests and ideology were not threatened; (2) at crucial points the chief executive was in a position to influence the selection procedure.

Board Composition and Ideology

As indicated earlier, there had been a slow shift in the managers' orientation, even though the board was still dominated by well-to-do businessmen plus a few doctors and lawyers (the board included no union leaders, professionals from other major institutions, or Democratic political figures). For example, one board member, former president of one of the two leading businessmen's associations in the city and vice-president of a national insurance company, strongly supported Leaf in the kinds of programs he represented. (His support, however, in this particular case was so assertive and his own base in the Chicago YMCA's Board so marginal that his support cannot be considered crucial. He was not fully involved in the search for a successor, for he was not on the executive committee, but he attended one executive committee meeting and pounded the table, saying "It has to be Leaf." He also had tried to rally a group to protest if the executive committee did not nominate Leaf.)

It should be noted that, when their direct interests were not involved, these businessmen did not feel bound to a definition of the Association which linked it with traditional programs alone. As long as the organization did not move in ideologically debatable directions (such as seeking too much contact with governmental agencies or with Democratic party politicians), board members would not oppose ameliorative attempts to solve problems.

As we have seen, Leaf's programs were opposed in some departments, for the local boards felt directly threatened by these new programs, which brought them, their staff, and their regular clientele into contact with delinquents. The members of the Metropolitan board were not threatened by such interaction, however, and the local boards were not consulted. Furthermore, neither board of managers nor staff defined issues in terms of traditionalistic versus innovative programs but rather in terms of traditionalistic *and* innovative program (the stress being placed on expanding old programs and finding news needs to serve). Since efforts to this point had been largely the result of private initiative in the welfare area, conservative opposition to government expansion in welfare areas was not aroused. Leaf's candidacy and ideology did not appear to the organization as a radical shift. In his interview with the executive committee, Leaf did suggest that the solution of many youth problems might require governmental aid and that the Chicago YMCA should not withdraw itself simply because government was involved. A few months after his succession, the organization did initiate a government-financed program with more than the usual degree of board dissent.

A political realist might argue that even though Leaf was not perceived as a radical alternative, a shift in the board's balance of power had to occur if he were to be elected. The whole matter is extremely complex, and there may be some truth in this assertion. That the personnel occupying powerful positions had changed is true. Some of the older, more conservative members had little influence on the election process, and there were more young, program-oriented men on the board. At least three of Leaf's influential supporters had withdrawn from board participation, however; so in this respect, the balance had not shifted significantly.

The political realist is partly right in assuming a shift, but this resulted from a change in the consensus of the board and executive committee members rather than through a change in their composition. As McClow shifted the organization's orientation toward innovative programs and a positive, inner city approach, he modified board members' views accordingly. The actual selection process was important in crystallizing this emerging consensus.

Although a shift in the board's consensus was functionally equivalent to a shift in the balance of power, this shift might not have been "actualized" without a shift in the mechanics of election. Senior staff members asserted that the executive committee had often played a relatively minor role in contrast to a "shadow cabinet" that was involved in most major decisions. The members of this group were more traditional and conservative than the total board. The "cabinet" included some of the board's more "substantial" men, precisely those who had long been associated with Maddy. The use of a formal, prolonged process forced the shadow cabinet to act through the executive committee, whose process required debate and consideration of alternatives. Because it was a creation of the board's consensus and informal orientation rather than a real deliberative body, the shadow cabinet had no identity or internal cohesion. Thus its members had no reason to oppose the more "rational" process proposed by the president. Once the new selection process had been set in motion, this traditional inner core lost its effectiveness. (It will be noted below that this kind of shadow cabinet disappeared as the organization shifted its political economy.) In a consensual society of gentlemen, such as this was, these men could not reimpose their point of view on the board, and with one or two exceptions they had no wish to do so.

The Role of the General Secretary

Although McClow had little formal power to influence this decision, events clearly indicate that he played an important informal role. Not only did he support a method that favored Leaf, but at key points he presented information and orientations favorable to Leaf. There were certain conditions that permitted this influence of an "employee" on the choice process.

First and obviously, McClow was alive and in office, a trusted and respected executive. Had there been no staff member with a long and confidential relation to the board, the executive committee members might have had to rely solely on their own resources and traditional procedures (McClow died three months later). Secondly, McClow was perceived as a successful executive. Had his tenure been marked by failure, the board would probably have disregarded his advice and discounted his perspectives (an organization's chief operating officer, unless he controls the vote, can choose his successor only when his own judgment is not under question).

Third, the board's structure and operation made it heavily dependent on the executive for administrative services. In some organizations, notably universities, boards often maintain their own secretaries and offices. When this is done, the chief executive may be less heavily involved in the informal shaping of the board's operation and in the procedure for selecting a new executive. In the Chicago YMCA, the chief executive's office adjoined the president's meeting room, and the general secretary usually served as secretary and administrative aide to the executive committee. He was not secretary, however, and was not present during most of the meetings during which the choice was made. His influence in this manner, then, cannot be considered decisive.

Finally, the chief executive could influence the board because he possessed more information about the board itself than any single member. For example, when some board members tried to reopen the question of Leaf's administrative ability, McClow could have suggested that they postpone action to allow further discussion. He had been informed, however, that a group of eight younger board members were prepared to support Leaf in the open board meeting; he knew that Leaf's chances for election in an open discussion were good. At this point and at others, his greater knowledge allowed him to shape strategies and influence choices. Though never directly persuading board members or holding crucial votes, McClow was nevertheless in a position to shape the situation within which a decision was to be made. Control of a situation is crucial to political power, particularly when the mechanisms for selecting a successor are not highly institutionalized. Since, other factors being equal, the full-time executive is likely to be more conscious than his board of the implications of different procedures, his greater rationality effectively gives him indirect control.

10

Priority Establishment and Centralizing Mechanisms

Once Leaf's appointment had been made, it was assumed that he would have a year and a half to learn his new responsibilities. The already close bonds between himself and McClow became closer as McClow conferred more frequently with Leaf. Suddenly, less than four months after Leaf became associate general secretary, McClow died, and the associate general secretary was quickly confirmed as general secretary. The selection process described in the preceding chapter had made its mandate explicit (that is, both the selection process and the views expressed by Leaf in that process had committed him to developing and accentuating both the YMCA's inner city role and its emphasis on program innovation).

In organizations not involved in a defined crisis situation, little attempt may be made to include an explicit mandate in the succession process. The mandate is rather an implicit commitment to maintaining the organization. Although the YMCA was not in a crisis situation, the succession process that had occurred effectively committed the executive committee of the board to continue in and accentuate the directions established by the previous general secretary, directions that Leaf had actively supported during his interview for the top office.

Apart from this explicit mandate, within the Association's broad constitutional framework, the general secretary was free to modify policy or change operating assumptions; he could begin to alter role definitions, budgeting priorities and the like. In fact, change occurred along two major lines. First, the Association generally stressed priorities bearing on the inner city program and program innovation, resulting in a change in the economy; second, the power of the professional staff and of the Metropolitan office staff increased with respect to lay boards and lay decision makers, and this constituted a change in polity.

191

PROGRAM DIRECTIONS, ORGANIZATIONAL
PRIORITIES, AND THE ECONOMY

The change in directions included a redistribution of the Association's resources to different programs and tasks. When a resource base is expanding and fund sources are changing slowly, it is possible that new directions and allocations can be grafted onto an organization's old economy without major shifts in allocation criteria (that is, an organization operating under "politics of abundance" conditions may add new program interests with little harm to older ones). On the other hand, in a "politics of scarcity," in which new directions must be financed from a stagnant or declining resource base, any change in allocation must imply a loss to some older interest, at least for the short run. (The concepts of the politics of scarcity and of abundance are elaborated in chapter 12.) Obviously, the latter case demands far greater statesmanship and is more threatening to organizational stability than the former.

Whichever the economy type, scarcities usually result from the sheer practical necessity of taking action in situations without either adequate time or energy for surveillance. Political leaders need decision-making criteria; they need guidelines for relating to the polity's various elements. With organizational change, these guidelines must also change, and they may change one group's power, influence, and status with respect to that of another group. Consequently, it is inevitable that one or another group seems to be slighted. Although the YMCA for the next several years existed within an economy of abundance and massively increased its resources, funds for certain purposes nevertheless remained scarce. Decision priorities had to be established.

The War on Poverty and the YMCA

The enlargement of the YMCA's inner city niche depended on both program innovations and the finding of new fund sources. On the one hand, the Association had to develop new means to reach and serve those groups that had traditionally been outside its concern. On the other, it was painfully obvious that the Association's traditional sources of funds, though not static, could not be enlarged sufficiently to effect a radical change in its traditional dependence on income from membership fees, business features, and endowment dividends. The "rediscovery of the poor" in America and the subsequent War on Poverty were to constitute a major breakthrough for the Association's economy. Although the Detached Worker Program and several programs of local departments had tilled the organizational soil for the War on Poverty, the potential opportunities represented first had to be evaluated and a decision process undertaken.

The first new program selected involved a contract with the Office of Manpower Training and Development, United States government, for the training and counseling of teen-age dropouts with few marketable labor skills. The enrollees often had records of delinquency as well as the usual gamut of attitudes and manners which would lower their probability of success on the job market. The program was directly funded between the participating agencies (the YMCA, the Chicago Youth Centers, and the Chicago Boys' Clubs) and the granting agency. (This contract was granted before the establishment of local poverty corporations, partially tied to local government, which were to become the main coordinators of local poverty efforts around the country.)

As senior staff viewed the prospects for establishing this program, two major problems emerged: (1) coordinating efforts with those of other agencies and (2) accepting massive federal support. First, in order to spread the program's effects and to increase coordination among agencies, the granting agency required the Association to participate with other agencies in administering and conducting the retraining program. Yet the three participating agencies had historically competed for funds within the Chicago area and had never developed any but the most casual relations in the past. Although senior staff shared professional interests, the respective boards were somewhat antagonistic. As one board member remarked, "I never thought I'd see the day when we'd sit down with the ———— board." And not only did the venture require commitment to a continuing interagency program, it also required that the Association resolve its ideological questions regarding the use of federal money.

The Detached Worker Program grant from the National Institute of Mental Health had been considered a research grant and had not been defined primarily as program support. Furthermore, it was carried out in conjunction with a Ford Foundation grant and with the University of Chicago. The new program, however, would be directly subsidized by the federal government, and the specter of federal control raised its head.

Program staff had formulated a proposal which could substantially benefit each organization. Underutilized buildings would be filled and rent paid for their use, buildings would be refurbished, and new staff could be hired without interfering with traditional programs. For the YMCA the program had double possibilities, because VISTA workers and others could be approached for residence occupancy. The question remaining was whether the boards of the two private organizations would approve the program.

In retrospect, agreement was easily obtained. A joint committee of the two boards met to discuss the proposal. From the YMCA, four board members were asked to participate. The board's president and the general secretary chose the four according to the following criteria. First, all were heavily involved; they were committed to the YMCA, devoted many hours to committee work, and were among the more knowledgeable board members. Second, they were respected by the other board members for their commitment and participation. Third, all knew and liked the growing inner city focus. The only point of difference among them was their ideological stance on federal programs: two were known to oppose an increase in federal funding and federal bureaucracy; the other two were believed either neutral or favorable to a federal role as necessary and beneficial.

The issue of federal growth and control did arise at the joint meeting, but the arguments favoring the program were so overwhelming that participants later reported that the issue was never in doubt. Those who in principle opposed participation with the federal government reported that they were swayed by the thought that, since the government was going to move in such directions anyway, the YMCA could do the work more satisfactorily than most agencies and that the money therefore would be well spent. Better for the YMCA to accept the task than to allow either public or inept private agencies to do it. In short, the basic commitment to the Association and its program in this case overrode the broad ideological principle. When the committee unanimously recommended approving the program, the board also approved it with little outward dissent. There was behind-the-scenes dissent. For instance, a bank vice-president, formerly president of the board of managers, complained bitterly about the program to the current president. The president reported that he told the complaining member to come to meetings and exercise his vote.

As described, the process seems simple and predetermined. Given the degree of financial benefit to the organization, a straight, vulgar, Marxist interpretation would seem to hold. This would be incorrect, however. Had the proposal been made without prior participation in both innovative programing and federal funding, there are indications that the new program would have been either defeated or slowed in its initiation. An examination of the income sources of the country's twenty largest YMCAs reveals that for 1962 and 1963 no others received as much federal money or participated as widely in such programs. Furthermore, many boards, including several in the Midwest, pointedly refused to participate. Their boards' ideology and their staff's compliance drew them away from poverty programs.

Clearly, the Chicago Association's prior experience had prepared it for negotiating with the government. First, staff and board members knew from their earlier experience that accepting federal funds did not, at least for the short run, result in accepting controls that were either unwelcome or too stringent. One senior staff member even posed the question: "Which is worse, federal funds or being beholden to major individual donors?" Second, a "taste" for new programs had been developed, and the federal government represented an external support source for such programs. Third, two former YMCA staff members were employed by that time on the federal end of the money pipeline. They were trusted by staff and board alike, and they could counsel on program and proposal development. Even though political pressure later proved necessary to obtain the actual release of funds, the Association had clearly begun to establish a rapport with the involved federal bureaucratic process. The process surrounding this first federal contract became the prototype of negotiation for later program development.

Not all other YMCAs totally refused to participate in the War on Poverty and related efforts. Many operated programs ranging from Headstart to Job Corps to adult education and homemaking classes. Still, however, there was substantial resistance in other cities. Some Associations absolutely refused to participate and others participated only nominally. The general secretary received at least one letter from the general secretary of another large Association denouncing the Chicago Association's participation in the poverty program. Although the Chicago Association appeared to have moved at least partially into a new niche within the community, in 1963 it was not clear how many other city Associations would attempt similar shifts. As long as funds were available, however, the Chicago YMCA appeared committed to a radically different inner city role.

Capital Fund Priorities and Budget Control

It is at least conceivable that the increase in federal funds could have been handled apart from the rest of the organization. A new "division for poverty programs" could have been created and the remainder of the organization could have pursued its normal course. Though conceivable, such a mode of adaptation was not really possible. Only if involvement in the War on Poverty had been undertaken with an overarching cynicism in high places could such a segregation have been possible. In fact the new general secretary's commitment to program development and his specific commitment to the inner city clearly indicated that the Association's involvement would not be cynical; the political economy would, to some extent, have to be reshaped to fit the changing conceptions of organization and mission.

We should, at this point, move back in time and consider those aspects of organizational change that were occurring without poverty money. Beginning with the changes attendant on the succession mandate, we should consider the decision premises, priorities, role definitions, and power balances that the general secretary moved to effect during his first two years in office.

One of his first actions was to attempt to restrict funds for capital expansion. This moratorium was proposed to give the Metropolitan office time to reexamine the policy of suburban expansion and to conserve the Association's capital resources. The general secretary reasoned that in the past the Association had approved capital programs for suburban development without knowing whether the community would really support the required fund drive or whether the department, once fully established, would be self-supporting. He could cite cases in which the Metropolitan office had paid a larger share of building costs than had been originally intended because the local departments had not been able to raise their full share. Further, he knew that poorly functioning suburban departments often became a drain on the Association's income. In either case, he thought money allocated to the suburbs might better be committed to more innovative uses.

A second aspect of the moratorium involved reexamining the current uses of income from special endowment funds. In the Association's accounting system, endowment funds were often kept in the name of the benefactor, or the benefactor's designate. In some cases these accounts had originally been established for specific purposes; yet their income had been commingled with other income and sometimes distributed without regard for their original purposes. Since the general secretary was committed to finding as many ways as possible to support inner city and "income unproductive" programs, he wished to learn whether some of these funds could be used for other purposes. Although the investigation did not reveal either large misallocations or substantial amounts of free funds, it did serve two purposes. First, the general secretary gained a better knowledge of his base for maneuvering. Second, it did indeed reveal funds that could be reallocated. In one case a fund generating an annual income of approximately $5,000 had originally been established to provide program scholarships for lower-income youth; yet in recent years the funds had not been used for this purpose. Such a fund could easily be used for incidental expenses attendant on inner city service. Furthermore, such reallocations provided symbolic reassurances of the possibility for moving away from the traditional fund usages.

Although the general secretary attempted to restrict expansion fund requests, the Association's political economy prohibited a full-scale moratorium. At best the announced moratorium notified departments that criteria for matching grants might change and permitted the board of managers and the general secretary to delay hasty action. Two important considerations forbade the imposition of such a moratorium for any long duration: the Association's dependence on the initiative of the local departments and the possible loss of capital funds from philanthropic sources.

The departments, as relatively autonomous centers of power and initiative, were free to propose expansion programs at any time. Although the Metropolitan office could refuse to match funds, local departments could proceed independently. A rigid moratorium might be interpreted as indicating that the Metropolitan office was no longer interested in supporting local initiative and expansion. This dilemma quickly became apparent when one of the most aggressive and well-run (even profit-making) suburban program departments proposed that the Metropolitan office support its expansion plans with matching funds. The first inclination was to refuse, but when the department's total financial record had been examined, particularly the records for the preceding two or three years, it became clear that this department could match its commitment without a further drain on central resources. The action taken in this case was to lift the moratorium but reduce the ratio of Metropolitan matching funds.

The possible loss of philanthropic benevolences also made a total moratorium, without regard for needs of matching funds, impossible to maintain. When an organization's resources are largely a function of market opportunity, its expansion opportunities are largely determined by the combination of its ability to raise capital and to serve or create market demand. Thus its arguments to a potential donor (an investment house) are usually based on its perception of market potential. Such an organization must define its own expansion possibilities. For the YMCA, with its broad goals and almost endless conceptions of population need, any philanthropic donor with a definition of need becomes a potential source for organizational expansion. To refuse a donor simply because of a preconceived plan would limit the Association's expansion ability. A more narrowly focused organization might do so, but to refuse such grants would usually violate the YMCA's historic style.

Soon after the general secretary took office, a wealthy Jewish business-man made a proposal: he would donate half a million dollars to the Association if it would construct and operate a teen-age center near the high school in a large suburb. The YMCA was very receptive to the pro-posal. The project was never carried through, however; Metropolitan staff believed that the businessman was subsequently pressured by the Jewish community to donate to sectarian causes. Nevertheless, such an opportunity to expand at little apparent cost, when combined with the YMCA's ability to define a need, obviated the moratorium.

The attempt to redefine priorities for expansion and matching fund policies did not produce a drastic shift in organizational policy. Given the commitment of existing suburban departments, to discourage local initia-tive and philanthropic gifts by a permanent moratorium on expansion funds would have been disastrous. From the changing balance of priori-ties, however, a new policy did emerge. First, the board of managers changed the ratio of funds that it would commit for local department's building purposes. Whereas during the preceding decade it had usually matched on a one-to-one basis, it now switched to a basis of one dollar of Metropolitan money to two dollars of local money. Second, the mora-torium effectively required that any departmental fund-raising drive be approached more hard-headedly and only when there was great probabil-ity of success, since it would otherwise not receive Metropolitan backing.

The reexamination of funding and expansion policies did not result in a refusal to back "risky" suburban ventures. With the general secretary's encouragement, the board of managers "bankrolled" several innovations in suburban programing. In the most dramatic instance, it supported a consolidated "station wagon" YMCA in the suburbs for youth. Program staff developed programs for teen-agers which utilized existing public and private facilities instead of building a new general physical facility. This program, which was in debt for the next few years, projected an image of need and vitality. In short, what the new Metropolitan office policy opposed was general expansion without strong financial support.

CHANGING THE POLITY

The general secretary might possibly have changed financial priorities and policies without changing organizational dependencies, power rela-tions, and individual departments' definitions of goals. In a decentralized and even pluralistic system such as existed, the Metropolitan office could offer incentives to the local departments and let them react or not, much as it had always done. The general secretary, however, defined his mandate more broadly than such a policy would indicate. Without attempting to change the formal definitions of organizational relations, he sought levers that promoted a more efficient use of, and coordination of, organizational activities while simultaneously redressing organizational power relations so that his preferred goals and directions would be more universally pursued.

No formal changes in constitution or basic principles were suggested; instead, obstructions to the new directions, beginning at the margins of the structure, were attacked. These attacks were made in two main areas. First, the general secretary wanted to modify the three-cornered relationship of Metropolitan office staff, local staff, and local boards so that the goals and policies of the total Association (or his definition of them) would be more firmly established in the local departments. Second, the board of managers required modifications to permit more direct confrontation with the Association's inner city role.

The Metropolitan–Local Department Nexus

The day-to-day operation of the Association's political economy interfered with emphasis on a vitalized, inner city program in several ways. First, the dual authority over the local executive secretary obviously inhibited the general secretary's role. If a local executive secretary gave primacy to his local board, and it opposed or ignored Metropolitan policy, that policy would be frustrated, at least in that department. Second, the local boards' composition and function had been historically insulated from Metropolitan influence. Thus the possibility of local boards' ignoring Metropolitan policy could easily occur. Furthermore, no easy mode seemed to exist for controlling or reshaping boards. Third, the emphasis on departmental autonomy effectively required each executive secretary to carry full administrative responsibility for facilities, personnel, and maintenance of his department. Under such a system there was little possibility of maximizing the benefits of economies of scale. Finally, the budgeting processes, as noted earlier, enriched the rich while impoverishing the poor. Without a modification of processes and a redirection of economies, some local departments, particularly in the inner city, would continue uneconomic and lacking in vitality.

From the general secretary's viewpoint, many executives were too subject to their local boards and, by implication, not adequately responsive to Metropolitan office policy directions. As he saw it, some executives were "unprofessional" and did not properly develop a board consensus which supported Metropolitan goals and program. Others, relatively passive, did not give their boards sufficient direction, at least with respect to broad organizational directives.

In one instance a proposal was made in conjunction with the United States Department of Justice to locate a halfway house for probationers and Justice Department counselors in one of the local facilities. The department in question was operating its residence far below capacity, and the program thus appeared economically beneficial to the department and appropriate to the reformulated goals of the whole Association. Whether or not the executive favored the program, he failed to prepare his board for it. When presented at a board meeting, the proposal was attacked by a lawyer active in trying to stabilize the local community. He presented two arguments: a malfunction in the program would harm the YMCA's image; and in any case, the program would introduce an undesirable element into the community. In the face of such opposition and lacking any previously established support, the proposal was rejected. Another department accepted the project, however, and it functioned with few difficulties.

In another case, a board avoided racially integrating its membership long after the Metropolitan office had made it clear that this was the Association's policy.

In still another case the Detached Worker Program requested access for its youth gangs to one of the larger inner city departments. In a dramatic confrontation (made so because the antagonists to the Metropolitan program solicited proxy votes from absent members), the local board voted not to allow them to use the building.

These three cases, all occurring within a two-year interval emphasized the difficulties attendant on the existence of multiple power bases and power lines within an organization. With the Detached Worker Program confrontation, a program that was legitimately part of the Association's program was refused access to an organization facility. In the other cases, local boards refused to implement programs and policies that were seen as useful and even vital aspects of the total organization.

Less dramatically, the general secretary observed cases in which individual board members treated departments as their private preserves. In one instance a powerful board member ordered the executive secretary to be available at specific times, even when he had previous commitments.

Change Mechanisms

In a centralized organization with power largely held by the chief executive officer, such reluctance and even refusal to follow organizational policy might have been met with wholesale reorganization and a change of personnel and power relations. For the YMCA, however, such a solution would have contradicted the Association's very constitution. Only if an organizational crisis demanded a radical reshuffling of lines could the constitutional principle of local autonomy be breached.

Instead, working within the constitution, the general secretary gradually altered power relations and definitions of responsibilities. Some actions were subtle and tailored to individual cases whereas others were more universalistic. In all cases, however, the actions were directed toward affirming the greater role of the Metropolitan office. Several policies and actions illustrate the directions of change.

Salary administration. When the general secretary assumed office, the executive secretaries' salaries were determined by the local boards. Each year when preparing their budgets for Metropolitan approval, each board decided individually how much to pay its executive. Consequently, there were wide variations in salaries paid to executives of comparable seniority, quality, and responsibility. The Metropolitan staff's personnel officer had long been concerned with the lack of salary standardization and, with the help of the board of managers' personnel committee, had designed a broad salary schedule applicable to all professional personnel. For executive secretaries the scale was based upon both length of time in position and scope of responsibility. The latter criteria were determined by grouping the thirty-seven departments into four categories. Within each category the departments were considered equal.

Since, in general, the Metropolitan office was interested in upgrading salaries, the Metropolitan schema indicated that several departments were paying their secretaries salaries below the recommended level. In the past, the general secretary had only recommended such salary levels. This time, however, when some boards rejected the recommended level, the general secretary threatened to subsidize the budget from Metropolitan funds to provide appropriate salaries. The executive secretaries knew of these negotiations and of the Metropolitan office's role. The general secretary explicitly recognized that the whole negotiation would link the executives more closely to the Metropolitan office; they "would know who their friends really were." The political point is obvious.

Executive appointments. Since the executive secretary played the key role in local department management, it was crucial that the men in these positions be oriented to the Metropolitan Association's goals. Yet under the principle of local autonomy, when a vacancy occurred, the general secretary merely recommended candidates to the board. Past procedure had been to recommend two candidates without specifying a preference. The new general secretary began presenting only one recommendation and indicating that this constituted his own preference. Although a board could theoretically refuse the candidate, the range of alternatives was foreclosed and the general secretary's control over the situation was increased.

The general secretary did not, however, move to the extreme of actually trying to appoint his own candidate. For example, when a vacancy arose in a large, successful suburban department, its board wanted to appoint the head program secretary. Although this appointment would place the appointee outside the expected career pattern, the general secretary preferred not to oppose the board. Past experience had proved it one of the better boards; its members were responsible and involved, and several had been generous contributors. Further, although the board's choice would not have been his, the general secretary did not consider the choice an especially bad one. Clearly, the general secretary was not trying to effect a radical change in policies and constitutional relations between the Metropolitan office and local departments.

A second course pursued by the general secretary was to fill positions with men whom he expected could and would take a professional and aggressive stance vis-à-vis their boards. Within the limits of his personnel pool and as positions became available, he would nominate candidates possessing the desired characteristics. Although such steps could obviously not be taken in wholesale fashion, executive secretaries who did not fit the model were slowly transferred into other positions.

Board relations. The nagging difficulty of board composition remained. Since board appointments were never seriously reviewed by the board of managers, the possibility continued that local boards would be antagonistic to Metropolitan policy. Again without formal policy changes or wholesale intervention, the general secretary began assuming a direct role by conferring with local boards and asserting his definition of their responsibilities.

In one case, when a board member and former board chairman complained that the executive secretary had not responded to a directive from him, the general secretary told the board member that the secretary followed only policies of the whole board and did not take orders from individuals. In another case, a board member attempted to block the appointment of a new board member who was closely identified with a fairly broad community definition of the local department (both the executive and the general secretary considered this man a good appointment); the general secretary directly confronted the recalcitrant member, who resigned shortly thereafter. In yet another case the general secretary took to task a board chairman who no longer seemed to be pulling his weight in a failing department.

In the main, the general secretary was expressing and operating upon the point of view that the local boards were really "advisory" boards, thereby suggesting that they were not as powerful as the phrase *board of directors* would seem to indicate. During the time of this study, general techniques for intervening in local boards had not emerged; when the opportunity arose, however, the general secretary lent his influence to directing board composiiton and policy.

Capitalizing on economies of scale. The attempts to intervene in board matters and to change the Metropolitan office's relationship to its executive secretaries can be classified as political acts directed at changing the operating goals of local departments and the relations of influence between the Metropolitan office and the executives. But the marginal attack on departmental autonomy also involved economic issues. As noted earlier the individual operation of each department resulted in the organization's losing certain economies of scale. On the one hand, there was little interdepartmental sharing of personnel with special talents. On the other, the independent operation of each department required each executive to divide his attention among the whole diversity of organizational activities, from working with his board to supervising building maintenance.

Since there was little sharing of personnel, no adjustments could be made between the staffs of underutilized and overutilized departments. For example, one department programed a dance for teen-age members but had only one or two staff members to supervise the three or four hundred youngsters who attended, whereas another department had several program staff members who never worked nights. More crucially, one department had an excellent cafeteria manager whereas several others were managed by (essentially) high-class short-order cooks. In both cases, short-term rotation and assignment of personnel among departments could have brought about more efficient utilization of resources.

Interdepartmental economies were achieved in several of the smaller departments. For example, whereas the larger departments had sufficient staff to employ a building engineer or business officer to supervise building maintenance, in the smaller departments the executive supervised custodial workers directly. The Metropolitan office persuaded several of the smaller departments to accept a single supervisor of maintenance personnel, thereby obtaining more detailed attention to custodial requirements. In accomplishing this change the general secretary was aware that, though it would free the executive secretary to "do what he is trained to do," it would also limit his autonomy. The principle of local autonomy was increasingly becoming part of constitutional history.

MARGINAL CHANGES IN THE BOARD OF MANAGERS

The transformation of the Chicago Association required more than simple changes in the local departments. Even though the organization had massively changed its economy and even though the board of managers had changed its orientation sufficiently over the years to be receptive to all manner of new problems and potential programs, still the board, too, required some redirection.

On the surface the board seemed to need few changes. Its orientation had already undergone substantial change. Furthermore, in the natural generational cycle of boards, new board members could be selected, in part, from among the business community's more progressive elements. Yet the logic of the general secretary's definition of his mandate required some changes in the board of managers as well. First, he was convinced that the board had to be restructured to permit greater conflict and debate; the consensus process had to be broadened to include more open discussion. In addition, the expanding definition of niche required greater liaison with the Democratic party and with labor groups; it also required a more powerful and prestigious board.

Consensus Process and Conflict Management

Had the board of managers been removed from the organization or involved primarily in fund raising, the general secretary might have been able simply to ignore its internal operations. Because of its dependence on the board for fund raising and its constitutional emphasis on lay involvement, however, the Metropolitan staff continually attempted to involve the board on basic matters of policy and direction. Even though staff in conjunction with key laymen could often define the alternatives for other board members, there was always the possibility that new lines of endeavor would awaken conflict and debate. Since the board tended to operate on a gentlemen's consensus basis, overt conflict could easily result in rejection of a proposal.

The nature of these difficulties as perceived by the general secretary deserves more explicit exploration. In his view the full board was operating in rubber stamp fashion. Members came to meetings, heard a bewildering array of reports, discussed the proposals casually and quickly, and usually approved the presenting committee's recommendation. He held two objections to this procedure. First, board meetings were so laden with trivia that major considerations could not receive a really broad discussion. Second and more important, if on occasion a board member disagreed sharply, he might effectively create a veto.

One incident in particular highlights the one-member veto phenomenon. During the McClow administration, it had been suggested that a cabinet officer of the United States government could be obtained as a speaker for the total Association's annual meeting. This controversial Democrat was intensely disliked by some board members, and when his name was presented at a board meeting, fairly casually, one member argued vehemently against the cabinet member's integrity and worthiness. Without further discussion, the suggestion was then pigeonholed. The new general secretary felt that the whole issue had been mishandled. First, it was unnecessary to bring the matter to the full board; second, once the matter had been introduced, one man's vehemence should not have been allowed to determine the action taken. This incident was particularly unwelcome because it reinforced the traditional, stereotyped picture of the YMCA as a conservative organization. Since the Chicago Association was moving into more controversial programs, Leaf wanted to make sure that one man's veto could not reject a program.

The consensus process could be influenced at several points. First, the general secretary could follow his own advice to executive secretaries; he could make certain that at least a few board members were prepared on every issue. Secondly, he could limit the agenda to allow more time at each meeting for presenting major programs and issues in greater detail. As of September 1964, no major open conflicts had occurred. Theoretically, however, the general secretary was prepared to meet them.

The consensus orientation resulted partly from the incentive basis of boards serving organizations such as the YMCA. As Wilson and Clark[1] point out, the boards of voluntary organizations (particularly of civic

1. "An Incentive Theory."

organizations) are largely based on solidary incentives. Especially in an organization with diffuse goals (such as the YMCA), the solidary value of belonging to the board would be damaged if debate and conflict were a prominent part of board proceedings.

The general secretary believed that he could develop a stronger, more prestigious board while simultaneously changing its traditional style. He hoped to achieve these effects through a more vital image of the Association.

Recruitment and Goals

Boards of directors serve several functions for organizations. They can set policy, lend prestige, contribute money, legitimate actions, and confer the organization's rewards on staff. They can "represent" the community or special constituencies. The board of managers was wealthier and more prestigious than the local boards of directors; a larger proportion of its members were listed in the *Social Register,* a larger proportion were ranked by the executive secretaries as earning above $18,000 per year, and the members were more likely to be senior officers of major firms.

Nevertheless, the general secretary had observed some problems. First, several members neither contributed money nor helped to raise it, even though, in the general secretary's view, they could well afford to do so. Secondly, as compared with other prominent organizations, the general secretary and other senior staff believed that the YMCA had been unsuccessful in recruiting "top executives." For example, several major national, industrial firms headquartered in Chicago lacked representation; and only one of the big downtown banks was represented. Finally, the board was too limited in its connections; it had no links with labor or with the Democratic party.

The general secretary did not argue that all board members should be big contributors, for he recognized the importance of program and other skills. Some members, however, contributed little in any area. His approach to this problem was, as usual, direct; he lunched individually with the board members in question, indicating that either a larger annual donation was in order or that the member ought also to raise money from his friends. One board member said that his invitation to join the board (fifteen years earlier) had indicated that he would not have to raise money; the general secretary told him that times, and with them the Association's needs, had changed. The board member's contributions increased.

The recruitment of more prominent board members was approached as a problem of demonstrating to such men the YMCA's relevance in Chicago. The general secretary believed that prominent men often did not join the organization simply because they viewed the Association as fairly traditional and relatively marginal. If they could be persuaded to see the YMCA as a vital community force, they would then join. Using a direct sales approach over the period 1961 to 1965, the Association added four men from top executive posts in heavy industry, and three men from banks.

Possibly the more difficult task was forging an effective link to labor groups and to the Democratic regime. Staff participation in various city groups (including city poverty groups) provided one bridge. Still, broader links to labor and the Democratic party were needed. One such link was found in a realtor who was influential in both Democratic party and in labor circles. His appointment not only opened new communication channels but also brought changes in the Association's traditional business practices. For instance, the YMCA usually financed new buildings from its capital endowment. The realtor successfully argued that the Association's capital appreciated at a faster rate in the stock market and that stock, therefore, constituted a better investment than a building. History may, of course, find him wrong, but the change in practice constituted a definite departure from the past, more conservative definition of financial management. The realtor followed his argument with a demonstration that, with a little negotiation, a lower interest rate could be obtained on a mortgage (by contrast with that obained on a loan negotiated by one of the senior and older members of the board of managers and board of trustees). Again, his negotiation represented a sharper approach to organizational practice.

The cumulative changes engineered by the general secretary did not represent an "all-or-nothing" break in the Association's political economy but rather constituted limited alterations in political relations, role definitions, board composition, and financial management which, as a whole, gradually began reshaping the Association and shifting it into a new niche. The foregoing description has made the process seem relatively painless. No palace revolutions were fought, no delegation from the local boards asked that the general secretary be fired. After describing the organization as it appeared several years later, I shall conclude by considering the forces that permitted this "easy" transition.

11
Three Years Later: Chicago Revisited

The undergirding assumption of the foregoing analysis has been that organizational change can best be understood in terms of polity responses to changes in economic and political constraints and demands. Polity choices may bring about changes in facility allocation and power distribution within organizations as well as new stances and changed external economic and political relationships, or a particular polity may block change. I have traced the organizational changes attendant on racial changes, increasing size of operations, suburbanization, and the advent (in the late fifties and early sixties) of both the civil rights movement and the War on Poverty. If my analysis of these changes is at all significant, then the responses and restructurings noted through 1964 (when I terminated the study's major field phase) should have developed even further as these same social forces continued to impinge on the organization. Conversely, a still different redirection in organizational niche and internal arrangement would have occurred only if major new environmental forces had developed.[1] Changes in the organization during the intervening three years were observed in the fall of 1967. Although three years is not long with respect to organizational life cycles, it is yet time enough to observe new trends and directions either reinforced or shunted aside. Changes in the Chicago Association during the three-year period largely reflected deepening of the new directions already discussed.

A quick indicator of organizational expansion is provided by a comparison of changes in yearly income from 1961 to 1966. The 1961 annual report lists total income of approximately $16 million; the 1966 annual report shows a total income 50 percent higher ($24 million). Of

1. The political-economy approach does not assume that all organizational change is based on environmental pressure. It does assume that one of the major impetuses for change is environmental pressure. Furthermore, only under special circumstances, such as internal slack or particular power arrangement combined with managerial attitude, does large-scale change occur in the absence of environmental pressure.

this $8 million increase, $3.7 million resulted from the YMCA's participation in twenty government-sponsored projects. The slightly more than $4 million increase from nongovernmental sources derived from increases in contributions, membership growth and service features in old as well as newly established departments, and increased charges for services and programs. These dollar amounts, of course, represent, and were correlated with, expanded facilities, programs, and staff. Most important, the increases in funds and associated programs were intimately related to complex changes in polity response and adaptation as role definitions continued to change, lay roles were placed under strain, policies were reexamined to support the emerging thrust of the organization, and various groups and individuals brought forth contending rationales and perspectives for organizational decisions and behavior.

Here I shall summarize three aspects of change which reflected major *shifts* in niche and structure. First of all, a more centralized as well as more hierarchical organization continued to develop. This trend issued from continued growth, an ethic of efficiency, and continuing emphasis on maximum mobilization to meet community need. Second, important changes occurred in expansion and funding policies. These changes reflected the Association's new relationship to its environment. Finally, the changes in polity and niche significantly affected the role definition of executives as well as basic commitments and loyalties to the organization.

CENTRIPETAL DECISIONS: THE SLOW DEATH OF LOCAL AUTONOMY

The principle of local autonomy had received legitimacy not only from its origins in Protestant congregationalism but also from its purported contribution to membership involvement, community identification with the YMCA, and executive and local board initiative. As noted earlier, inroads on local autonomy had developed from many sources, particularly the growth of standardized centralized services and the development of Metropolitan subsidies (which created financial dependency), as well as the general secretary's activities with respect to salary administration, and manipulation of board attitudes and board recruitment.

During the period 1964–67, two developments further solidified the death of the local autonomy principle: (1) the power of centralized services was sufficiently increased that, for some services, the "staff" supervisor in the Metropolitan office had a "line" relationship to local personnel; (2) each local department became part of a district, headed by a district coordinator. The latter change in organization has already had radical consequences for the internal hierarchilization of the Association, the mobilization of resources, and the spread of YMCA programs.

Centralized Services: Cafeteria Operation

The "operator syndrome" (chapter 6) had emerged partly because an executive secretary had responsibility for managing a diversified enterprise. He was "in charge" of everything from program supervision to residence management and building maintenance. Just as the personnel director's appointment years earlier had resulted in standardization and some centralization of personnel policy, the appointment of an executive director of food services presaged a centralization of decisions over cafeteria management. The executive hired had had an extensive career in institutional and catering food management. Executive secretaries retained nominal control of their cafeterias (for example, they formally hired their own cafeteria managers); the executive director for food service, however, was made responsible for screening job applicants and making recommendations to the executives. Furthermore, all pricing, service, and operating problems were to be shared with the executive director of food services, who also was given control of purchasing. Since the income of the cafeteria was to benefit the local department and since repairs, capital renovation, and hours of service had to be tailored to the local department, the executive secretary still seemed to be in charge.

It was quite clear, however, that greater expertise and centralization were increasing the Metropolitan office's effective power. In one "showdown" between an executive secretary and the Metropolitan food service manager, it was clear that the latter's recommendations on personnel and prices would carry the day. Whether in the long run the new position and structure would prove effective was not known. In the meantime, however, another functional area had been centralized.

The centralized food service furthered the general management philosophy which, as it developed, legitimated incursions into local autonomy. Annual reports and staff memoranda increasingly referred to "decentralization of the creative functions of management (staff development, lay leadership, and program innovation) and increasing centralization of the support for creative functions (business features, accounting, purchasing, finance, etc.)." Some memoranda discussed "releasing the executives for the tasks they were trained to do." Such rhetoric justified an approach to the management of local departments different from the principle of local autonomy. Although some executives might welcome freedom from the humdrum of cafeteria management or building maintenance, nevertheless it was clear to all that the executive was becoming less of a master in his own department.

The District Concept

Although centralization of services diminished the executive's autonomy, it did not change his relation to the general secretary. He was still officially an assistant general secretary. Beginning in 1963 attempts were made to coordinate local departments, increase sharing of facilities and staff, and offer more imaginative joint programs. Regional coordination gradually issued in a district subpolity.

The concept of a district with its own director was first implemented in an inner city area covering roughly six square miles and containing three departments. One of the Association's elder statesmen, a widely respected "operator," was asked to direct the district. The venture was initially treated as frankly experimental; the departments agreed to specific sharings, but there was no attempt to fix authority or to coordinate many of the executives' most important tasks, such as fund raising. By January 1967, however, when the Near North District took on its title, it was sharing fund raising, one business office, maintenance, one storeroom, and a single program staff. Shortly thereafter the total Association split into twelve districts, each composed of three or four departments.

Each district coordinator was selected from among the executives of departments within the district. All executives interested in directorships (nearly all of them applied) were interviewed for the job by a screening committee. Although some executives opposed the district concept, if it was nevertheless to be developed in spite of their preferences, they could still appreciate the advantage of becoming coordinators. The coordinators finally chosen were usually the executives of the districts' larger departments. They were thus usually slightly older than the other executives and had more experience, larger salaries, and (supposedly) greater competence.

The district structure concept emerged as a response to several problems. First, the general secretary had found it increasingly difficult to supervise thirty-nine departments (two new ones had opened since 1964) while playing an active part in interagency and governmental relations. Although the district coordinator's was officially a "staff" responsibility, it would nevertheless reduce the problems ultimately needing the general secretary's attention. Second, the creation of districts would eliminate service gaps in geographic areas bordering the departments. Third, there would be increased sharing of facilities. Fourth, the larger, wealthier departments would begin to take responsibility for the smaller, poorer ones; the latter's departmental boards would have a broader base from which to draw financial support and expertise. Finally, the stronger, more imaginative executives would work with the poorer, less imaginative ones.

Some potential benefits of the district structures were immediately evident. For example, the hotel's board of directors had never held a current expense campaign, since the hotel always made a profit. As part of a district, however, its wealthy and influential board could probably be induced to campaign for other deficit-ridden departments (whether they actually did so was not observed).

Another example: One district coordinator was asked to recommend a plan of rejuvenation for a small, struggling department that had fallen far behind its income projections and had personnel problems to boot. The district recommended both program changes and personnel reallocations. The Metropolitan staff approved the plan.

To some extent, the creation of districts interposed a layer between the general secretary and the executives. This process had actually begun in 1964, when the general secretary discontinued the general secretary's cabinet. Instead, all professionals met in a larger quarterly meeting, and Metropolitan staff met as required by the general secretary. With the creation of the districts, the coordinators began meeting with ten or twelve Metropolitan personnel; a new monthly cabinet, less cumbersome than the old fifty-man cabinet, emerged.

The main question posed by the district position was whether it was truly "staff" or "line." At the time the districts were formed, there was no desire to create either new superboards or a large administrative structure. Within six months, however, a "line" relation was clearly emerging. Local departmental budgets, for instance, were presented as district budgets, and each local department's budget had to be approved by the district coordinator.

Whether or not implementation of the district concept would accomplish all its purposes, it was clearly beginning to reshape the relations of local departments to each other and to the Metropolitan office. The shape of the polity was altered, and a constitutional principle (local autonomy) though not openly voted upon,[2] was effectively repealed.

2. The district concept had been discussed in open staff meetings. And while many (not all) executives and some of his closest advisors had opposed the formaliza-

Although it was hoped that this centralization would eventually produce increased resources, such as higher cafeteria profit and greater mobilization of boards, the institution of centralized food service and the creation of districts were intended largely to achieve more effective utilization of resources in hand (personnel, money, and facilities). From 1964 to 1967, however, increasing emphasis was placed on expanding the organization's financial base and on a new set of policy priorities for using funds.

FUNDING POLICIES AND THE BOARD OF MANAGERS

The composition and operating procedures of the board of managers had begun changing as early as 1962. While still largely a businessmen's board, it had increasingly incorporated key professionals, such as leading accountants, and men with solid labor connections. Still excluded were members whose *major* ties were to political offices and organizations. Indeed, the president of the board argued against such recruitment. He felt that the Association's independence might be compromised by such a move and that it was more important to have board members with influence on political figures than to have actual political officeholders on the board. As the editor of a major newspaper, his own influence was substantial; he was supported by several other board members who had considerable prestige on both the local and national scene.

There also had been a conscious restructuring of the board of managers to bring increased vitality into committees and to facilitate an "action agenda" in board meetings which would allow discussion of critical issues. Information is incomplete, but a detailed analysis of the restructuring process would, I believe, amplify the linkage of the political-economy framework to the micropolitics of group and committee restructuring. The board of managers could, on its own, aid staff in restructuring financial operation; it could also engage in more direct fund raising. From 1960 to 1967, for instance, the board of managers' campaign goal increased from $50,000 annually to $400,000. The appeal for this money was based largely on inner city needs. (Indeed, throughout the Association fund raising was increasingly based on inner city rather than traditional program appeals.) In addition to a revitalized

---

tion of districts, in the last analysis the general secretary made the decision, participant democracy notwithstanding. Some of the effects of this decision on individuals are discussed below.

board of managers, the general secretary believed that the board of trustees also needed energizing. As managers of the Association's real estate, "trustees' policies" could impede the mobilization of resources. In 1966 the average age of this board's members was just under eighty, and the youngest member was sixty-nine. Many had little or no contact with the Association's ongoing operation; it was necessary, then, to find a means to realign the board of trustees. Again, without overt challenge, means were found to influence the perspectives of new recruits.

Several kinds of funding policies (the subsidy and deficit arrangement between the board of managers and local departments, the system of charging local departments for Metropolitan services, and the policies and priorities of capital financing) had been changed since 1964. These changes were designed both to provide more funds with less strain to poorer (particularly inner city) departments and to maximize the growth of total resources available for new facilities.

Subsidy and Loan Rules

Under the Association's fund accounting system, a department with income expectations below its approved budgeted expenses (or with expenses above its approved budget) could meet its deficits in several ways. First, it could cut expenses. Second, Community Fund subsidies to the Association could be allocated to the specific department (indeed, departments had a regular claim on portions of Community Fund money and these were part of expected income). Third, a special subsidy or grant might be arranged from the board of managers' income. In some cases (if, for example, a department was operating under special circumstances or running an experimental program), an outright grant could be given. The usual procedure, however, was for the department to apply to the board of managers for a loan, to be supplied from endowment funds. In turn, the board of managers charged the department 4 percent interest (see chap. 5).

This system, which weighed heavily on struggling inner city departments, was eliminated in 1965. Over $1.6 million of noncollectible, internal, current deficit and capital loans were written off; the endowment and capital worth of the Association was reduced by the amount of the back debt. This action was, of course, completely a matter of internal bookkeeping, but as a consequence the burden was considerably lightened on deficit departments.

From this point on, deficit subsidies and Community Fund subsidies were granted as outright gifts from the board of managers, raised either through their own drives or from endowment income. Each executive was still expected to stay within his budget, and fiscal irresponsibility remained an organizational sin; but, one part of the organization was no longer supporting another part's investment.

Financing Metropolitan Services

In the past, Metropolitan office expenses had been paid from endowment income and from fees charged to departments (for example, separate fees were charged for bookkeeping services, membership development and public relations, and insurance). No one had a true picture of total Metropolitan expenses because the cost of various services was kept in numerous separate accounts; office space and upkeep were provided in the downtown building owned by the Association (the building made only a small profit but provided free rent and upkeep for between eighty and one hundred employees). However, salary and wage figures alone came to more than had been charged to the departments.

During the first phase of change the Association moved to a flat fee, 4 percent of departmental income, for Metropolitan services. Even though Metropolitan overhead exceeded this figure, the new procedure simplified the accounting system. The next move projected raising the fee, in 1968, to 7 percent. All departments would be charged 7 percent, but inner city departments with financial problems would receive subsidies. The new system would thereby effectively relieve the board of managers of subsidizing administrative costs for outer rim departments.

Priorities in Capital Expansion

Of all the policy changes with respect to money handling, accounting and investment, the most far-reaching in their effects were those determining criteria for expansion and modes of fund raising. A moratorium on matching funds had been called in 1963. When a new suburban department had attempted to collect what it had thought was a pledge for matching funds, the Metropolitan office suggested that the department borrow from local banks (four banks in that area eventually loaned $100,000 apiece to complete the capital fund drive). Definitive expansion policies were yet to be formed, however.

By 1967 the board of managers and the general secretary were taking two related positions on suburban expansion. First, when approached by a suburban area, the Metropolitan office would fund a staff person to that area for two months only. At that time, local funds had to take over or the staff person would be withdrawn. Second, capital drives would not be subsidized by the board of managers.

These policies influenced several townships to begin paying YMCA workers from public funds. Furthermore, the Association defined criteria for establishing departments (multiple community services, a 150,000 population potential, etc.) in an attempt to avoid entrapment in uneconomic suburban ventures. (It became apparent that, even without financial support, suburban areas wanted to affiliate with the Metropolitan Association, largely because it offered substantial organizational strength and expertise.)

The decision to use outside financing constituted a radical step which raised many questions. How much indebtedness could the Association afford? Which projects would be funded through private, outside sources and which through government (3 percent) mortgages? Who had responsibility for approving these loans? All such questions involved the board of trustees and its traditionally conservative stance of refusing outside financing. Since at least two newer members of the board of trustees were sympathetic to its inner city orientation, the newer policy changes were in process by late 1967.

All the accounting changes discussed above were linked to a basic redirection of funds toward the inner city. If suburban expansion were to occur, it would have to be financed locally. In the past, suburban expansion had actually been financed from depreciation reserves of all the local departments (most of which were in the city) as well as from the board of managers' endowment fund. The new orientation clearly effected substantial redirection in fund use.

Other changes in accounting rules were less clearly related to the Association's perceived changing niche and concept of itself. For instance, the retirement of the comptroller (a man employed with the Association for fifty years) resulted in the hiring of a new comptroller with more experience in managerial accounting. It became clear that the complicated fund accounting system was masking liquidity problems. A true statement of the income and budget situation was needed. A new reporting system was devised which permitted simpler presentation of required information. The new system did not redirect funds; rather it clarified the funding situation, increasing the Metropolitan staff's ability to survey the economy of the local departments.

EXECUTIVE PERFORMANCE AND ORGANIZATIONAL LOYALTY

The funding policy changes and those affecting internal polity both emerged from and contributed to a general reshaping of organizational goals and orientations. These changes had consequences for executive performance and for staff and board commitments. The new political economy changed the demands on executives and evolved a new image of the exemplar YMCA and the exemplar staff member. The new image was not a matter of changing formal role definitions; instead, it emerged out of the change processes. At the same time, questions regarding organizational loyalty and legitimacy were raised.

Under the older system, the "operator" executive was virtually independent (see chap. 6). He was directly responsible to his board and the general secretary, but as long as his budget was balanced, few demands would be made upon him. The new political economy, however, brought a new set of demands. First, the executive secretary was expected to move into community programing (a building-centered program was considered inadequate if it ignored the unreached and unwashed). Second, any department operating a stable cafeteria and residence without adequate community service programs was considered inadequate. One executive who had stabilized a deficit operation would, under the old system, have been a hero. The general secretary's attitude, however, was "I expect you to do institutional management out of your back pocket." It was necessary but no longer sufficient to be a good "operator."

Indeed, the new exemplar was expected to anticipate and to lead in the process of community change and problem solving. Executives unable to adapt to the new system were threatened with dismissal:[3] in one case one of the better "operators" who did not adapt had become increasingly isolated. Even middle-class suburban departments with burgeoning programs were expected to find social-problem pockets for outreach service.

For many secretaries, especially younger ones serving the inner city, the new approach suggested exciting possibilities. New programs meant innovative departures from the traditional, quick and large salary increases, organizational prestige and publicity, travel to other cities for

3. Among the more cynical YMCA secretaries it was said that, historically, YMCA personnel were fired only if found seducing the board chairman's wife. The general secretary had long argued that the YMCA subsidized—indeed, even rewarded—incompetence. The new demands presented not only a new exemplar but sanctions behind it.

consulting purposes, and a sense of being "where the action is." For others, however, the new system not only created a new set of demands but also challenged the value and legitimacy of their work and, indeed, devalued the Association's traditional activities. One suburban executive commented that he and his staff considered the meetings of the total Association irrelevant to them; these meetings always seemed primarily concerned with new government programs. Another executive faced the difficult task of trying to convince his laymen that their "traditional" activities in the suburbs were useful and good, even though all the fund-raising hoopla in which they participated emphasized inner city programs.

For many senior personnel, conformity to the goals, program, and new organizational design (districts) of the new system affected their basic organizational loyalty and was not simply a matter of commitment to a new set of ideas. In open-ended interviews with executives in 1961 and 1962 the question of commitment to the Association's general program was never raised; organizational loyalty was assumed. By 1967, however, loyalty could no longer be assumed. Executives used such phrases as, "He's the boss; I was in the army and I believe in doing what the boss wants" or, "I give him what he wants."

Wholesale defections did not occur. The Chicago Association was the highest paying in the country (thirteen of the country's thirty-seven top salaries were in the Chicago Association); senior executives had substantial investments in their positions. Nevertheless, where for some the new political economy offered excitement and challenge, for others it left a "bad taste in the mouth," and for still others it constituted a road to failure. The fact that the new political economy could be expressed in terms of Christian service and organizational vitality was probably important in minimizing the transformation of disenchantment into dissaffection.

POSTSCRIPT

The years from 1964 to 1967 saw other processes develop which represented a rationalization of the new political economy. Interagency coordination and program development efforts, for example, were formalized in 1967 by the creation of an Inter-Agency Development Corporation, jointly funded by several agencies and devoted to proposal writing and funding of joint programs. At the level of organizational symbols, titles were changed to represent the newer conception of professional roles and the newer image of the YMCA's mission. Executive secretaries became executive directors, and the general secretary became the general director; to minimize the institutional quality of the organization departments were called "centers." The word *center* was designed to highlight a more community-oriented, "outreach" approach. The new federal relations also produced certain funding difficulties. Congressional appropriation committee proceedings were scanned by executives, and executives testified in Washington; government audits and overhead contributions had to be taken into account.

Although old constitutional principles had been destroyed (or at least shaken), newer ones were not well established. For example, although the norms and rhetoric concerning the power and autonomy of local boards of directors had been severely shaken, the newer norms seemed still in flux and were only dimly perceived. Similarly, though the principle of local autonomy had vanished, the new principle of collective responsibility and enterprise desired by the general secretary still existed largely in his mind and was only partially institutionalized in the new district concept. The specifics of the new constitution remained to be seen.

At the same time that the Chicago YMCA began experiencing change in its political economy and community niche, Associations in other cities (to a greater or lesser degree) were experiencing similar pressures to change. Depending upon the political and ideological values of their elites, their linkages to other organizations, and their demographic settings, greater or lesser niche shifting occurred. In some cities the élite were so firmly against the federal government that even when they initiated imaginative programs, they insisted upon avoiding federal funds. In other cities a program might be started with federal money, shift to private, and then shift back.

Although not all Associations participating in poverty programs accepted federal money, in all Associations the new programs challenged traditional styles of work and goals.

The variety of programs indicated a deep commitment to service out of the normal byways of the organization. Some YMCA board meetings took on a strong community-action and conflict flavor, and new kinds of indigenous leaders were elected to them. The sedate solidary groups were breached. Delinquent gangs were searched out and seduced into making organizational and program demands. Fee structures were lowered—indeed, memberships were given away. Tutoring classes and literary programs were introduced. Although the YMCA rarely became the leader of civil rights activities, it did make itself available to civil rights organizations and offered to cooperate where it could.

YMCA programs shifted from preventive to group rehabilitative. Although few YMCAs moved to individual counseling or psychotherapy, the attempt to change group and individual functioning became a salient aspect of organizational operation. Furthermore, the web of political and interorganizational dependency tightened. The new urban climate was less hospitable to the older style of autonomous functioning. Where the YMCA's niche had been characterized by a commitment of the conventional middle class, its broader niche would tie it to the agony of urban change.

In most communities, new and vital relationships to other public and private agencies and to clientele groups began to emerge. On the one hand, the new urban niche of the Association led it to work with lower-class clientele previously outside its scope. On the other, it led to a new set of organizational and funding relations.

The involvement in poverty programs gradually affected the national polity. For example, federal involvement presented a conflict issue for national meetings, and just before the 1964 national election a hot debate was resolved in favor of the appropriateness of using federal money.

Even more important for the long run was whether this new source of funds would change the relationship of local Associations to the national YMCA. Partly financed by the Chicago Association, a Washington office of the YMCA was established to aid local associations in processing proposals and gathering information on new programs. Some attention was also directed toward having one contract for a given program written for the total Association. If this were done, a centralized funding function would necessarily be assumed by the national Association.

The directions of change would also affect the training and recruitment of professionals, as well as the traditional geographic and political boundaries between local and state Associations.

Although my primary concern has been the impact on the political economy of the Chicago Association of the civil rights and poverty movements, the political economy of the National movement would clearly be affected also.

12

Epilogue: The Importance of Political Economy

The Chicago Association's transformation was of no mean proportions. Goals, values, and traditional operating modes were sharply questioned, a new model of the moral exemplar emerged, and new uncertainties were introduced. Although the whole organization was restructured, many local departments retained their traditional set of programs, clientele, organizational relationships, and constituency commitments.

One question raised, but not answered, by the foregoing analysis concerns the relative ease of transformation. Certainly, when nation states undergo massive change in political economy, they experience massive economic dislocation, large-scale social movements, political conflict, and even revolutions.

Clearly the Association's transformation was not without conflict; yet it remained within reasonable bounds. There were no mass resignations, nor even any serious number of individual resignations. There were few attempts by departments to disaffiliate from the Metropolitan Association and few major conflicts between local boards of directors and the board of managers.

Within a political-economic context, I can speculate about the relative ease of transition. The explanation will focus on the participation incentives offered to different groups, the operation of a politics of abundance, and the development of a compatible rhetoric to justify change.

CONFLICT AND CHANGE

I have asserted that the level of conflict evidenced in the Association's transformation was relatively low. This assertion is based on a very rough estimate of the degree of conflict within the Chicago Association as compared with that in other large-scale organizations (for example, union-

221

management conflict,[1] conflict within social movements,[2] or conflict in correctional institutions[3]). Conflict does appear more pervasive in this case than in the organizational histories described in Chandler's *Strategy and Structure*. Obviously a solid observational basis for such comparative statements is lacking; nevertheless, a crude, qualitative analysis both illuminates the dynamics of conflict within the Association and suggests the directions that political economy would take in analyzing conflict processes.

Four general, though interrelated, propositions are useful in explaining the kinds and level of conflict found. First, when an organization uses several kinds of incentives (solidary, material, and purposive) to attract and hold member commitment, the *amount* and *balance* of incentives offered for each organizational segment and each member's relative gratification or deprivation contributes to the conflict level for that segment. Dissatisfactions can be either individual or aggregated into group demands. The second proposition holds that overt conflict varies directly with aggregated dissatisfactions.

The amount and balance of incentives offered individuals and the aggregation of demands is related to the overall incentive *stock* of the organization. A third proposition holds that in a politics of abundance (as opposed to a politics of scarcity) the distribution of rewards, whether consciously manipulated by élites or proceeding as part of the "normal" functioning of the system, mitigates the depth of conflict. Fourth, especially where purposive incentives are an important component, to the extent that change can be cloaked in a rhetoric consistent with the central values of participants, conflict will be mitigated. Where multiple, incompatible goals exist, however, a harmonizing rhetoric will be difficult to develop.

Incentive Theory and Organizational Conflict

I have earlier discussed (chap. 4) as a central constituting principle, the kinds of incentives offered to attract and hold member commitment. Each of the major organizational types offers a different combination of incentives. One consequence of different incentive bases is that, with re-

1. For a useful general survey, see Walter Galenson and Seymour Martin Lipset, eds., *Labor and Trade Unionism: An Interdisciplinary Reader* (New York: John Wiley & Sons, 1960).

2. Zald and Ash, "Social Movement Organizations."

3. Mayer N. Zald, "Power Balance and Staff Conflict in Correctional Institutions," *Administrative Science Quarterly* 7 (1962): 22–49.

spect to a similar issue or kind of change, each lends itself to different levels of conflict.

One illustration clarifies the impact of incentive base on conflict expression. A person who accepts his employer's right to hire a Jew to work next to him may react vigorously when his country club's membership committee proposes a Jew for admission. Two components of this example have particular relevance for understanding conflict within the YMCA. First, the same issue may differentially threaten an organization's constituting principles. Introducing Jews into a non-Jewish country club threatens the club's essential solidary nature. Apart from recreation, country clubs offer status homogeneity and prestige. Introducing Jews (or Negroes) breaks the club's sense of mutual similarity, social ease, and social status. Furthermore, the very introduction of conflict breaches the solidary incentive basis.

Second, organizations having different incentive bases also create a differential set of "comparison levels for alternatives" for their members.[4] If a Jew is introduced into a work situation, the discontented employee must consider his job alternatives; his employment is likely to be of greater salience and less easily replaced than his country club membership. In general the large-scale organization offering material incentives, if it offers adequate salary and security compared with alternatives, has a greater hold over its members than the organization based on solidary incentives. In general, solidary (and for that matter, purposive) organizations are more dependent upon their members than are their members upon the organization.

If this analysis is correct, organizational élites in solidary and purposive organizations will be more concerned with the disruptive effects of change on member commitment than will the élites of organizations based on material incentives. Members of the former willl convert a change issue into a conflict issue more readily than will members of the latter.

The professional staff and the board members of the Chicago YMCA were bound to the organization by different incentives. Staff were *recruited* through a combination of purposive-solidary and material incentives. It is extremely difficult to isolate the solidary-purposive component from the "package" offered by the Association. With the exception of a rare missionary who embodied the YMCA's older social gospel commit-

---

4. John W. Thibaut and Harold H. Kelley, *The Social Psychology of Groups* (New York: John Wiley & Sons, 1959).

ment, most professionals in the traditional mode were attracted by the
YMCA's combination of good work and clean living with nice people
and surroundings. Even more important, YMCA employment offered a
potential career to the staff. Few staff members refused promotions because of commitment to a specific kind of work (boys' work, for instance). Material incentives (salaries and fringe benefits in a comfortable
setting) were the dominant incentives, with solidary and purposive incentives secondary components.

Since material incentives dominated, staff accepted goal and program
changes with minimal discontent, expressed largely through informal
grumbling rather than overt opposition. When staff did oppose a change,
they were more likely to utilize covert sabotage (delay and apathy) than
direct attack. This is, I feel, the norm for expression of discontent in
organizations offering material incentives. Thus, large-scale businesses
usually find executive-individual conflict occurring via informal and covert routes.[5] (This proposition holds only when individual discontent is
not aggregated through group solidarity—see below.)

Material incentives submerge conflict because individuals are exchanging compliance for money and fringe benefits. This exchange is the heart
of the constitutional principle. Indeed, Metropolitan staff believed that
executives claiming inability to act in a specific situation because of local
board opposition were often simply shifting their own (illegitimate) opposition to a legitimate oppositional center.

Board members were bound to the organization through a combination of purposive and solidary incentives. In a sense, as in many organizations of this type (Kiwanis clubs, Rotary, hospital boards), a public
purposive rhetoric cloaked and legitimated a private, solidary incentive
base. The relative weight of solidary versus purposive incentives would,
of course, vary for any single board member.

Staff were perpetually concerned to maintain board commitment and
involvement. During the period of change, the boards' traditional authority to make policy and set goals issued in a situation in which basic
changes and issues reached the level of board decisions. These potential
conflict issues had to be considered by the departmental boards and the
Metropolitan board of managers; yet many executives and board chairmen feared losing member commitment and did not want conflict issues
to arise.

5. Tom Burns, "The Reference of Conduct in Small Groups: Cliques and Cabals
in Occupational Milieux," *Human Relations* 8 (November 1955): 467–86.

This dilemma resulted, first, in a notable reluctance to pose critical issues to local boards. Second, the desire to avoid disruption of solidarity permitted a vocal minority (or even a lone dissenter) to veto a new program. The solidary base often effectively vetoed change. Third, in dealing with a potential conflict issue, executives and key board members, preferring to avoid conflict, would often not discuss the merits of the issue, but rather present the issue and its resolution as the result of decision processes by a higher authority (the board of managers). An organizational issue thereby became a fait accompli. Fourth (in a few cases), boards vetoed programs and changes proposed by the executive, the Metropolitan staff, and the board of managers. In such actions, the board's power appeared to be substantial. Yet continued and significant opposition from any department usually produced either a change in executives (the Metropolitan staff would argue that staff leadership of the board was lacking) or a change in the local board's composition or organization. Thus, although the means were less direct, the general secretary and the board of managers could control local boards and their directors as well as local staff.

The detail in this discussion should not obscure its major contention that, as contrasted with business corporations, the Chicago Association historically had created relatively independent decision centers which, due to the incentive ties of board members and the traditional ideology, could conflict with decisions and thereby impede the rate of centrally directed change. In recent years the process of change eventuated in a diminution of the power of the independent centers.

Aggregation of Demands

Individual discontent is transformed into organizational conflict when the individual has power or when he combines his power with others who are discontented. First, an individual, through his power (control of financial resources, constituency linkages, charismatic leadership, knowledge, authoritative position), can contest the rules, policies, and goal definitions of other key decision makers or members of the élite.

Second, individuals can mobilize others with similar discontents. Factors that increase collective identity (as career blockage, homogeneity of statuses, high rates of communication) even cause organizations offering largely material incentives to experience expressions of collective discontent and organizational conflict. Whether the focus is on businesses or social movements, the expression of internal discontent is dependent upon the conditions for communication and the development of collective identity.

One reason that a greater degree of overt conflict between staff members (especially the executives) and the Metropolitan office failed to occur is that the staff members were not a functioning group. The executives had individual rather than collective relations with the Metropolitan office. Working and living in all parts of the metropolitan area, they lacked a separate club or organization for focusing discontent or attention. Since they were not uniformly opposed to the new policies, there is little reason to believe that such an organization would have been a channel for conflict or opposition: the conditions for collective expression, however, would have been present.

This situation may be contrasted with that of other organizations in which conflict has occurred on goal and program issues. Correctional institutions, prisons, and hospitals experience conflict in which different groups clearly take differing positions on an issue. Within the YMCA, conflict lines lay between departments and the Metropolitan office rather than between personnel groups. The local departments formed the basis for identity. Individual discontent could, of course, have produced an exodus; yet few staff resigned. A politics of abundance helped to minimize such defection.

A Politics of Abundance

The foregoing has examined the effects of different incentives offered to organizational segments. We shall now explore consequences of the *amount* of incentive offered.

The terms "politics of abundance" and "politics of scarcity" refer to political consequences of the *state* of the economy (the extent to which "adequate" or "inadequate" resources—money, prestige, services—are available for distribution). The adequacy of distributional resources (incentives) is, of course, ultimately based on the social definition of a person's "just due"—what he receives compared with what he believes he should receive.

Although these terms are widely used and easily understood, there has been little systematic analysis of the concepts and their consequences. Myron Weiner, for example, titles his book, *The Politics of Scarcity: Public Pressure and Political Response in India;*[6] yet the index provides only one reference to scarcity. David Potter's perceptive essay on Ameri-

6. Chicago: University of Chicago Press, 1962.

can history and character, *People of Plenty*,[7] includes a chapter on the consequences (for national politics) of abundance that is relevant here.

These concepts can be stated in terms of game theory.[8] A politics of scarcity almost always involves a zero-sum game in which one person's or group's gain requires another's equivalent loss; competitive strategies are obviously encouraged and political élites must mediate between competing claims. The politics of abundance, however, resembles a non-zero game in that alternatives exist through which *both* parties can achieve results above zero; cooperative strategies are thus encouraged and élites need not penalize one person or group to reward another or to change allocations.

Politics of abundance and of scarcity emerge not only from the absolute state of the economy, but also from the direction of economy change. The economy may be growing or contracting. A growing economy encourages expectation of a larger payoff (at least among those who believe that the economy is growing). On the other hand, a decreasing economy raises the fear of loss (a large but declining economy may occasion less immediate anxiety or discontent than one that is small to begin with).[9] Both absolute and relative increases and decreases in payoff must be evaluated.

Scarcity and abundance have several consequences for organizational change. First, organizations changing in a system of scarcity are likely to experience greater conflict and discontent than those in an economy of abundance. Members being deprived (and believing that they are being deprived) are generally more resistant to change than those either being passed by (though not directly deprived) or who are increasing their payoff, although not as rapidly as some others. Second, élite strategies of change vary according to whether the organization is operating with scarcity or abundance. In an economy of abundance, élites may attempt

7. *People of Plenty: Economic Abundance and the American Character* (Chicago: University of Chicago Press, 1954).

8. Anatol Rapoport, *Fights, Games and Debates* (Ann Arbor: University of Michigan Press, 1960).

9. This analysis is fairly crude. It has long been noted that people lacking resources and existing in an economy of scarcity respond to decline with hopelessness. Some would argue that (1) persons experiencing an increase in their resources just prior to a setback are most likely to express "left wing discontent," whereas those forced to relinquish a higher share experience "right wing discontent"; (2) expression of discontent requires that persons have had *some* resources (the totally downtrodden do not express discontent). A fully developed analysis of the politics of scarcity and abundance would take into account the timing of deprivation and discontent expression and the effects of differential reward positions on modes of conflict expression.

organizational changes without directly attacking outmoded or traditional practices, arrangements, and personnel. On the other hand, in a situation of scarcity, change usually requires replacing obsolescent parts and redistributing resources from one party to another.

During the first years of change, the Chicago Association was clearly operating with a politics of abundance or, at minimum, the prospect of abundance. New fund sources were acquired and new programs initiated without attacking or eliminating older modes. Furthermore, throughout the period of this study the Chicago Association paid higher salaries than other comparable organizations in Chicago and, more important from the career viewpoint, higher than YMCAs in other cities. Indeed, the general secretary argued that no man valued by the Chicago Association should leave Chicago for another position *only* because of a higher salary. Although some executive personnel accepted general secretaryships in other cities, they sometimes did so at a lower salary. (The top position in a city association was a scarce resource in the sense that, with a young general secretary in Chicago, an executive desiring to manage a city association was forced to work outside Chicago.)

A politics of abundance would characterize the regime either until revenues failed to increase or until an attempt was made to change the entire organization to fit the new conceptions. Exactly such a change was occurring in 1967, with greater conflict than previously. For example, an executive secretary who had proved inadequate in building programs and had failed to adapt to his changing community was given (by the general secretary) six months to find employment elsewhere. The executive mobilized his board to appeal the decision to the president of the board of managers, only to be reminded by the general secretary that he could be fired outright.

To recapitulate, as long as organizational change followed the paths of abundance and growth into new areas, change could be easily instituted. A polity of scarcity, however, especially with the pluralistic and multicentered polity of the Chicago Association, was certain to foster conflict. By 1967, increased central control enabled the general secretary to confront issues that, at an earlier time, might have been skirted.

Ideological Consistency as a Problem in Scarcity

During the 1950s and 1960s, students of political extremism have used the concept of status politics to illuminate political movements lacking immediate economic ends. This concept of status politics encompasses two rather disparate ideas. One, not of interest to this study, is that of rank. The notion of rank is operative when a group identifies with a leader or set of ideas in order to claim a different rank within a society's group prestige system. The second notion posits a competition among groups who wish to define normative order. Joseph Gusfield, for example, interprets much of the temperance movement as an attempt by certain groups to define sin and morality in the face of immigrant groups' challenges to Protestant American society.[10] Although the two concepts are not unrelated (a rank change alters deference patterns and the social conception of worthiness), the second notion bears greater relevance for this study.

Simply put, ideologies are part of and shape normative orders. Especially in organizations with purposive incentives, the relative compatibility of symbol systems becomes a major source of potential strain. As new goals and concepts are incorporated by an organization, they initiate a process in which the new is made more or less compatible with the old. If the new ideas *appear* incompatible, then the operative political process resembles, in essence, a politics of scarcity (when ideologies are incompatible, a zero-sum game is in process and competitive strategies are the primary order of the day). In such organizations as mental hospitals and correctional institutions, the acceptance or rejection of a new treatment modality may depend on the extent to which it appears to conflict with other norms concerning order and custody. The ability to harmonize a new concept with the traditional view of purpose and means may issue in an easy organizational transformation: the harmonious ideological definition then resembles a politics of abundance.

In the Chicago Association the new programs and styles were largely justified in terms of such overarching YMCA values as "finding needs to be met" or being relevant to "the times." Partly because the innovators were more articulate and partly because the new programs and goals appealed to general humanitarian stances within the society, defenders of the traditional encountered difficulty in mounting a counter-ideology. One was, of course, available to them: people participating in traditional programs could not be served in the same building at the same time with those served by some new programs. Such a position, however, would have possessed little moral force in a society conducting a war on poverty.[11]

10. Gusfield, *Symbolic Crusade.*

11. In "Ideology as a Culture System," Clifford Geertz argues that ideological metaphors must receive cultural validity if they are to be accepted. They must be

In the Chicago Association, conflict was contained precisely because new programs were justified in terms of a traditional set of overarching values and because the one potential counterideology lacked moral force.

Before examining the general utility of a political-economy framework, I might mention one more factor which encouraged the ease of transformation. In chapter 4 I noted that the substratum of personality modalities and attitudes was relevant to political functioning. I also cited Roy Grinker's observation that George Williams College students traditionally accept authority and are relatively unintellectual. These personal attributes also seemed prevalent in the Chicago Association, and both would clearly contribute to the acceptance of change when it was initiated by legitimate authority.

THE IMPORTANCE OF POLITICAL ECONOMY

This description of the YMCA's history, structure, and current processes of change has had two purposes: it is first an organizational ethnography; equally important, however, it also demonstrates the usefulness of a political-economy framework for analyzing organizations. To fulfill its first purpose, this study used sociologically relevant categories to describe an organization, common in American cities, that is marked by an interesting amalgam of organizational characteristics. The description stands or falls on its verisimilitude and on its interest and usefulness for other scholars' theories and comparative analyses. The descriptive material needs no long summary or amplification.

The second purpose, to demonstrate the usefulness of a developing political-economic framework for analyzing organizational change, began to emerge well after the field phases of this study were launched. Since the framework and "theory" are still being developed, it is useful to restate the framework's main components, to note the directions in which it must be elaborated, to assess the extent to which the study has demonstrated the utility of this approach, and finally, to evaluate its limitations and relations to other methods of studying organizational change.

The political-economy framework was initially developed because organizational analysis seemed inelegant and diffuse when used to study the causes and dynamics of organizational change. Any general social system's approach to organizational change must include a host of vari-

---

integrated with other elements and values. In the YMCA, "helping delinquents" is more consistent with "need" than are "swimming classes." Geertz's essay is published in David Apter, ed., *Ideology and Discontent* (New York: Free Press, 1965).

ables, some of which will be political and economic, to explain change. My focus on the political-economic variables was intended to provide a more *efficient* and *illuminating* approach than would otherwise have been possible with a more general framework. This approach postulates that economic and political forces, structures, pressures, and constraints (1) are among the most significant motivators of change and (2) are the key factors shaping directions of change. The political-economy approach is *efficient* because it concentrates investigation on two key processes and structures and their interrelation; a general social-system approach would not have pinpointed the dynamics of change as easily.

This approach is *illuminating* because it allows a greater explication of political and economic processes and structures within organizations than most sociologists have heretofore provided. It forces the researcher toward a more finely wrought conceptualization of organizational polity and economy than has been the norm. Nearly all sociologists interested in organizations utilize some concepts of power and exchange as well as their synonyms and related terms. Without explicit focus on polity and economy as the central objects of analysis, however, a rich set of distinctions and analytic units has not been developed. In this study the examination of succession processes in political terms and the analysis of accounting rules and constitutional principles were made possible by and coherent through the concept of a political economy. Furthermore, the over one hundred years' history of the YMCA in America has been illuminated by examining the YMCA's economic base and political structure.

As a first step in developing such a set of concepts I have turned, wherever possible, to the fields of economics and political science. The concepts used by these disciplines (at the most general level) are often applied to whole societies or to nation-states. But since political scientists are centrally concerned with the aggregation, structure, mobilization, utilization, and limitation of power, and economists with the consequences of differing exchange systems and terms, it has been useful to scan these disciplines for concepts and ideas applicable to organizations. No claim is made that this volume presents a "complete" political-economy approach. For other studies, different concepts or aspects of polity and economy might be elaborated. For example, there has recently been an interest in the judicial and internal legal systems of corporations. What appeals system, if any, do employees or members have? What rights are vested in the individual and how are individual rights protected?[12] For a battery of concepts relevant to analyzing an organization's legal system, the student might well turn to that part of political science which examines judicial processes and comparative legal structure.[13]

Let us briefly elaborate the elements of the analytic framework. As noted, the political-economy approach examines the interplay of political processes and structures with economic processes and structures. The polity is an organization's power system—the systematic manner in which power, influence, and authority are distributed, mobilized, utilized, and limited. Power is utilized to achieve or to maintain a set of goals, attitudes, and values. These ends may be either personal or collective.

The Polity

Several analytic components included in most analyses of polities are: (1) the distribution of power, (2) the processes of demand aggregation, (3) organizational constitutions, (4) critical transfers of power, and (5) external alliances and linkages.

Amount and distribution of power. Most polity analyses include a description or prediction of the distribution and "amount" of power in the system. Quite commonly used are such polar terms as centralization-decentralization and federated-corporate. Less common are references to absolute "amount" of power (power is often perceived as a fixed quantity). Yet careful students of power within nations and organizations, such as Tannenbaum, Huntington, and Parsons,[14] find the concept of absolute (rather than relative) amounts of power crucial for analyzing different polities. The amount of power refers primarily to the degree to which resources and energies are directed toward or engaged in the influence process. The amount of power may be affected by a social system's changing economy. For example, if an organization experiences a growing interdependence through increased mechanization and moderniza-

12. William G. Scott, *The Management of Conflict: Appeal Systems in Organizations* (Homewood, Ill.: Richard D. Irwin, 1965).

13. I must admit that academic disciplines do not coincide neatly with analytic distinctions. Comparative jurisprudence, for example, has been the province of lawyers and anthropologists; few political scientists have concerned themselves with the topic. Few in any discipline, however, would deny that legal and judicial systems constitute a part of polity.

14. Arnold Tannenbaum, "Control in Organizations: Individual Adjustment and Organizational Performance," *Administrative Science Quarterly* 7 (1962): 236–57; Samuel P. Huntington, "The Political Modernization of Traditional Monarchies," *Daedalus* 95 (Summer 1966): 763–88; Talcott Parsons, "On the Concept of Influence," *Public Opinion Quarterly* 27 (1963): 59–62.

tion, a relatively powerless segment of the organization may increasingly affect other parts (at minimum it has potential power). Within organizations a unit may gain power by developing crucial services for other units. This can be done with no decrease in the overall power, within their traditional spheres, of other units.

Both the centralization-decentralization and federated-corporate concepts focus on the relation of the "center" (executive office) to the "periphery" (constituent units). It may well be, however, that sophisticated polity analyses will require other concepts more descriptive of polity processes. In this study, for example, I was driven to notions of pluralistic and dual polities. The former term referred to a situation in which many groups and levels (local boards of directors, Metropolitan staff, executives, the board of managers) had overlapping jurisdictions of influence. The dual polity concept was used to describe the growth of a national organization independent from, but not controlling, the local Association. It may be that some organizations are best described as gerontocratic oligarchies, and others as modernizing democracies. Both terms interject elements of ethos into the description of power systems; they introduce notions of goals and directions. Furthermore, recent work on international relations focusing upon multination coalition systems (rather than on polarized nation-state systems) may provide a wealth of insight into organizations' power systems.[15]

The development of a vocabulary for analyzing power systems is crucial for two major aspects of the political-economy approach. First, the power system is a central factor in shaping an organization's economy. Without an understanding of polity structure and its implicit ethos it is, I feel, extremely difficult to understand the direction of organizational change. Secondly, and of immediate relevance, the distribution of power shapes the processes by which demands are aggregated.

Demand aggregation. Organizations, like nation-states, change in response to demands for change. Since the political-economy approach takes as its distinctive (though not sole) advantage the illumination of change, great attention must be given to the internal polity processes as well as the external economic and political processes which issue in pressures to change. Organizational change does not normally occur because an ivory-towered leader scans the organization and its environment in a search for problems. Indeed, depending upon the amount and distribution of power among members of a polity (from large customers to board

15. Morton Kaplan, *System and Process in International Politics* (New York: John Wiley & Sons, 1962).

members to unionized labor), a process occurs in which demands for change develop within specific organizational sectors. The response to demand aggregation depends not only upon the resources and power of the demanders but also upon the distribution of responders' power. One still unmet task of a political economy approach is to develop a typology of change processes based upon their relation to the power structure and ethos of change.

Our concern can be phrased more dramatically. In some organizations change occurs in response to an upswell of sentiment and emerging internal social movements; in other organizations change emerges through a set of limited agenda committees, slowly creating consensus on potential directions; still other organizations undergo change at the snap of one man's fingers. The analysis of this variety is the task of political economy.

Organizational constitutions. One aspect of a polity is its constitution (a system of norms which limit, constrain, and guide the actual system of power, as well as the economy's operation). Constitutional norms consist of norms binding individuals into the organization, binding together the organization's parts, relating the organization to the larger society, and shaping the expression of collective concern. (See chapter 4 for a somewhat more elaborate development.)

Analysis of constitutions is critical to political economy for two reasons. First, differences in constitutional principles underlie variations in political economy. Whether one is interested in aspects of constitutions as dependent or independent variables, constitutions are crucial for understanding organizational changes over time, as well as differences among major types of organizations. Second, constitutional norms provide the context within which organizational élites confront change. Organization leaders, however bold, must consider the consequences of violating constitutional norms when they pursue a given course of action.

In this study of the YMCA, major attention has been given to constitutional principles surrounding the rights and duties of units and groups (departments, boards, and executives) and to incentive relations and their consequences. Other studies might give greater emphasis to constitutional principles binding organizations into the larger society. One might wish to examine norm changes with respect to shifts in the functional problems of the larger society. For example, many organizations are currently experiencing different demands as a result of the Vietnam war and Negro unemployment (group integration). Or one might examine the manner in which general societal norms and values condition group relations within an organization. Michel Crozier has studied the massive impact of French family and peer life on bureaucratic behavior,[16] and O. Kendall White has demonstrated how the internal norms of Protestant denominations originating in Europe were adapted to norms of American society.[17] Sociology has barely scratched the surface of difficulties raised by either of these two potential study areas.

Transfer of power. Of interest to most political economists are those key decisions and processes which result in transfers of power, changes in the élite perspectives, and redistribution of power. Succession processes, generational cycles, and new patterns of coalition are central to analysis of political life. It is unthinkable that sociologists and political scientists should ignore such critical processes within organizations. Unfortunately, however, while several social scientists have recognized these phenomena, those working in the area have generally refrained from pushing toward more general conceptions of the processes they were examining.

Transfers of power are important both as *culminations* of change processes and as *forerunners* of new directions of change. Succession processes and outcomes are intimately related to a polity's fundamental structure and to economic structure and change. Similarly, the outcomes of these processes result in new mandates for organizational change.

External political linkages. During the last decade sociologists have become increasingly concerned with interorganizational relations. At one level they have examined nonmonetary, interorganizational exchanges.[18] One agency, for example, may refer cases to another. From the viewpoint of the sending organization, the referral facilitates achievement of goals (eliminating an overload, finding a better service for their clients, etc.). From the viewpoint of the receiving organization, the referral offers them appropriate clientele and an adequate work load to justify their services. Such exchange relations are properly treated as part of an organization's external economic relations.

A second type of external relation involves the forging of alliances, the creation of "umbrella" organizations to further the ends of participant organizations, and the development of external linkages through organi-

16. *The Bureaucratic Phenomenon* (Chicago: University of Chicago Press, 1964), especially chap 8, pp. 213–36.

17. "American Religious Organizations: A Study of the Influence of the Cultural Constitution" (unpublished paper, 1967, Department of Sociology and Anthropology, Vanderbilt University, Nashville, Tenn.).

18. One of the first of these studies was Sol Levine and Paul E. White, "Exchange as a Conceptual Framework for the Study of Interorganizational Relationships," *Administrative Science Quarterly* 5 (March 1961): 583–601.

zations or individuals. These linkages do not involve direct exchanges but are properly considered political. They provide a means of concerting policies and promoting mutual ends and have three major consequences for organizations. First, the alliance may commit an organization to programs and stances which, in turn, shape its goals and directions. Second, these alliances and linkages serve as a channel and means for gaining resources. Third, they form the basis for a network of interorganizational influence. Although some linkages and alliances are relatively clear and open (for example, a Protestant denomination's membership in the National Council of Churches),[19] others are relatively unclear and delicate —and so are their consequences.

The Economy

The analysis of organization polities is most useful in describing the organizations' internal polity structures and processes and in understanding their responses to environmental change. Economy analysis examines both the effect of changing supply and demand schedules on organizational change and the internal economy's effect on polity structure.

The internal economy. Economies are systems that produce and exchange goods and services. An economy is a system of distributing and allocating resources to produce goods which satisfy needs. An organization's internal economy is its system for *allocating* resources (factors of production) in order to produce an output which satisfies clients' and funders' desires (that is, an output at a "price" that leads clientele to exchange resources).[20] An internal economy is also a system that distributes resources (including incentives). The distribution of resources obviously has great impact on the actual operation of the polity.

Three aspects of internal economies merit systematic attention: (1) the division of labor, technologies, and interunit relationships, (2) mech-

19. See James R. Wood, "Protestant Enforcement of Racial Integration Policy: A Sociological Study in the Political Economy of Organizations" (Ph.D. diss., Vanderbilt University, 1967), pp. 28–32. Wood notes that Protestant denominations joining the National Council of Churches for ecumenical reasons found themselves committed to civil rights action.

20. This definition of internal economy deemphasizes the central aspect of the generic definition of the field of economics given in chapter 1—economics as the study of exchange systems. Exchange relations are obviously important for inducing contributions to the organization whether of labor or of goods. Once labor and goods are obtained, however, the organization controls resource allocation largely through mechanism of legitimate authority; the price mechanism, so essential to market exchange of economic goods, is less relevant to understanding *internal* allocation of nonhuman resources.

anisms and criteria for allocating resources and assigning costs, and (3) incentive economies and their consequences.

1. Division of labor, technologies, and interunit relationships. Basic to any economy, whether free market or centrally controlled, are considerations of specialization and (closely related) role differentiation and division of labor. Specialization and differentiation within an organization are, in turn, largely functions of the state of the arts (technology) for producing a specific good, the variety of "products" offered by the organization, the scale (size) of the organization "required" both to produce and to distribute production to the "market," and the organization's geographic dispersion. Each of these factors has consequences for the amount of role and unit differentiation (combination of roles into organizational segments with identity and internal structure), as well as independent effects on the political structure and difficulties facing organizations. For example, difficulties in supervising and maintaining organizational loyalty vary directly with geographic dispersion. Similarly, greater complexity (holding size constant) requires more supervision and administrative personnel.[21] Further, the less routine the tasks, the more discretion must be left to lower-level personnel.[22] In addition, a unit's weight in organizational counsels varies directly as it controls, or is perceived as involved in, the organization's functionally most difficult subtasks.[23] Greater routinization and stabilization of output processes facilitates increased centralization and reduces coordinating problems, and so on.

Although aspects of the internal economy affect the polity, they, too, are affected by the external economic environment and polity and by the internal polity. For instance, which of several alternative technologies is adopted is a function not only of the state of knowledge, but also of the amount of competition, political pressures, and the orientations and distribution of power among managers.[24]

Two general propositions summarize the relation of the economy's "shape" to the polity and to organizational change. First, factors influ-

21. William A. Rushing, "The Effects of Industry Size and Division of Labor on Administration," *Administrative Science Quarterly* 12 (September 1967): 273–95.

22. James D. Thompson and Frederick L. Bates, "Technology Organization and Administration," *Administrative Science Quarterly* 2 (March 1957): 325–43.

23. Michel Crozier, *The Bureaucratic Phenomenon;* Charles Perrow, "Analysis of Goals in Complex Organizations," *American Sociological Review* 26 (April 1961): 335–42.

24. I am indebted to Rolf Schliewen for this point.

encing the shape of the economy (division of labor, attributes of technology, nature of raw materials, and size) are determinants of polity form (amount of hierarchy, distribution of power, and conflict potential).

Second, as any one component of the internal economy changes, the potential is created for changing the organization's polity.

2. Mechanisms for resource allocation—budgeting and accounting. Since internal pricing mechanisms are found only in the largest modern corporations, allocation of resources (land, labor, and capital) within most organizations must be accomplished through budgets and internal accounting procedures. In modern business corporations, new developments in managerial accounting have transformed traditional allocation criteria (check rules for ordering stock, rule-of-thumb criteria of labor cost relationship to expanding capacity) into analytic choice procedures. Although several sociologists have emphasized the relation of technology and tasks differentiation to polity, few have examined the relation of accounting rules and procedures to resource allocation and organizational power.[25] This is an exceptionally fertile field for sociological analysis, one whose surface has barely been scratched by this study.

A paradigm for investigation can be suggested. Resource allocation in organizations is a complicated function of traditional rules, intergroup bargaining, mechanics for deciding conflict, and élite perception of new areas for growth, change, or defense. One level of investigation would be an examination of the *structural mechanisms* for reaching decisions. For example, following Louis Pondy's lead,[26] we might study institutional structures and the organizational rules used to reach decisions on allocating resource capital for investment and major facility change.

A second level of investigation is suggested by the *history and development* of the accounting and allocating rules themselves. For example, what factors encouraged the development of charging units a fixed interest cost on loans or allocating costs in a given ratio to different functions? On what basis do social-movement organizations determine staff salaries or the proportional split of membership income as divided between national and local units (in the National Association for the Advancement of Colored People, for example, or the American Civil Liberties Union)?

25. But see Reginald S. Gynther, "Accounting Concepts and Behavioral Hypotheses," *The Accounting Review* 42 (April 1967): 274–90. For an empirical study see Harvey M. Sapolsky, "Decentralization and Control: Problems in the Organization of Department Stores" (Ph.D. diss., Harvard University, 1966).

26. "Budgeting and Inter-group Conflict in Organizations," *Pittsburgh Business Review* 34 (April 1964): 1–3.

A third level of investigation would be the *consequences* of different allocational procedures. Who benefits? Which functions are supported and which slighted?

For many stable organizations, it will become apparent that allocation rules are compounded of traditional cost accounting procedures with a percentage increase or decrease, depending upon total income projected for a given year (or whatever period is used). Crecine, studying municipal government, has found that department heads request and receive a budget based on last year's expenditures plus or minus the percentage increase projected by the municipal executives' financial office.[27] Only as new programs are initiated or old programs expanded is this formula changed. For other organizations (particularly those in rapid flux), resource allocation and criteria for allocation will constitute central concerns of political economy.

3. Incentive allocations. One component of resource allocation is the distribution of rewards and sanctions to motivate role performance. It was asserted earlier that one central normative principle of organizational constitutions is a set of exchange terms. What is to be gained by joining an organization? Even within major categories, organizations differ in the amount of incentive resources they control,[28] and their ability to retain and motivate members will depend upon their "stock," or "supply." Moreover, the incentive necessary to maintain a member's motivation may differ from that necessary to obtain his initial membership (for instance, a person joining an organization for purposive values may stay because of solidary relations).

Major organizational changes usually effect changes in the balance of incentives, thus creating difficulty in maintaining participant motivation (a dynamically growing organization is, of course, generally increasing its ability to supply fundamental incentives). Conversely, a changing stock of incentives affects political control. Incentive analysis provides a linkage between the political-economy approach and social psychological approaches.

The structure of external change. The foregoing has had to do with

27. "A Computer Simulation Model of Municipal Resource Allocation" (Ph.D. diss., Carnegie Institute of Technology, 1966).

28. Incentive allocations are here treated as a problem of internal allocation. On a different analytic level, they might be treated as an external allocation problem. A radical distinction between personality and role occupant would lead one to argue that incentives function to motivate personalities to occupy roles. This distinction does not seem to have important consequences for empirical studies.

major features of organizations' internal economies. It is unnecessary to examine in detail the economic environment of organizations. All must obtain resources from their environment to survive. Whether the objects of analysis are social-movement organizations, religious orders, military organizations, city governments or business corporations, all organizations must obtain resources and offer a product. They must find or maintain resources and supplies and "satisfy" consumers. Organizations vary in their relative concentration of these supplies and buyers.

Economic concepts are applicable to all kinds of organizations. For example, some social movements, such as one that favors euthanasia, may have a relatively fixed demand level: regardless of environmental factors it is virtually impossible to alter the movement's number of supporters. Some social movements may have widely varying demand levels; they will experience wide variation in support, depending upon the ebb and flow of hostility toward the movement and on dramatic events surrounding it. All organizations are affected by secular trends in demands for services and new opportunities which help explain directions of organizational change. Organizations also experience fluctuation in the inflow of revenues (support) for the organization if the short-range demand is elastic.

It is precisely in analyzing organizations' reaction to the supply-demand equations that analytic economics has been most compelling. With but a minimal imagination the basic notions of economics can be applied to other than profit-making organizations.

CONCLUSION

The framework used in this volume has provided a set of descriptive categories and an interpretive framework for ordering this analysis of the dynamics of structure and change within the Chicago YMCA. At this stage the political-economy approach is a framework, not a theory.

But at least two generations of social scientists have been nurtured on a model of the scientific enterprise that perceives formal theory and experiment as science's exemplar. Some philosophers and historians of science (such as the late Norwood Russell Hansen) would argue, however, that these models are only formalizations of "truths" emerging from a much looser pattern of discovery.[29]

Even if the hypothetical deductive method constitutes a late stage in

29. *Patterns of Discovery: An Inquiry into the Conceptual Foundations of Science* (New York: Cambridge University Press, 1958). See also Thomas F. Kuhn, *The Structure of Scientific Revolutions* (Chicago: University of Chicago Press, 1960).

the establishment of scientific truth, few would deny its value for clarifying the logical status of concepts and providing economical explanations. The political-economy framework can be used to generate specific predictions and in one case has already demonstrated its predictive values.[30] Thus, ultimately, I think the framework will prove useful as a relatively tight and coherent theoretical approach and as a generator of illuminating and enriching concepts.

For this particular study the framework has been of immense value in linking together the organization's structure roles, strains, and policies (chaps. 4–7). Thus the operator syndrome and the constitutional principle of local autonomy were linked to the diverse enrollment economy and local dependencies of the Association in America (chaps. 2 and 3) and in Chicago (chaps. 4–7). Furthermore, key policies relating to expansion and race relation were shown to be outgrowth of basic goals, economic dependencies, and definition of the situation.

The Association's economic problem of developing a stable resource base became combined with a pragmatic interdenominational polity to issue in the transmutation from evangelism to general service. Furthermore, the essentially federated national polity permitted and encouraged local adaptation and change even as an independent national center grew and then declined. For the Chicago Association the political-economy framework led us to see the interpenetration of accounting rules and the distribution of resources with constitutional principles and problems of change. Using a political approach we examined the succession process and the change in polity definition attendant on moving into a new organizational niche.

The political-economy framework is not a substitute for decision theory, the human-relations approach, or the concept of organizational rationality. For analysis of *organizational* change, however, it does claim to subsume these others. If, for example, organizations are conceived as rational instruments, the political-economy approach suggests that their rationality depends upon specifying rationality for what groups, or élites, with what kinds of incentives and normative legitimacy as support.[31]

---

30. I.e., James R. Wood (see n. 19).

31. See Harold Wilensky, *Organizational Intelligence* (New York: Basic Books, 1967) for a set of cases in which information, the sine qua non of rational decision making, is distorted by organizational polity processes.

INDEX

243

headquarters on West Side of Chicago, 172; major supporter of YMCA, 172; represented on board of management, 97

Selznick, Philip, 15, 142; general framework for organizational analysis, xv; total organization as subject of analyses, 15

Senior citizen: YMCA programs for, 87–88

"Shadow cabinet": more conservative and traditional than total board, 189; influential inner core of board, 189. *See also* Board of managers

Short, James F.: study of Chicago YMCA's Youth Gangs Project, xiv

Simon, Herbert: study of decisions and perceptions of middle-level managers, 14

Social change: effect of on YMCA, 163–65 passim; value of case study, xiii

Social gospel: only in student organizations, 66

Social problems, YMCA: as affecting goals and polity, 166; changing political attitudes of businessmen, 166; concern over fate of city, 166; growth of civil rights movement, 166; suburbanization, 166

Social psychology: approach to organization change, 12 n; broad directions of organization change outside scope of, 9, 10; focus on power and exchange influence, 11 n; traditional position of, 10

Social scientists: Detached Worker Program conceived by, 176

Sociological analysis: relation of accounting rules to resource allocation, 238

Sociological literature: social movement organizations separated from formal organizations, 7–8

Springfield College in Massachusetts: affiliate, YMCA, as trainer of public parks workers, 71

Star Lecture Series, 44

"Station wagon" YMCA, 198

Stinchcombe, Arthur: definition of constitution, 22 n

Strodtbeck, Fred L.: study of Chicago's Youth Gangs Project, xiv

Suburban departments, Chicago YMCA: advantage of affiliation with Metropolitan association, 216

Suburban expansion, Chicago YMCA: capital drives not subsidized by board, 216; different views on, 215–16; funding from public monies, 216

Succession processes: as central to analysis of organizational life, 235; "Crown Prince" systems, 179; determined by inner circle of decision-makers, 180; literature on, 180; mandate of, 192; no openly competing groups in formal organizations, 180; political analysis, difficulty of, 180; relation to fundamental structure of polity, 235; rules governing, 23; structure of, 179–80; underlying political processes in, 180; vary according to basic constitution, 179

Chicago YMCA: choice reflection of power balance, 180–81; constitutional norms in, 179; description of main contenders, 184–85; effect on organizational goals, 180; frequency of, 180; full discussion of new role of YMCA, 185; ignoring of political character of, 180; importance of particular personality, 180; invisibility of power struggle, 180; manipulation by professionals, 183; mechanisms of choice, 181; no traditional influence by chief executive, 183; as opportunity to evaluate policy, 181; participants in decision of, 181; political aspects, 181; power of bureaucratic staff on, 179; sectional interests and allegiances, influence of, 180

Sullivan, Captain: founder of YMCA in United States, 29

Sunday, Billy: as religious director of Chicago Association, 78

Supervision, Chicago YMCA: by board of managers, 108; difficulty in interpersonal relations, 133; effect of geographic dispersion on, 237; by general secretary, 110; growth of, 104; as power for Metropolitan office, 109, 134; requirements of, 132

Sweet, William Warren: formation of benevolent societies, 29 n